RAILWAY
BREAKDOWN
CRANES

The Story of Steam Breakdown Cranes
on the Railways of Britain - Volume 1

Peter Tatlow CEng, MICE

Noodle  Books

RAILWAY
BREAKDOWN
CRANES

The Story of Steam Breakdown Cranes
on the Railways of Britain - Volume 1

Peter Tatlow CEng, MICE

© Peter Tatlow and Noodle Books 2012

ISBN 978-1-906419-69-1

First published in 2012 by Kevin Robertson
under the **NOODLE BOOKS** imprint
PO Box 279
Corhampton
SOUTHAMPTON
SO32 3ZX

www.noodlebooks.co.uk

Printed in England by the Information Press Ltd., Oxford.

Front cover (main picture) - *One of the once relatively numerous Cowans Sheldon 15-ton steam breakdown cranes, examples of which were supplied to fourteen different British railway companies in the 1890s. No RS1025/15 was one of a total of ten cranes for the Midland Railway delivered between 1893 and 1901 and is seen here at Willesden Jct awaiting scrapping. (MS Welch)*

Front cover (insert) - *The final development of Cowans Sheldon's original concept of is the 25/30-ton crane for the LNWR of 1908. No RS1020/30 is carrying out bridge works on the Northampton to Rugby line around 1962. Upon withdrawal, it was added to the National Collection, although now preserved in private hands. (MS Welch)*

Pages 2/3 - *Ex-LSWR 36-ton Ransomes & Rapier steam breakdown crane, built in 1918, from Eastleigh on 24 March 1963 clearing the single line between Highclere and Burghclere on the Didcot, Newbury & Southampton route. A diesel hauled freight train for Southampton Docks had de-railed in a deep cutting on the single line the previous day. (SC Townroe, courtesy Colour-Rail)*

Rear cover - *Long jib 36-ton cranes were introduced by the GW in 1908. Ransomes & Rapier steam breakdown crane No. 2 outside A Shop at Swindon on 23 August 1971 with its jib raised as it prepares to carry out a lift. (Author)*

Note - Many of the drawings in this book have been reproduced to a scale of 4mm to 1 foot. However as will be seen, due to the size of the cranes involved some are to the very limit of the printed page. Where a scale-bar is shown, the modeller is advised to verify the dimesions.

Peter Tatlow, CEng, MICE

Note on the Author

Peter Tatlow is well known for his contribution to railway research over 50 years. An interest in railways and railway modelling has been his main pastime since he can remember. Born during the age of the 'Big Four', some of his earliest memories are of journeys undertaken during World War II. Following military service in the Royal Engineers, he joined the Chief Civil Engineer's Department of the Southern Region of British Railways. He left BR over ten years later having qualified as a chartered civil engineer and then worked on the design and construction of bridges, in both the United Kingdom and overseas. He is now retired from full-time employment.

His interest in railways and modelling has led to his writing numerous articles in the prototype and model railway press and in specialist journals on a wide range of subjects including locomotives, coaches, wagons, travelling cranes, bridges, train ferries and civil engineering activities.

His books include:

A Pictorial Record of LNER wagons, OPC, 1976, reprinted twice.
A History of Highland Locomotives, OPC 1979.
Highland Railway Miscellany, OPC 1985.
Historic Carriage Drawings, Volume 3 – Non-Passenger Coaching Stock, Pendragon 2000.
Harrow & Wealdstone Accident, 50 years on, clearing up the aftermath, The Oakwood Press, 2002, reprinted 2008.
St John's Lewisham, 50 years on, restoring traffic, The Oakwood Press, 2007.
Return from Dunkirk, Railways to the rescue, Operation Dynamo (1940), Oakwood 2010

Recently he has revisited the subject of his first work with *An illustrated history of LNER wagons* in four volumes, the first three of which were published by Wild Swan in 2005, 2007 and 2009.

Dedicated to members of breakdown gangs and crane-men of the railways.

This photograph ideally illustrates the development of cranes and the distinction between the generally earlier ones covered in Volume 1 and the later usually larger cranes to be considered in Volume 2. It was taken by a Mr Atherton of Craven Bros at Newton Heath, probably on the occasion of the delivery of their crane sometime in 1931. On the left is a Cowans Sheldon 20-ton crane supplied to the Lancashire & Yorkshire Railway in 1902, which is about to be replaced by one of a pair of brand new 36-ton cranes for the LMS from the Craven stable. Bearing in mind that the latter is positioned further from the camera, one can gain some idea of their relative size. Whilst the carriages of both are mounted on four axles, in addition the Craven crane has a 4-wheel relieving bogie at each end to distribute the greater weight while in train formation, as will be explored in Volume 2.

Contents

Preface   8

Introduction   9

    Crane makers
    Crane carriage
    Crane superstructure
    Wheel arrangements
    Boilers
    Engines & Machinery
    Jibs & lifting tackle
    Match wagon
    Stability
    In service alterations
    Numbering
    Liveries
    Use of the tables

1.   **Early Days**   27

    Appleby 5-ton cranes for Midland Railway
    Appleby 10-ton cranes for LSWR
    Forrest 20-ton crane for North British Rly
    Chaplin 20-ton crane for Taff Vale Rly
    Dunlop & Bell 15-ton crane for LSWR
    Smith (Rodley) 15-ton cranes for GNR

2. **Early Cowans Sheldon Cranes**   39

    Cowans Sheldon 10/12-ton cranes for GER
    Cowans Sheldon 15-ton cranes
    Cowans Sheldon 15-ton cranes for CR
    Cowans Sheldon 15-ton crane for HR

3. **Standard Cowans Sheldon 15 ton Cranes**   57

    Standard 15-ton cranes – curved jib (Mk 1)
    Standard 15-ton cranes – swan-necked jib
    (Mk 2)

4. **Further Cowan Sheldon Cranes**   85

    Cowans Sheldon 15-ton steam-driven hand
    crane for FR
    Standard 20-ton cranes
    Standard 25/30-ton cranes

5. **Early Competition**   97

    Jessop & Appleby 20-ton crane
    Craven Bros 20 & 25-ton cranes
    Stothert & Pitt 20-ton cranes for LSWR

6. **Railway Built Cranes**   115

    GER 12-ton hand cranes converted to
    steam power
    LNWR 20-ton crane
    GER 20-ton cranes

7. **Long Jib Cranes**   125

    Ransomes & Rapier 36-ton crane for GW
    Stothert & Pitt 36-ton crane for GW
    Ransomes & Rapier 36-ton crane for
    LNWR
    Wilson 12-ton crane for GW

8. **Poor Rivals**   145

    Cowans Sheldon 35/36-ton cranes of
    1911-14
    Craven Bros 35/36-ton cranes
    Cowans Sheldon 35/36-ton cranes of
    1916-17

9. **Ransomes & Rapier Consolidates Its Position**   171

    Ransomes & Rapier 35-ton cranes for GER
    Ransomes & Rapier 36-ton cranes of 1918
    & 1927
    Cowans Sheldon 36-ton crane for LSWR

10. **Further Smaller Cranes**   177

    Cowans Sheldon 25-ton cranes of 1917-19
    Cowans Sheldon 20/30-ton crane for
    Met Rly
    Ransomes & Rapier 30-ton crane for LER

11. **Unusual Duo**   197

    Cowans Sheldon 45-ton cranes for
    LNER of 1926

12. **Use of cranes on breakdown**   201

    The early days
    Introduction of steam cranes
    Tool & riding vans
    Breakdown gang
    Calling out the breakdown train
    Operating breakdown cranes

13. **Civil engineering activities**   217

    Interim conclusions   231

Appendices

    Mechanical details   232
    Speed of motions   233
    Lifting performance   234
    Glossary of terms   235

Acknowledgements   236

Colour Section   237

Preface

As young boys, to give our mother some respite, my brother and I were made to have an hour's rest every afternoon. To assist us while away the time, we were permitted to take a book to read. One of my favourites was my father's copy of the Revd Edward Beal's *Scale railway modelling today*, published shortly before the Second World War. Perused carefully, this would be guaranteed to keep me quiet for an hour. Amongst the author's favourite topics was modelling breakdown equipment and he included a drawing of a rather crude interpretation of a steam breakdown crane. Later, my father was considerate enough to make a model of this, largely in cardboard.

As a teenager, I recall being fascinated by the clearing up of the line following the horrendous smash at Harrow & Wealdstone in October 1952 and this has already been the subject of a publication. Following military service, I started work in Chief Civil Engineer's Department of British Railways, Southern Region in the New Works Drawing Office at Waterloo in October 1957. Soon after, another serious accident occurred at St John's Lewisham on 4 December 1957, again the topic of another of my efforts.

In 1960 Hornby-Dublo introduced a red-coloured die-cast metal steam breakdown crane in 00 Gauge at a scale of 4mm to 1 foot. The die-cast process permitted some fine detail, but compromise was necessary in the matter of the winding handles, propping girders and over-length relieving bogies to enable the mounting of the automatic coupling. It was stated at the time that this was based on a Cowans Sheldon example from the Eastern Region of British Railways, but there were no immediate answers as to its capacity and allocation. This challenged me to find out more about it, and incidentally launched me into research of breakdown cranes and broader field of railway matters. About two years later, I concluded that Hornby's model was a hybrid. Its No, 133, was Cambridge's 45-ton crane of 1940, but the jib was too short. I suspect that the example modelled was originally intended to be the 45-ton version of 1940, but in model terms the long jib led to difficulties in negotiating 15 inch radius curves and the solution was to substitute a shorter jib, probably from the 1926 version, and match wagon on a standard 17ft 6in underframe. The same compromise will be found in Triang Hornby's later attempt to represent in plastic British Railway's Cowans Sheldon 75-ton steam crane.

So the need to answer some simple questions regarding a modelling project led, not for the first time, to a long running investigation into the fascination and intricacies of railway breakdown cranes. At this early stage I was employed on the railway and my work was soon to involve the use of these beasts in the renewal of bridges. Although a decade later I was to move on to building bridges in pastures new, my interest in and research into breakdown cranes continued unabated.

As part of this, enquiries of the then still in business crane-makers soon revealed that another person was also researching the subject with a view to publishing the results. So it was that I at first corresponded with, and subsequently met, John S Brownlie. In July 1970, there was some discussion of my joining him in a joint venture, but he was already far advanced in the preparation of his manuscript, whereas I was only just starting out. Although we were both keenly interested in the same specialist subject, we had rather different approaches and proposed treatment of the material gathered. In particular, I had a more graphical outlook on the matter to aid the railway modelling fraternity, together with considering accidents, whereas he was more interested in some of the underlying, some might say obtuse, political aspects and majored on the history of the crane makers. As a consequence, I was likely to want significant changes and additions to his proposals. It was reluctantly decided, therefore, that we should go our separate ways in a race I was unlikely to win. In due course his work duly appeared self-published as *Railway steam cranes* in 1973, while in the meantime I had been drawn towards other aspects of railway research, initially into LNER wagons.

A proposal for a book devoted solely to cranes supplied to British Railways was launched in 1996. This was initiated by Alan Earnshaw, of Trans-Pennine Publications, to be jointly contributed to by him, David Carter and myself. Progress was slow and regrettably Alan passed away in March 2009 with the work incomplete.

Nonetheless, my interest has continued intermittently throughout and, after a gap of over forty years, I feel it is time to place my offering in the public domain. I am therefore grateful to Kevin Robertson of Noodle books for taking on this work.'

Peter Tatlow   Hampshire 2011

***Opposite page** - The first design of steam breakdown crane supplied to British railways in any significant number was the Cowans Sheldon 15-ton crane in the 1890s. This example was delivered to the Midland Railway in 1893 and photographed at Derby Works when new. (BR, LMR, author's collection)*

Introduction

Crane makers / Crane carriage / Crane superstructure / Wheel arrangements / Boilers / Engines & Machinery / Jibs & lifting tackle / Match wagon / Stability / In service alterations / Numbering / Liveries / Use of the tables

Clearing the line in early days of the not infrequent derailments and collisions before the introduction of steam cranes would have been carried out by jacking and packing, for which purpose jacks were often carried on the running plate of locomotives; dragging by a locomotive; and the occasional use of hand cranes. All had their limitations of capacity and dragging in particular risked damaging both the vehicle and the permanent way.

The safe and efficient use of hand cranes called for considerable skill and experience by the supervisor and the team of labourers to operate the winding handles to raise and lower a load and often to slew the superstructure on the carriage. The crane would be positioned by a locomotive. The jib would be raised by the hoisting rope or more likely chain to a limited number of fixed radii and could not be adjusted while under load. In particular, as loads increased, so did the skill and coordination needed of the team in taking the strain of a heavy load as the brake was released without the load overcoming the muscle power available and running away.

It seems the advent of bogie vehicles rendered hand cranes inadequate in capacity and reach, with dragging futile and re-railing ramps and 'jacking and packing' becoming increasingly difficult for breakdown

work. As a consequence, a notable difference in the managements' attitude to investing in adequate cranes occurred during the 1890s, when many companies began to acquire steam breakdown cranes. In a limited number of cases, however, this had been anticipated, namely by the Midland Railway, LSWR and North British Railway.

Originally, of course, all cranes were hand-operated and it will be convenient to describe these first and then add steam power and note the developments from there, leading up to the very latest designs. As there is a common misconception that all rail-mounted cranes are breakdown cranes, the other types, often in use by the engineer on his permanent way work, will be outlined, but no attempt will be made to describe them in any great detail.

To prevent misunderstanding, therefore, it would be wise to define breakdown cranes as taken for the subject of this work. It will consider cranes primarily designed and developed for the purpose of dealing with railway accidents and derailments and usually employed on the standard gauge (4ft 8½in) railways of the mainland of the British Isles. These cranes were usually under the control of the locomotive department, although occasionally they were under the ownership of other

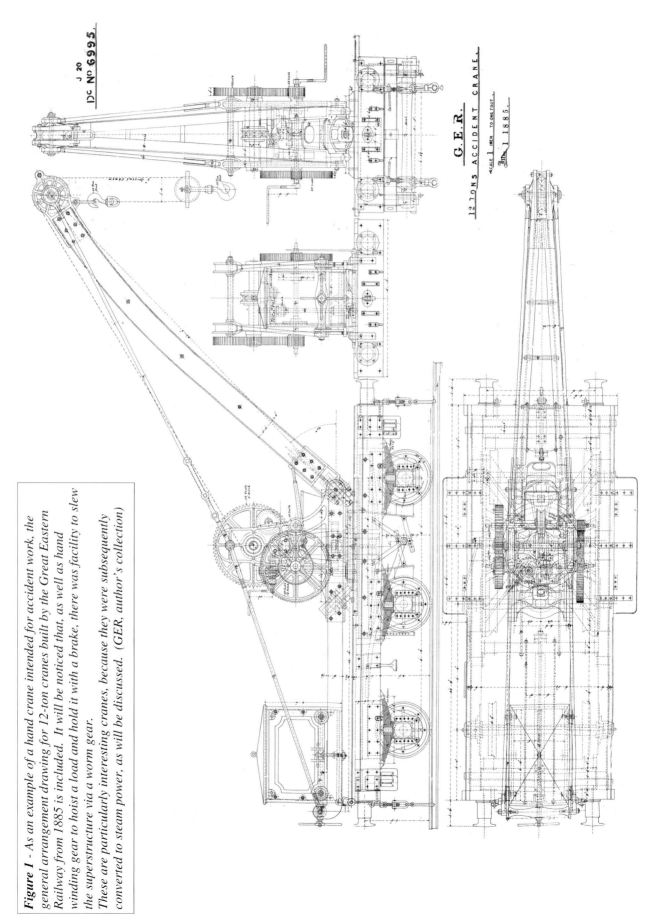

Figure 1 - *As an example of a hand crane intended for accident work, the general arrangement drawing for 12-ton cranes built by the Great Eastern Railway from 1885 is included. It will be noticed that, as well as hand winding gear to hoist a load and hold it with a brake, there was facility to slew the superstructure via a worm gear.*

These are particularly interesting cranes, because they were subsequently converted to steam power, as will be discussed. (GER, author's collection)

G.E.R.
12 TONS ACCIDENT CRANE.
SCALE 1 INCH TO ONE FOOT.
Jan. 1885.

J 20
Dc Nº 6995

The land mark development of relieving bogies to distribute the weight of larger cranes will be considered further in Volume 2. This view of LNER 45-ton Cowans Sheldon crane of 1940, BR No. RS1058/45 at Eastfield, shows the arrangement of 4-wheel bogies attached to each end of an 8-wheeled carriage. (J Templeton, author's collection)

departments, such as the Civil or Electrical Engineers. The military authorities also found a use for this type of crane and, although some were retained in Britain for training and local purposes, most military cranes found their way overseas in due course. Naturally, it will be necessary to make references to developments that initially appeared on cranes built by British makers for overseas railways and occasionally those built by foreign companies.

Cranes are usually referred to by their maximum capacity, such as 15- or 45-ton, but this only represents the crane's maximum capacity when fully propped and falls off rapidly as the radius increases and even more so if 'free on rail', as will be discussed below (p 21).

Whilst in the early days the limited number of hand cranes may have been used for a variety of purposes, it is necessary to distinguish between both hand and powered cranes intended primarily for different functions and in due course allocated to the appropriate department. As well as breakdown work, this included bridge work; permanent way renewals; the erection of signals; around engineering works; and mobile cranes for use in goods yards without adequate fixed cranes.

For instance, engineer's travelling cranes are designed for work six or seven days a week and can frequently lift their full design load of 6 to 15 tons 'free on rail' allowing them to travel slowly under their own power, albeit at a reduced radius, with the same load as when propped. Initially steam-powered, cranes have over the years developed to be diesel-mechanically, diesel-electrically or diesel-hydraulically driven. For use in confined situations and to avoid obstructing the adjacent track, tail-less and telescopic jib cranes have also been developed.

Locomotives equipped with a crane, usually referred to as crane locos, have developed along different lines and will not be considered further here. Cranes have sometimes been ordered and built specially for bridging work and with driving of piles in mind, and subsequently

utilised for breakdown work.

The steam was usually created in a vertical boiler mounted near the rear of the crane, although at least one early type of breakdown crane had a horizontal locomotive-type boiler. The engine had two cylinders, one usually bolted to the outside of each side frame plate, which drove a crankshaft carried across the crane. Three or four motions were provided, which were driven from the crankshaft by gearing and intermediate shafts. They are derricking (raising the jib); hoisting or lifting (often with gearing at two lifting speeds); slewing (rotating the crane on its carriage); and travelling under its own power. Not all early breakdown cranes were provided with the self-travelling motion, relying on an attendant locomotive instead, but from about 1905 all were able to travel under their own power at a speed of 2 to 4 mph, or more.

Early breakdown cranes, with a lifting capacity of about 15 tons, were usually mounted on a six-wheeled carriage and weighed between 35 and 45 tons, resulting in an axle load of about 12 to 15 tons. When travelling in train formation, stops on the carriage were raised to engage with the superstructure or chains attached to prevent it swinging out of alignment during the journey. The jib was either secured on a support at the front edge of the carriage or rested on a support on the match truck, on which it slid laterally while negotiating curves.

The 20-ton and some of the larger 15--ton cranes weighed 50 to 60 tons and therefore required four axles. The usual arrangement was to have the one or two driven axles fixed in the carriage frame, and provided with outside bearings. The other two axles were mounted in a bogie, usually with inside bearings, similar to a locomotive bogie. Alternatively, the two middle axles were fixed in the carriage and a radial axle, with inside bearings, provided at each end. When 35- and 36-ton cranes weighing 65 tons or more were introduced five axles became necessary, usually with three axles fixed in the carriage, while the other two were similarly in a four-wheel bogie at one end or the other, or the radial axle arrangement.

Later 36- to 75-ton cranes had four axles. These were fixed in the carriage, but also had a four-wheeled relieving bogie at each end, so spreading the load over eight axles when travelling. These will be the considered in Volume 2. There was one notable exception, but this made no attempt to achieve a high route availability, instead being mounted on just a pair of 4-wheel bogies.

British crane makers have always also built cranes for overseas, leading in certain respects to alternative features of design. Generally the differences in practice between cranes for the British market and those overseas stem mainly from the more commodious structure gauge to which their lines were constructed and hence loading gauge that could be accommodated and, when rail section and strength of under-line structures permitted, associated with much higher permitted axle load and total weight in train formation.

This book therefore confines itself to those cranes built for British railway companies, together with such other cranes as were stationed, albeit briefly, at sometime in Britain and which could pass the main line companies' loading gauges and weight restrictions. Cranes supplied to Irish railways have been excluded, not least because the track gauge was wider, which has an effect on design, as will be explained.

The arrival of hand powered rail-mounted cranes for use on the railways of Great Britain seems to have gone unannounced however an early example of a Great Northern Railway (GNR) crane of 1855 is preserved by National Railway Museum at York. Steam power was first applied to a Scotch derrick around 1839 to 1842 by James Taylor. It is claimed that a steam driven crane able to hoist, derrick, slew and travel was designed by WW Hulse of Whitworth's staff around 1852 and built in the years following, while Couvreaux's machine of 1855 was probably the first ever rail-mounted steam crane with power operated jib motion. Others, such as Appleby, Taylor and Russell independently developed these ideas into the commercial rail-mounted steam crane, soon to be followed by J Brown & Co, Alexander Chaplin, Cowans Sheldon and Stothert & Pitt.

Cowans Sheldon supplied a batch of 5- and 10-ton steam cranes to the East India Rly in 1866 and a 4-ton one to the North Eastern Railway (NER) in 1872. Alexander Shanks & Son of London were advertising such in *Engineering* in Jan 1866, while six manufacturers, including G Russell & Co of Motherwell, James Taylor & Co of Birkenhead, Shanks and Appleby Bros of London and Leicester exhibited their wares at the Paris Exhibition a year later.

The elements of a sound railway breakdown crane are as follows:

a)   For maximum stability it should possess as much weight as the maximum permitted axle load will allow.

b)   In working order, with its jib at minimum radius at right angles to the track, the centre of gravity of the whole crane transversely must be as far back as is consistent with safety when the crane is un-propped and unloaded. When in travelling order, i.e. with

the jib resting on the match truck ready to travel over the line, in order to keep within the allowable axle loading, the centre of gravity of the whole crane, longitudinally, should ideally coincide with the centre of the wheel-base.

c)   It is preferable to have only two points of propping on each side of the crane.

d)   The axle journals should be of large size, with the bearing surfaces arranged on the outside of the frame.

e)   To relieve the springs of excessive loading during lifting operations and to help stabilise the crane, screws or wedges should be provided over each wheel bearing.

f)   The length of the carriage should be the minimum practicable to enable it to approach as close as possible to the load to be lifted.

g)   Placing the centre of rotation of the superstructure as near the centre of the carriage as practicable will minimise the need for the crane to approach the point of lift from one particular direction.

h)   The fixed wheel-base of the carriage should be as short as possible to enable it to traverse tight curves.

i)   The crane should be designed in such a manner that all stresses are calculable.

j)   The crane should be designed in its details so that on arrival at site of operations it can be quickly set to work and, hence, unless absolutely unavoidable, no removable counter-weights should be employed.

Motions:

a)   Lift/Hoist

b)   Derrick/Luff (not usual on hand cranes)

c)   Slew

d)   Travel (if self-propelled)

Apart from small specialist components, such as in bearings and boiler fittings etc, the majority of the crane was fabricated from ferrous metals. Earlier ones will have employed cast and wrought iron; however as developments in the bulk production of steel occurred, hot rolled and cast steel will have been adopted. Whereas rolled steel sections and plate for structural work is generally recognised as becoming the usual structural material from the 1880s with the completion of the Forth Railway Bridge, the introduction of steel castings was more gradual. This was due to the casting of steel, as opposed to iron, being long fraught with many difficulties, making it very costly, which in turn will initially have limited its use to the critical elements. Nonetheless, steel castings were being made on a fairly large scale by the late 1860s, and were widely adopted by the turn of the 19th/20th century.

Crane Makers

Alexander Chaplin & Co Ltd, Govan. Alexander Chaplin & Co was established in 1849 and the Cranstonhill Engine Works erected in Port Street, Glasgow in 1857 for the manufacture of various items of engineering plant, including marine and railway equipment and the repair of steam boilers. Steam and later electrically powered cranes of various types were made, including steam travelling cranes from about 1860. In 1891 the firm built a new engineering works in Helen Street in Govan. In due course the business was acquired by Herbert Morris, see below. Only one steam railway breakdown crane appears to have been built for a British company, viz: a 20-ton crane for the Taff Vale Railway in 1884.

Appleby Bros. Charles James Appleby was one of the Victorian Engineers now recognised as the pioneers of steam cranes. He was born on 23 February 1828, the son of James Appleby, one of the iron masters at the family owned Renishaw Iron Works of Appleby and Co. Following his training in Renshaw and other engineering establishments in the Manchester area and a spell in Russia, in 1858 Charles started working on his own account from offices in London, when public works contractor's plant, including cranes of various types, and other equipment were produced. In 1862 he was joined by his elder brother, Thomas H Appleby, the company trading from then on as "Appleby Brothers". To develop their range of products, in 1866 they established two works, one in Leicester (The London Steam Crane and Engine Works) and the other in Emerson Street, Southwark, south of the Thames, in London. Joseph Jessop, who had supervised the construction of their new Leicester works, became the resident partner of the Leicester works. The Emerson Street works, which were near to the London offices of the Appleby Brothers, were specifically designed for working on new inventions and on other experimental works, under close supervision, and for conducting a large export trade.

On 30 June 1876, TH Appleby resigned from the partnership, leaving his brother, CJ Appleby, as the sole proprietor of Appleby Brothers. In 1878 CJ Appleby established a new works in East Greenwich, closing the Emerson Street works the following year, and on 3 March 1880 the partnership with Joseph Jessop was dissolved. Joseph Jessop then took over The London Steam Crane and Engine Works in Leicester, and, joined by his son George, established the new and independent firm of Joseph Jessop and Son. Prior to this, during the Appleby partnership, some production from the Leicester works had been carried out in the name of Joseph Jessop.

In 1886 Appleby Brothers became a limited company, CJ Appleby, who had a small share holding in the new limited company, being retained as a consultant. Three years later, however, the limited company failed and was put into liquidation by the High Court, resulting in the closure of the East Greenwich works. Nonetheless, a continuing demand for Appleby Brothers machinery led Charles Appleby to revive the Appleby Brothers partnership, with two of his sons, PV and EG Appleby.

On 21 February 1896 the new Appleby Brothers partnership merged with Joseph Jessop and Son to form Jessop and Appleby Brothers (Leicester and London) Ltd. In 1906 Jessop and Appleby Brothers Ltd in turn combined with the Glasgow Electric Crane and Hoist Co Ltd and traded as Appleby's Ltd. A similar expansion took place the following year (1907) when Appleby's Ltd absorbed The Temperley Transporter Company. Appleby's Ltd only survived until January 1910 when it went into voluntary liquidation. The company was refinanced under the new name, The Appleby Crane and

Transporter Co Ltd and later in the same year this was taken over by Sir William Arrol. After the takeover, the Glasgow Electric Crane and Hoist Co works became Sir William Arrol's new Crane Division and, in 1912, Sir William Arrol sold the old Appleby Brothers works, in Leicester.

Cowans Sheldon & Co. Founded in 1846, this Carlisle based engineering firm established a world leading reputation in the construction of rail and dock cranes. The firm was simply known in the city as *the crane-makers*. Cowans cranes were exported across the globe to countries including Argentina, Australia, Bolivia, Canada, China, Egypt, India, Iraq, Japan, Nigeria, South Africa and Russia. Generations of young men from the city took up engineering apprenticeships at the Cowans Sheldon.

In 1857 Cowans Sheldon moved from Woodbank, Upperby to the St Nicholas site on London Road that had once been the St Nicholas Leper Hospital. By the following year the first railway crane had been produced and was used by the Carlisle & Maryport Railway. During the two World Wars the company boomed due to the high demands placed upon heavy engineering for both the war effort and home front.

In 1969 Clarke Chapman of Gateshead bought the firm, thus returning to the Geordie roots of its four founders who had moved west to Cumbria. Following a merger in 1982 with John Boyd the firm was renamed Cowans Boyd. The omens for the firm, however, were not good due to the decline of Britain's heavy industries. Many British manufacturers and engineers disappeared during this period, Cowans Boyd following and in 1987 the St Nicholas works closed. Thereafter, work was transferred to Saltmeadows Road, Gateshead.

The builder's plates for the 15-ton cranes supplied to the Caledonian Railway in 1886 were oval in shape, the larger attached to the frame of the carriage on both sides and another smaller set on each side of the crab. Thereafter a more elaborate shape was adopted, but again of two sizes at similar locations. The larger plates, again on both sides of the carriage were in cast iron about half an inch thick and 2ft 4in long by $10^5/_8$ inch tall with elaborately shaped edges, as shown.

The works plate from Works No.2545 from the 20-ton crane supplied to the Lancashire & Yorkshire Railway in 1902. (Author)

Along the top edge was **COWANS SHELDON & Cᵒ Lᴰ**. Beneath came the Works number preceded by: **Nᵒ**. In the centre was **NOT TO EXCEED** load (**20**) **TONS**, below which the maximum load of the crane was inserted. Finally across the bottom was: **CARLISLE** and the year of construction. In addition some cranes also had a similar styled smaller plate mounted on one or both of the crab sides, reading **COWANS SHELDON Co/LIMITED/ ENGINEERS/CARLISLE/**date (**1893**).

From 1921 the arrangement of the text on the same outline of plate was changed to a simpler three line entry. The company name **COWANS SHELDON & Cº Lᵀᴰ** was still across the top, but the middle line now read: Works number, **ENGINEERS** and the year of construction with just **CARLISLE** across the bottom. The capacity of the crane at various radii and conditions were tabulated on a duty plate attached to the cab-side, crab, or frame. The final form of builder's plate will be discussed in Volume 2.

The revised arrangement of works plate thought to have been introduced with Works No.4193 of 1922, a 36-ton crane for the LSWR. (Author)

Craven Bros. Cravens of Vauxhall Works in Salford, was established in 1853 by the brothers William and John Craven, four years later establishing their works near to Osborne Street and developed a reputation as makers of high quality heavy-duty cranes for industry and railways. In 1900 it became necessary to expand into additional premises in Reddish, from where it became known for electrically powered travelling gantry cranes etc. Difficult trading led to the closure of the Osborne Street premises in 1920. In 1928 the business was divided with the crane division being sold to Herbert Morris of Loughborough, the work being transferred to Loughborough in 1931. The machine tool division at Reddish remained in business until 1966. Nonetheless, with the transfer of the crane division, the firm's long established and high reputation continued under Herbert Morris, trading as: Cravens Bros Cranes Division Ltd.

Craven Bros works plate from one of the two 20-ton steam cranes supplied to the Caledonian Railway in 1907. (Author)

Dunlop & Bell. Dunlop & Bell Co Ltd of Liverpool were marine engineers, producing engines and steam winches for ships and colliery winding engines. They were one of the major engineering employers on Merseyside, but the depression that swept Britain from the early 1920s hit their business hard, finally closing in 1932. Like Chaplin's only one railway breakdown crane appears to have been

built for a British company, viz: a 15-ton one for the LSWR in 1885.

Forrest & Co. Forrest & Co, Port Dundas, Glasgow, formerly Forrest & Barr of Canal Street Engineering Works, Glasgow, engaged in general engineering including the construction of some locomotives. The future locomotive engineers, the brothers Dugald and Peter Drummond served their apprenticeships with them. It was Dugald who some twenty years later, having risen to be Locomotive Superintendent of the North British Railway, placed an order for a 20-ton steam breakdown crane. No other breakdown cranes were supplied to British railway companies, but Forrest did build a 5-ton crane for use at Oban Pier and a 2½-ton crane for Kyle of Lochalsh.

Herbert Morris. An enterprising salesman, Herbert Morris (1864-1931) rose from being a salesman of pulley-blocks in London, in 1889 acquiring an interest in the Sheffield company of Shardlows which manufactured lifting gear. In partnership with Frank Bastert, a German engineer, he rapidly expanded the business, trading as the Sheffield Crane Works. To provide room for expansion and with the benefit of good transport links in the Midlands, a move of the factory to Loughborough was commenced in 1897 with the construction of the Empress Works, from where a range of cranes, hoists and winches were produced. In 1920, the company expanded further with the construction of the North Works besides the old Coltman factory. During the early 1930's the company took over several rival businesses, including: Alexander Chaplin and Co. Ltd; Craven Bros (Manchester) Ltd; Vaughan Crane Co of Manchester; Royce Ltd of Trafford Park; and Holt and Willets of Cradley Heath. The business became a public limited company in 1939 and is still in business as Morris Material Handling.

Jessop & Appleby. See Appleby Bros above.

Ransomes & Rapier. Robert Ransome, a Quaker ironmonger in Norwich moved to Ipswich in 1789 to make plough shares and cast iron bridges. In due course the firm became Ransomes, Sims & Jefferies. In 1846 it transferred to Orwell Works to produce railway materials, agricultural machinery, traction engines, thrashing machines and steam ploughs. The railway equipment business grew to such an extent that the firm split with the railway work taken up by Ransomes & Rapier which moved in 1869 to Waterside Works, a rail and water connected 13 acre site. Even then, a year previous, consideration was being given to the need for cranes that could travel at main line speeds to the scene of an accident or derailment and promptly clear the line. This had led the company to establish a reputation for the reliable cranes it had supplied to numerous railways throughout the World. As well as producing rail-mounted cranes, the company made overhead gantry cranes, turntables, traversers, hydraulic buffer stops, capstans, permanent way components, pumps, special wagons, drag lines and later road mobile and lorry cranes.

During the First World War it produced shells, guns and tank turrets. In later years the company's name was sometimes abbreviated to Rapier and applied such at the jib head. The company merged with Newton, Chambers & Company of Sheffield and the NCK excavator division to form NCK-Rapier in 1958. Ransomes and Rapier closed in 1987.

Ransomes & Rapier works plate for the Great Western Railway's 36-ton crane of 1908. (R Cooke)

Thomas Smith & Sons (Rodley) Ltd. Smith, Balmforth & Booth first built hand cranes in 1840 for a variety of applications such as in quarries, and later at wharfs on nearby canals. Around 1847 Booth left the partnership, setting up in premises next door, trading as Joseph Booth & Bros. In 1861, the sons of Smith and Balmforth went their separate ways, when the former bought out the latter and thereafter traded as Thomas Smith & Sons (Rodley) Ltd, at Old Foundry, Rodley, near Leeds.

At this time Booth announced a comprehensive range of steam and hand operated cranes, becoming popular with public works contractors. It produced its first steam excavator by attaching a shovel to a 3-ton crane in 1887. Incorporated in 1918, the firm was able to adapt to the introduction of the internal combustion engine, but suffered commercially during the Depression of the 1930s. Eventually it was forced to join up with Clyde Crane & Engineering to become Clyde Crane & Booth Ltd.

After World War 2 there were a number of amalgamations in the crane business, which came to a head in the late 1960s when Clarke Chapman took over several companies. Cowans Sheldon had already merged with Clyde Crane & Booth and Leeds Engineering and Hydraulics when it in turn was absorbed by the Clarke Chapman Crane and Bridge Division. In the meantime Smiths had been acquired by Thomas Ward in 1939 and the full circle was completed early in 1978 when Thomas Smith & Sons (Rodley) Ltd was acquired by Clarke Chapman.

Stothert & Pitt Ltd. The engineering company of Stothert & Pitt was founded by George Stothert in 1785 in Bath, where it built a variety of engineering products ranging from dock cranes to construction plant and household cast iron items. By 1815 an iron foundry had been set up, the company by now being managed by the founder's son, also George. Robert Pitt joined the company in 1844 as a consequence of which the firm became Stothert and Pitt. In 1851 it exhibited a hand crane at the Great Exhibition. The firm became a limited company early in the 20th century, when it began building electric cranes, self luffing dockside cranes and rail cranes for export to the colonies.

During World War 2 it designed and built tanks and miniature submarines for the War Office, as well as armaments. The firm was sold to the Hollis Group in 1986 and, following the collapse of Maxwell's empire, a management buy out was undertaken in 1988. Unfortunately, this failed and the company closed down

and within a year all manufacture ceased, the name and intellectual property rights only going to Clarke Chapman.

JH Wilson & Co Ltd. John H Wilson & Co Ltd, of Sandhills, Liverpool from about 1860 and from 1900 at Dock Road, Seacombe, Birkenhead, was an iron-foundry and engineering business producing machinery for the shipping industry and contractors' plant, including steam cranes and grabs. On the railway by the beginning of the 20th century it was developing a line of permanent way cranes, one of which appears to have been designated for breakdown work by the GW despite being of only 12 tons capacity. About 1935, however, the Dock Road works was taken over by Manganese Bronze & Brass Co.

Crane Carriage

The crane's carriage was a strongly built structure fabricated from rolled steel sections and plates upon which the rotating superstructure was mounted, while beneath it provided the guides within which the axle-boxes slid, or to which the bogie or radial axles were attached. Between these were either, in early days, two or three sets of stirrups within which to slide the propping beams, or later the transverse fabricated boxes within which the telescopic propping girders were temporarily or permanently placed.

These girders could be drawn out either by hand, or, in the later type of cranes, by a suitable ratchet mechanism, to provide a much improved propping base and to prevent the crane overturning when lifting a heavy load sideways to the track, but only while the crane was stationary. An enhancement was the fitting of a jack on the end of each girder which could be screwed down on to packing to speed the process and improve the security of support. It is a matter of debate as to whether a third set of propping girders warranted the extra cost, as the opinion has it that the girder nearest the load took the majority of the load anyway.

Rail clips were provided on the buffer beams of the crane, which could be clipped to the head of the rail and tightened up to improve the crane's stability. Below the carriage on self-propelled cranes there was a train of gears, together with clutches to enable this to be engaged or disengaged by means of hand-wheels on the side of the carriage frame from the gears keyed to one or two of the axles.

Brakes, operated by a hand-wheel on each side of the carriage, were provided. Vacuum brakes, although seldom fitted, were desirable in case it was necessary to propel the crane to the scene of the accident, and should this be on a falling gradient and a coupling broke it could result in the crane running away with serious consequences. Nonetheless, cranes were frequently equipped with through vacuum brake pipes.

Buffers and draw gear, often provided by the purchasing company, were fitted to the headstocks at each end of the crane or relieving bogie. Of necessity these were usually self-contained because the space behind was often occupied by components of the crane's machinery, which would have precluded through draw gear and the buffer projecting behind the end plates of the headstock. It was with time realized that buffers mounted on hinges enabled these to be folded back sideways to improve the portée in critical situations when space was tight.

Crane Superstructure

The crab sides of the superstructure on smaller cranes consisted initially of cast iron. Soon, however, these were replaced by two steel plates, usually at 5 foot centres, with angles riveted to the edges to stiffen them, while double plates each side were more usual on the larger cranes. Bearings to carry the various shafts were bolted to the crab frame plates which were extended backwards to carry the boiler while the forward cheeks supported the foot of the jib. Alongside the boiler a coal bunker over a water tank was usually fitted to the left (when looking forward) and a taller water tank to the right, while heavy cast balance weights were fitted either below or behind the boiler.

The crab frame plates were attached to a cast iron or steel, or fabricated bedplate. Earlier cranes had a central pillar fixed to the carriage and passing up through the superstructure with the load being taken through a small number of rollers. In this case the bedplate was supported and rotated on rollers bearing on a roller path on top of the crane carriage. The pillar design, however, was improved upon by the incorporation of the live-roller slewing ring, based on swing-bridge practice, only taking off as capacity significantly exceeded 15 tons. In this solution, numerous tapered rollers between upper and lower roller paths took both the direct compressive forces of the vertical load plus the downward component induced by the moment couple, the uplift being resisted by tension in the short king pin in the centre, instead of the bending in the tall central pillar.

Wheel arrangements

For the purpose of this book, the well-known Whyte's notation for describing locomotive wheel arrangements has been adopted for the crane, assuming jib leading, to distinguish rigid axles from those with some lateral flexibility by means of a bogie, pony truck or radial axle. The outer digits represent wheels with some capability to articulate on rounding curves, while the middle digit represents the wheels on rigid axles, which may or may not be powered. A simple 4-wheel crane will, therefore, appear as a 0-4-0, while a third axle extends to 0-6-0 etc. A common arrangement of bogie at the front thus becomes a 4-4-0 and later 4-6-0, or at the rear 0-4-4 and 0-6-4, while pony trucks at the front and rear is rendered as 2-4-2, or 2-6-2 etc. As jib lengths increased, however, the

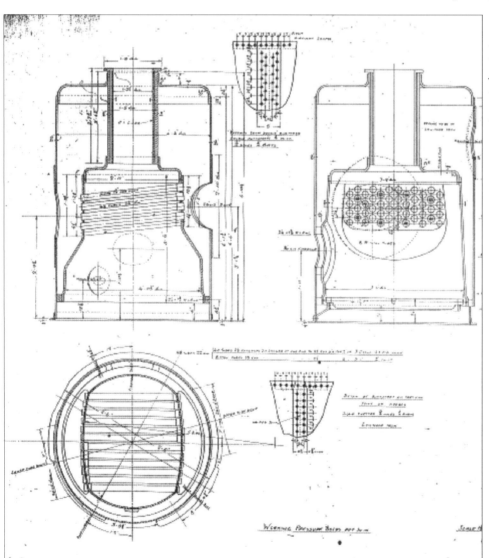

Figure 2 - *Spencer-Hopwood coal-fired vertical boiler as fitted to the LSWR's 36-ton Ransomes & Rapier crane of 1919. (Ransomes & Rapier, courtesy Roger Cooke)*

bogie at the rear afforded a smoother passage. Relieving bogies, which will be explored in Volume 2, are indicated by the addition of RB, thus 4-8-4RB.

Boilers

The limited space available on a rail-mounted crane for raising steam rather constrains the form of boiler to be adopted. Although Cowans Sheldon and Ransomes and Rapier are known to have fitted a small horizontal boiler typical of a locomotive to their earliest cranes, the vertical cylindrical type, often referred to as a donkey boiler because of its association with secondary purposes on ships, soon became the norm. Demand for steam on breakdown cranes is intermittent, so it was necessary to provide a boiler with the ability to raise steam at short notice to satisfy the demands of the engines running at full throttle and speed. Having arrived at the site in the train formation hauled by a locomotive, the most onerous demand was raising the jib from its rest on the match wagon, to its working position at short radius. While on site propelling itself any significant distance could also create a heavy demand on the boiler.

Various versions of patent boiler have been tried, but in the end the squat Spencer-Hopwood type became standard, in the British context usually up to 4ft 6in diameter and about 6ft 6in tall, or more depending on loading gauge limitations. Coal firing was universal on British main lines, with just one exception of a crane returned from overseas following military duty. Over the years, boiler pressures rose from 60 to 150 lb/sq. in.

A removable extension chimney, to carry the products of combustion clear and help the fire draw when in operation, extending above the gauge line was usually provided, but frequently soon discarded. A few cranes were fitted with chimney raising and lowering gear, but this too was sometimes removed, either because it was over-complex or because it projected beyond the minimum tail

Top - The outer shell of a Spencer-Hopwood boiler from Ransomes & Rapier 45-ton crane of 1940 raised above the inner, while undergoing restoration on the East Somerset Railway in 2011. Note the holes for the cross tubes to the middle left and man-hole on the lower right. The flue rises from the crown. (Roger Cooke)

Left - Rear view of a Cowans Sheldon 36-ton crane showing its boiler undergoing a washout. The chimney was still in situ, albeit in the lowered position, while the two access holes to the tubes and crown are apparent. (Author)
Top - A closer view of the water tubes across the furnace. On the left hand side the cast iron counterbalance weight rather constrains access for maintenance. (Author)

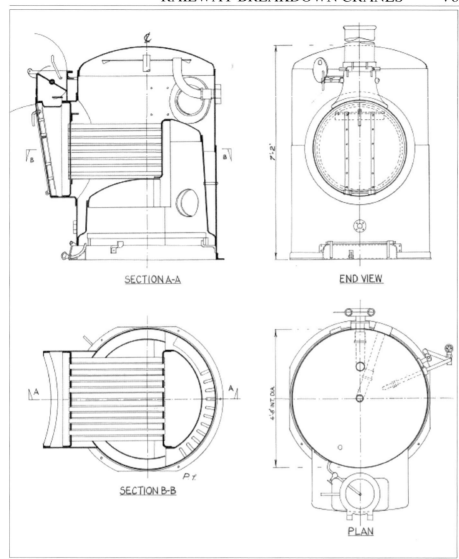

SECTION A-A

END VIEW

SECTION B-B

PLAN

Figure 3 - Turner boiler. (Author)

radius and in certain situations the additional space occupied might have been critical.

Cochran & Co. Cochran & Co was established in 1878 at premises in Duke Street, Birkenhead as a general engineering and ship building works. A partner in the firm, Edward Compton devised an efficient vertical cylindrical boiler with a domed water space above the fire grate, intended principally for secondary duties on ships. A flue to one side led to one end of a series of horizontal smoke tubes between vertical plates after which flue gases were conducted out through the side of the boiler to a smokebox and vertical chimney. Doors in line with each end of the tubes gave access for maintenance. Such was the popularity of the Cochran boiler that within three years four other firms were licensed to produce these, including Ransomes, Head & Jeffries of Ipswich. Despite this, later, they were producing what was termed a Cochran-Hopwood boiler for such work, see below. With the expansion of the business generally, but especially in boilers, a fresh site had to be found, resulting in move in 1898 to Newbie Works on the banks of the River Annan on the Solway Firth, near to the town of Annan.

In time the nature of the work moved towards boilers and pressure vessels. In 1968, the company was taken over by John Thompson of Glasgow and traded as the John Thompson Cochran Group, in turn taken over by Clarke Chapman Ltd, from which the Northern Engineering Industries Ltd (NEI) was created in 1977. In December 1996, Cochran was established as a separate limited company, operating as a business unit of Rolls-Royce Nuclear Engineering Limited. Cochran became known as Cochran Boilers Limited. The firm is still in existence, albeit now a subsidiary of boiler maker Shanghai Huanuan Boiler Vessel of Hong Kong.

A close-up of Cowans Sheldon 15-ton crane showing the inclined cylinders and disc crank wheel on LMS No.RS1021/15 in BR days, together with the canopy, steam turbo-generator set mounted on the crab side and vacuum brake pipe added. (JS Brownlie, courtesy C Capewell)

Spencer-Hopwood. WH Spencer & Co of Hitchin and successor Spencer-Hopwood produced a squat version of its patented Spencer-Hopwood boiler for use on breakdown cranes where the height of the loading gauge, at least in Britain, precluded taller boilers. This was a vertical cylindrical boiler with an internal water jacket. To improve water circulation, there was directly above the fire grate a nest of marginally inclined small diameter transverse water tubes between slightly curved tube plates. In the outer shell, in line with the tubes were oval shaped pressed steel doors on both sides affording ample space for cleaning the whole interior of the boiler. As well as being able to clean the tubes, it was possible to renew the plain ones if not the stay tubes. The slope of the tubes and wide water spaces at their ends ensured the rapid circulation without the risk of over-heating or priming, it being claimed that steam could be raised from cold in about 35 minutes without fear of damaging the boiler. Spencer-Hopwood Ltd was taken over first in 1929 by Sir WG Armstrong & Co Ltd of Scotswood Works. In 1937 it was then sold on to Robert Stephenson and Hawthorns Leslie Ltd, who produced the boilers first at their Darlington works and then from 1946 at their Forth Bank, Newcastle-on-Tyne, works. Other companies also recognised the advantages of this design and produced similar boilers.

ER & F Turner. ER & F Turner, general engineers of Greyfriars Works, Ipswich, manufactured multi-tubular type boilers which were unusual in that, although vertical boilers, they featured a very shallow locomotive-style smokebox that projected backwards through the rear of the crane's canopy and upon which was mounted the chimney. Inside, the space above the fire grate was extended at the front end to provide the inside tube plate from which a substantial number of smoke tubes passed through the water to reach the smokebox at the rear. A door in the smoke box afforded facility for cleaning the tubes in the usual way. This type of boiler is known to have been fitted to two 36-ton Ransomes & Rapier cranes for the GWR in 1908 and 1912 and another for the LNWR in 1909. Although boiler manufacture ceased upon the outbreak of the World War 1, the firm is still in business as Christie & Turner to produce a wide range of machinery and plant, used in the processing of human foods, animal feed, biomass, waste recycling, minerals, chemicals and pharmaceuticals.

Nicholson Boiler. The Nicholson Patent multi-tubular boiler with a side-mounted smokebox attached to one side with a chimney on top was fitted to a pair of 15-ton cranes supplied to the Great Northern Railway in 1892. Little more is known about its design. In view of the disparity in dates, it seems improbable that the patentee is the same John L Nicholson of USA, who in July 1928 took out a patent for the thermic siphons, as fitted to Bulleid locomotives in the 1940s. It is thought that the Nicholson boiler would have been of similar construction to the Turner boiler, which itself was similar to the original Cochran boiler of the time (which is not to be confused with the later Cochran-Hopwood boiler which is quite different).

Engines & Machinery

The steam from the boiler was conducted via a regulator to the steam chest and usually slide valves mounted inside the crab sides. These, frequently of the link motion type, admitted steam to a pair of either inclined or horizontal double-acting cylinders more often than not situated one on each side outside of the superstructure side frames. Steam chests and valve gear outside the crab sides were only occasionally applied in later years. When it was, the trunk guides to the cross-head were usually replaced by single slide-bars and Walschaerts valve gear could be employed. Exhaust steam was led back to the chimney directly above the boiler without the benefit of a blast pipe to enhance the combustion of the fuel in the firebox. The cylinders drove disc cranks and a transverse shaft from which gear wheels actuated the various motions.

The speeds of motions achieved by the engines, where known, are tabulated in Appendix 2.

Jibs and Lifting Tackle

The jibs of breakdown cranes tended to follow a particular form. Rather than the simple straight strut type jibs, to contain the overall length and in turn the length of match wagon to act as an under-runner, and yet still to be able to reach out over the load and/or debris, the jib was usually turned over at the end in one way or another. The short jibs on the early cranes of up to 15 tons were often of double lattice construction throughout. 15- and 25-ton cranes were usually fairly short, about 22 to 26 feet from the foot to the jib head pulley, and were often box girders built up from steel plates, albeit sometimes with lightening holes. Early jibs were usually slightly curved towards the outer end with a straight length down to the foot. Shortly before the turn of the century the swan-necked jib tended to replace the curved one.

Later larger cranes and longer tapered jibs, now invariably of the swan-necked style, required greater attention being paid to efficient design in order to achieve lightness and adequate strength. On the 35- to 45-ton cranes, vertical plate sides braced together with transverse flats, angles or tees were usual. Nonetheless, some makers continued to adopt built-up jibs fabricated entirely from angles and tees with plating and reinforcement only at points of concentration of load, at the jib head and foot. It was usual to attach a wearing plate on the underside of the jib in the region where it was likely to bear on the jib support of the match wagon. This meant that any chafing between the two was not impairing the structural integrity of the lower flange of the jib.

On early cranes the derricking tackle passed round a pulley towards the outside of the top of the jib, or even fitted in between the side plates. As the length of jibs increased, to reduce the weight of chain, bridles were introduced first at the lower end of the derricking tackle. Later, the fixing was moved above the top of the jib structure and on long jibs bridle rods fitted at the top as well, see page 125(GW R&R 36T). Provision needed to be made in the design of the crane to accommodate the bridle gear and for its supports while the crane had its jib lowered.

The purpose of a jib is, of course, to support the lifting hook and to this end one or more pulleys for either chain or steel wire rope lifting tackle would be accommodated at the jib head, often together with a securing point for the dead end of the chain or rope. Sometimes a further pulley was required to redirect the hoisting chain or rope when a straight run down to the winding drum was not possible.

All early cranes were fitted with chain for hoisting and derricking. As capacity exceeded 20 tons and developments in the production of steel wire rope became available, this superseded chain as being more flexible and lighter. Rope is more compact, therefore taking up less space on the pulleys and winding drums, without which higher capacity and long jib cranes would have been impractical.

From the jib head the hoisting chain or rope fell to a hook, usually passing round one or more sheaves in a block from which was hung a hook. For smaller and earlier cranes this would be of the single form of hook, while larger cranes usually had a double sided hook, known as a rams-horn frequently with a single hole through the root of the stem through which the pin of a shackle or lifting beam could be passed. The stem of the hook was suspended from the block usually with a ball-race to enable it to rotate freely relative to the pulley(s). The size of chains precluded more than one pulley, whereas steel wire ropes often passed round two or three. To improve the maximum height of lift two pulleys could be spaced out laterally, thereby permitting the support to the hook to be raised between them.

Whether in chain or steel wire rope, the arrangement of both derricking and hoisting tackle was described in terms of the number of "parts", i.e. the number turns of chain or rope, and the number of these "winding", i.e. the number of chains or ropes which were attached to the derricking or winding barrel and hence acted upon when that motion was engaged. With chain the number of parts seldom exceeded two, with only one winding. Rope, on the other hand, could go up to twelve parts, still with only one winding, although two were often winding and in one instance three were winding.

Match Wagons

Very often the company purchasing new and expensive cranes was tempted to economise by pairing the crane up with a second-hand vehicle, usually retired from revenue-earning service, to act as a match wagon. As the crane was frequently long-lived, it was not unusual for a replacement to be found during the crane's life.

At first it was not unusual for the match wagon to merely act as a guard truck under, but not supporting the jib projecting from the crane while in train formation. Later of course it also acted to support the jib towards its outer end and thereby relieve a small part of the load of the crane. It is important to support the jib as high as the loading gauge will permit, because the lower the jib when at rest, the greater the force needed initially to raise it to the working position and therefore the hardest work for the derricking gear to set in motion.

The inclusion of the match wagon, whether supporting the jib or not, meant that it was an ideal vehicle upon which to load up the numerous bits of equipment inevitably associated with breakdown work. The most obvious items were propping girders and counter weights

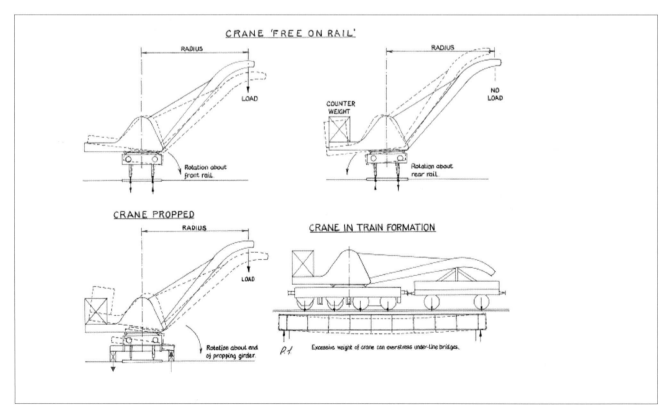

Figure 4 - Stability of rail-mounted cranes. (Author)

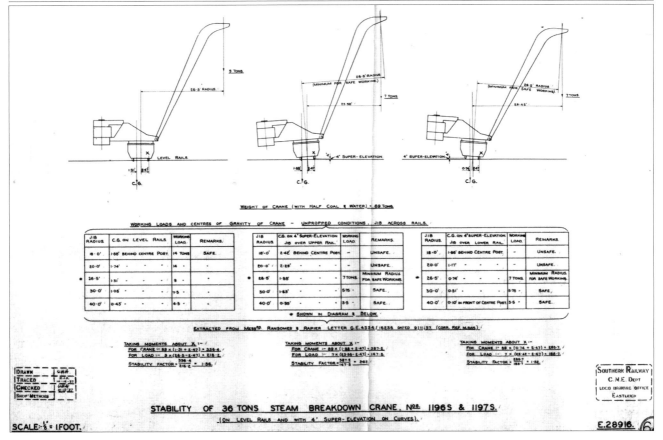

Figure 5 - *An official SR drawing showing the effect of super-elevation of the track on the safe lifting capacity of a 36-ton crane. (SR, author's collection)*

were placed there by design to reduce the axle loads of the crane. Other equipment included timber packing for positioning under the ends of the propping girders, lighting equipment and various slings, shackles and hooks for special purposes, etc.

The lateral and longitudinal movement of the jib relative to the match wagon as it and the crane traversed a curve of any magnitude or the shocks to be absorbed by the buffers called for careful consideration. On short jib cranes little problem arose if the crane's superstructure was locked to the carriage while it was in train formation, even if supported by the jib rest on the wagon: allowing the jib to slide across the top surface usually sufficed. As the length of jibs increased, however, the lateral displacement of the jib relative to the match wagon could become a problem. A partial solution was to allow a small degree of movement of the crane's tail, sometimes spring controlled, which due to its relatively short length to that of the jib had a proportional beneficial effect at the tip of the jib. To this end, some companies provided jib rests with one or two transverse rollers mounted in a small wheeled cradle which was free to move laterally across the jib rest, subject to a small degree of spring control in some cases. An even better, more modern, solution of articulating the jib foot will be discussed in Volume 2.

Stability

The ability of a crane to lift a load without toppling over is a function of the overturning moment induced by the load and the restoring moment of the crane, considered about the point at which the crane is likely to tip, known as the fulcrum. The overturning moment consists of the load multiplied by the horizontal distance from the point at which the load is being lifted to the fulcrum, while the restoring moment is made up of the self weight of the crane multiplied by the distance from the crane's centre of gravity to the fulcrum. The sum of the moments of the load and all the individual components of the crane, including with and without water and coal, are taken about the fulcrum. The fulcrum is either at the centre of the rail head nearest the load, when working 'free on rail', or at the tip or centre of the jack, if fitted, at the end of the propping girder, when blocked up. Not only must the crane be stable when lifting a load, whether propped or not, but it also has to be stable in the reverse direction unloaded when 'free on rail'. The moment applied by the load, or lack of it, has the effect of displacing the centre of gravity of the crane and to be safe the resultant force must remain within the propping base, whether the centre of the rail, or at the end of the propping girder, plus a small safety allowance.

When the crane arrives on site it will be standing on its wheels in a condition known as "free on rail". As such its ability to lift a load is severely restricted, particularly at right angles to the rails, by the short distance between its lines of support, i.e. the width between the rails. On British standard gauge, as all the cranes considered by this book, 4ft 8½in plus the width across the rail head, normally about 2¾ inches, giving a total of just less than 5 feet. Matters can be improved by adding a counter-balance to the tail of the crane. There is a limit, however, as to how much counter-balance can be

added due to the tendency for the crane to tip backwards when there is no load on the crane.

The carriages of all large rail cranes and particularly breakdown cranes are provided either with telescopic propping girders, or vertically -hinged outriggers. While travelling in train formation to and from the scene of operations, these are stowed away within the loading gauge. On site, the lifting capacity of the crane is severely restricted by the possibility of overturning when supported only on its running wheels, but it is able to propel itself, or be hauled by a locomotive at slow speed, with the jib raised and carrying a load. On the other hand, whilst stationary the crane's performance can be significantly improved by drawing out the propping girders, or swinging out the outriggers, and wedging, or jacking, on to a firm support to increase the propping base.

Rail cranes of any size, therefore, are usually fitted with a means of extending the propping base. In Britain, with the exception of the final batch of breakdown cranes supplied for use in this country and which will be considered in Volume 2, all cranes have been provided with propping girders, whereas overseas, hinged outriggers tend to be the norm. Whilst the use of either vastly improves the crane's lifting performance, the crane has to remain stationary until the load is either released or the radius reduced to safe limits, after which the propping girders, or outriggers can be stowed and the crane slowly moved. Two or three pairs of girders are usually provided and should be drawn out and supported on both sides.

Rail clips on the headstocks of the cranes were also provided and these could be clipped over the rail head, when of course they would also help to prevent movement of the crane. They may have been beneficial on earlier smaller cranes, but in the extreme they will merely pull the track out of the ballast and one has to wonder just how much faith should be placed on them with larger cranes. If nothing else, however, their tightening would indicate approaching the limit of stability and they would also act to prevent a crane running away should the brakes fail!

Heavier cranes can, of course, lift heavier loads, but the total weight, maximum axle-loads and size are usually constrained by the line's civil engineer and are dictated by the standard of track, strength of the under-line bridges and clearances to lineside structures. The number

36 TONS STEAM BREAKDOWN CRANES.
Nᵒˢ 1196S & 1197S.

INSTRUCTIONS TO CRANE DRIVERS.

WHEN THIS CRANE IS WORKING ON A STRAIGHT LINE OR ON A CURVE WITH THE PROPPING GIRDERS RUN OUT THEY MUST REST ON SOLID PACKING ADJUSTED TO BRING THE CRANE LEVEL BEFORE LIFTING IS COMMENCED.

WHEN WORKING ON A STRAIGHT LINE OR ON A CURVE WITHOUT THE PROPPING GIRDERS IN USE THE SAFE LOADS WILL BE AS FOLLOWS :—

JIB RADIUS	SAFE LOAD	
	WITH RAILS LEVEL	WITH 4" SUPERELEVATION
18'- 0"	14 TONS	UNSAFE
20'- 0"	14 ,,	UNSAFE
26'- 6"	9 ,,	7 TONS
30'- 0"	7½ ,,	5¾ ,,
40'- 0"	4½ ,,	3½ ,,

WITH A SUPERELEVATION OF 4" THE CRANE JIB MUST NOT WORK AT A LESS RADIUS THAN 26'- 6" WITHOUT LOAD TO AVOID BACKTILTING.

SOUTHERN RAILWAY.
C. M. E. DEPT.
LOCO DRAWING OFFICE
EASTLEIGH

E. 28918.

Opposite page - Man posted to the rear of the crane during a critical lift to warn his supervisor when the wheels start to lift off the rail. *(SC Townroe, author's collection)*

Above, Figure 6 - *The resultant instructions issued to crane drivers. (SR, author's collection)*

of axles can be increased, but this will increase the size of the crane's carriage, which in turn will limit how close a crane can approach the load to be lifted end on, a dimension sometimes known as the 'portée'. The eventual solution for larger cranes was to be the adoption of relieving bogies, attached to each end of the carriage and capable of flexing transversely relative to it when negotiating curves. The bogies helped to spread the load, and could be removed at the site of operations. These, however, will form the basis of most of the cranes to be considered in Volume 2, when the details will be further explored.

The duties of a crane as calculated by the crane manufacturer and shown on the duty plates duly displayed in prominent positions on the crane will include an appropriate stability factor. The lifting performances of cranes, where known, are tabulated in Appendix 3. Super-elevation of the track through curves, sometimes known as cant, has an adverse effect on the crane's stability and therefore needs to be taken into account by reducing the maximum load or, if the load cannot be reduced, temporarily removing the cant.

In the early days crane makers usually only indicated and displayed on any notice plate the maximum load the crane was designed to make when fully propped up and at some, usually unstated, limiting radius, leaving the crane operatives to feel their way on what loads could be safely lifted at greater radii and/or when free on rail. In due course these values were calculated, either by the maker, especially for new cranes, or the owning railway's engineering staff and displayed on new cranes and sometimes on existing ones. More particularly these figures came to be noted on the diagrams for each type of crane. However, not all agreed on these other values, perhaps because the cranes in questions were by then showing signs of their age. Indeed the radius at which the maximum load could be lifted, and even the maximum load, were occasionally marked down.

During actual breakdown work the need to clear the line and reopen it to traffic as soon as practicable often led to the crane supervisor undertaking lifts well beyond the stated capacity of the crane. In doing so he would take many factors into account. He would be aware that the stated capacities include a small safety factor. Furthermore, they will have been calculated for the worst condition, such as at right angles to the track and experience may have indicated that at other positions he might get away with it. But of course in the end the responsibility rested with him. For this reason a wise supervisor would post a man at the rear off-side of the crane from the lift to warn him when all but the last wheel was lifting off the rail, or the loosely-fitted rail clips were tightening. Another common trick was to place the blade of a shovel under the rim of a wheel on the side away from the lift, since the handle could be seen moving long before the wheel could.

In Service Alterations

Over the years most companies carried out many minor alterations and additions to their cranes, some of which were unique to the company concerned, especially the earlier cranes which tended not to include basic creature comforts. With time the provision of some form of shelter from the elements for the driver and his controls became almost universal, as was the removal and discarding of any chimney extension piece.

Automatic vacuum and/or air brake through-pipes were often fitted to the crane and match wagon, together with any attendant packing/tender wagons, to maintain continuity between the locomotive and fully braked vehicles in the rest of the breakdown train, such as tool and mess/riding vans, the latter usually being fitted with a guard's compartment. It was seldom practicable to fit automatic brake gear to the crane itself and even accommodating the pipe retrospectively often meant routing it outside the carriage frame for at least part of the way due to the solid obstruction presented by the base casting within.

In earlier times, the propping girders were often of one through length and when not in use, carried in or under the match wagon. These were heavy and awkward to manhandle and many such cranes were altered to accommodate shorter length beams under the carriage, from where they could be drawn out. Again the plain propping girders were blocked off a pad of baulk timbers by means of folding wedges. As cranes grew in size, screw jacks were fitted at the ends of the propping girders of some cranes from new, whilst others had jacks added retrospectively. Another alteration carried out on a few earlier cranes was the replacement of hoisting and/or derricking chains by steel wire rope. Some cranes were fitted with paraffin, acetylene or electric lighting units to illuminate the work at night. More recently, as a safety precaution, steps were taken to enclose moving parts by fitting guards.

Boilers were in need of regular and expensive maintenance and would frequently be replaced on a crane more than once. This could often result in a change in type and small differences in size, leading inevitably to alterations to the connecting pipe-work and a disruption to any housing or framework in the vicinity. Towards the end of a crane's life, the condemnation of its boiler often led to its withdrawal from service.

Match wagons were not past alterations and additions, frequently as a result of local initiatives. Although some early match wagons were fitted with 3-link couplings, these were usually exchanged for the screw type and not necessarily in connection with provision of through vacuum brake pipe. Many of those early match wagons equipped with grease-lubricated axle-boxes will have had these up-dated to oil boxes. Additional grab handles and steps to assist the gang to access the wagon were often added, particularly in later years. Further tool boxes, hooks upon which to hang lifting hooks, shackles and other impedimenta found their way on the wagon. Later, once steam had been eliminated as regular motive power, water columns were no longer maintained, leading to the need for water tanks to be added, or provided by means of additional vehicles to ensure an adequate supply for the crane's boiler.

Cranes were usually overhauled in the companies' locomotive works. In due course, under BR's stewardship, shops specialising in this type of work were established. Known examples include Derby 1 Shop roundhouse (now a listed building, recently refurbished) and where they were weight tested outside; Ashford (Kent); Swindon; and Doncaster.

Numbering

LMS

The LMS had initially numbered their breakdown cranes in the MP series, although the Northern Division in Scotland also applied a Plant Number. In May 1941, however, the LMS instituted a system-wide comprehensive scheme for all mobile cranes, in which all forms of steam-driven rail-mounted cranes were prefixed 'RS' followed by a four digit number and finally the maximum load capacity. Nonetheless, most cranes seemed to have continued to carry the small cast iron plates bearing their MP number. Match wagons were allocated with own numbers, usually in the departmental lists, although not always displayed on Scottish examples. Upon being separated from its territory south of the border and joined by the ex-LNER network in the north to create the Scottish Region, the LMS system was perpetuated with ex-LNER cranes being renumbered in the ex-LMS system, but without reference to what was going on south of the border. Paradoxically this led to one or two duplications of numbers! Match wagons were merely prefixed DM, or DE for former LNER vehicles.

LNER

Individual areas of the LNER initially followed their own patterns. The NER had numbered their cranes in the CME series and continued to do this on the North-Eastern Area. The Southern Area adopted the SB series for their breakdown cranes, while in Scotland either the 77xxxx, for the Southern Scottish Area, or 88xxxx series for the Northern Scottish Area was used for departmental stock, separate numbers, usually consecutive, being allocated to the crane and match wagon. In 1938, however, the company imposed a new system of six digits on the whole network, commencing with 9 for all departmental stock, whereby the second digit indicated the area to which a vehicle was allocated and for cranes the third was always '1' followed by 5, 6 or 7, viz:

901xxx North-Eastern Area
941xxx Southern Area, ex-Great Northern territory
951xxx Southern Area, ex-Great Central territory
961xxx Southern Area, ex-Great Eastern territory
971xxx Southern Scottish Area, ex-North British territory
981xxx Northern Scottish Area, ex-Great of Scotland territory

Again individual consecutive numbers were given for the crane and match wagon and match wagons prefixed DE after nationalization.

GWR

The GW had, since the first decade of the 20th century, been numbering all their travelling cranes in a sequential series starting with No. 1 for the crane stationed at Old Oak Common. Following grouping they fitted in the cranes inherited from their constituent companies, presumably in the gaps as best they could. This they continued after nationalization merely by adding the prefix DW.

SR

Sometime after grouping in 1923, the SR renumbered all its service stock, including travelling cranes, followed by the suffix S. The series started with ex-LSWR vehicles and continued with the SECR and the LBSC. Match wagons carried the same number as the crane, merely suffixed by the letters SM. A problem, nonetheless, arose with the two 36-ton cranes supplied to the LSWR after World War 1, which had a pair of recovered locomotive tender frames permanently coupled together. In this case one was given the crane number, while the second was given the next number, both suffixed SM. Following nationalization most stock had the suffix replaced by the prefix DS, while from June 1952 the match wagons were accorded their own individual number within the former SR departmental list.

British Railways

At first the regions continued individual policies in numbering new cranes, together with cranes transferred from one region to another. The Western Region maintained its existing scheme, while the Eastern, North Eastern and Southern regions added their new cranes into the BR departmental vehicle series. The London Midland and Scottish regions continued the LMS system of 1941, as discussed above. The Eastern and North-Eastern regions renumbered their cranes in February 1956 with a three digit number allocated according to the section to which each was stationed, although at least one failed to comply, viz:

They then added either DE 330, for those on the Eastern

Region	Section	Numbered from
Eastern	Great Northern	101
	Great Central	121
	Great Eastern	131
North Eastern		151

Region, or DE 331, for the North-Eastern Region, as a prefix to cranes of pre-nationalisation origin from February 1965.

As the users of by far the largest proportion of specialist rail-mounted service vehicles, the Civil Engineering Department introduced in 1974 the Civil Engineering Plant System (CEPS) of numbers. Under this scheme, the first two digits indicate the type of machine, the third the sub-type and the fourth the maker. As far as cranes are concerned, the first letter 'A' indicated that they were owned by the Director of Mechanical & Electrical Engineer, rather than the Regional Civil Engineer, DR showed that they were reportable under TOPS. Makers were accorded: C – Cowans Sheldon; R – Ransomes and Rapier; and V – Cravens Bros. Those steam driven cranes were numbered in 95xxx series and diesel 96xxx.

Liveries

Short of finding a written paint specification and before the days of colour photography, it is very difficult to be precise about the liveries carried by cranes. Not much information on the painting styles of cranes has come to hand and, where known, any specific details for individual cranes will be found with the discussion of the particular cranes concerned. It will be noted, however, that, as the cranes were the responsibility of the locomotive department, the liveries applied to cranes not infrequently follow the scheme adopted by the owning company for its locomotives.

Some generalizations, however, may be noted as follows:

British Railways

The first repaint of cranes following nationalization usually found them in black, sometimes lined mixed traffic livery of red and slate grey, to which the two forms of totem might be applied, and lettered in straw and/or white. Jib heads were frequently painted white. Notice and works plates were usually in white with a red background. As in previous times, individual depots were not past adding their own embellishments, such as picking out the cylinder wrappers in green, painting the jib in grey, or whatever.

Instructions were issued for the red livery in July 1959, but cranes probably did not appear in this until the following year. It and the subsequent yellow livery will be considered further in Volume 2.

GWR

GW breakdown cranes are thought to have been painted either black or dark grey, probably similar to its wagon grey, with white lettering. GW cranes were noted for being adorned on the side of the water tanks/coal bunkers with one or more large cast iron notice plates with elaborate instructions on the safe working of the cranes.

LMS

Monochrome photographs suggest that at least some LMS cranes were likely to have been black, but it is equally clear that by the late 1930s and following World War 2 steam breakdown cranes on the Northern Division in Scotland had the crimson lake lined locomotive livery applied with coach insignia. Yet the match wagons may have remained in the goods wagon livery, although slate rather than light to mid grey. There is, however, no evidence to indicate for how long this may have been applied.

LNER

The livery worn by the pre-war LNER cranes is unknown. No evidence has come to hand to indicate that they were ever painted Oxford blue, as applied to Engineer's vehicles. It is more certain that the 45 tonners supplied at the beginning of World War 2 were black with red lining and lettering in white or straw. The maker's name was applied along the jib sides in large cut out aluminium letters.

LSWR / SR

By 1905 the breakdown cranes were being called the 'Red Rover', no doubt because they were rushing over much of the system dealing with incidents, but did it also indicate its colour? Less exotic tones were applied to SR cranes, as a duller Admiralty battleship grey with white lettering.

Midland Railway

From subtle differences in tone apparent in some photographs of MR cranes, it is clear that the side angles or edges of the jib; crab sides; and ends of the carriage were darker than the remainder, while a pale line divides the two. Lining can also be distinguished around the fly wheel and the adjacent circular casting; lower steps to the carriage and the solid W irons to the fixed axles. Bearing in mind the suggestion that crane liveries often follow that of the owning company's locomotives and that this is the Midland Railway, one can speculate this may have been black edging and straw lining to crimson lake.

Use of the Tables

In the **tables** the dates it is thought a crane was allocated to a depot are shown in upright letters where this is known for the start of its spell there. More often a crane has been reported as being at a depot on one or more individual dates and, when more than one, sometimes may be assumed to have resided there in between. Such spot dates are therefore shown in italics. These are offered in the belief that some readers like to know where cranes were based, but the accuracy cannot the guaranteed. It should also be born in mind that from time to time cranes went away to main works for an overhaul, while at other times cranes may make positioning moves on the way to or from planned works such as bridge works, or standing in at an important depot while its crane was away at works.

Often in pre-grouping days the name ascribed to a locomotive shed to which a crane was allocated was somewhat generalized. Following grouping confusion can arise if more than one railway was present in that town or city. Furthermore, over the years, the names of depots sometimes changed. The names used in the tables have been adopted in an attempt to avoid such misunderstanding even if such a title had not been adopted until a later date. For instance, the Midland Railway's depot in Carlisle has been referred to as Durran Hill to avoid any confusion with the LNWR's Upperby, or the Caledonian's shed at Kingmoor.

It should further be noted that the GW kept a number of breakdown and other cranes under the control of the Locomotive Engineer, later M&EE, Department at Swindon, although when the occasion demanded they seem to have been made available for breakdown work. The Midland and NER on the other hand also had breakdown cranes at Derby and Darlington which seem not to have ventured forth on the main line.

1. Early days

Appleby 5-ton cranes for Midland Railway / Appleby 10-ton cranes for LSWR /
Forrest 20-ton crane for North British Rly /
Chaplin 20-ton crane for Taff Vale Rly / Dunlop & Bell 15-ton crane for LSWR /
Smith (Rodley) 15-ton cranes for GNR

Appleby 5-ton Cranes
for Midland Railway

The Midland Railway acquired four or five 5-ton two axle steam cranes from Appleby Bros of London and Leicester around 1875 of a type advertised at the time as 'permanent way or accident cranes'. Unlike perhaps some of their contemporary ilk, these were mounted on wrought-iron carriage with full running gear of sprung suspension, buffers, hand brake and draw gear to permit their running in a train on the main line. Many of the design features to become usual practice on all subsequent breakdown cranes were already apparent, such as the centrally mounted machinery with a pair of inclined cylinders driving a cross shaft from which gearing drove the various motions, including travelling under its own power; a boiler, with coal supply alongside, at the rear acting as a counter-weight; a curved jib; double fall hoisting chain; and a rams-horn hook; and rail clips.

Four speeds of hoisting were claimed, presumably by two trains of gears and a double purchase block, whilst lowering a load could be achieved by either the operation of the brake or driving it down with the engines in reverse. A worm drive was adopted for the derricking motion. Slewing was achieved, if necessarily simultaneously with other motions, by double friction clutches leading to a single wide roller under the jib foot, rather than a spur gear. The drive for the travelling motion was by means of a shaft passing down the centre of the king post, by bevel gears to a cross-shaft and sprocket wheels and chain to the rear axle, but which was capable of being disengaged while in train formation.

No information on their allocation has come to light, nonetheless, their number would suggest a fairly

One of four or five 5 tons capacity steam cranes supplied by Appleby Bros to the Midland Railway in 1874 or 1875. Many of the features to become standard on breakdown cranes in the future are already apparent, such as the boiler, water tanks and coal bunker at the rear; double cylinders driving a transverse shaft; worm-driven derricking gear; self-propelling gear; rail clips; tail lock; and rams-horn hook. (John Steeds collection)

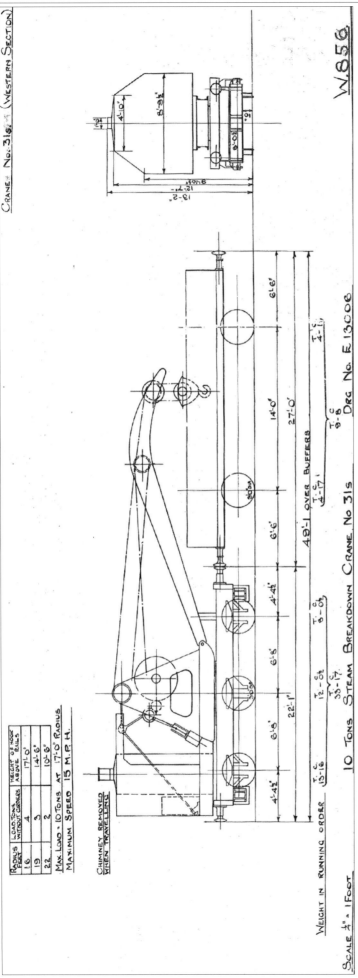

CRANE+ No. 31s•+ (WESTERN SECTION)

W.856

10 Tons Steam Breakdown Crane No 31s   Drg No. E.13006

WEIGHT IN RUNNING ORDER   33-17.

SCALE 4" = 1 FOOT

RADIUS FEET	LOAD TONS. WITHOUT OUTRIGGERS	HEIGHT OF HOOK ABOVE RAILS
16	4	17'-0"
19	3	14'-6"
22	2	10'-6"

MAX. LOAD = 10 TONS AT 17'-0" RADIUS

MAXIMUM SPEED 15 M.P.H.

CHIMNEY REMOVED WHEN TRAVELLING.

wide distribution to a prepared plan, as will become apparent in subsequent acquisitions. They are presumed to have been withdrawn prior to grouping. In March 1869 the Midland Railway kept breakdown vans at Derby, Birmingham, Bromsgrove, Gloucester, Leicester, Kentish Town, Peterborough, Nottingham, Sheffield and Leeds. From this, one may presume that some of the more important locations may have included a steam crane. In 1952 Colonel Harold Rudgard recollected using a 5-ton crane in his youth to re-rail a Matthew Kirtley double-framed locomotive, but whether this was one of the Appleby cranes is uncertain.

Appleby 10-ton Cranes
for LSWR

The Midland Railway cranes were followed in 1875 and 1880 by a pair of 10-ton three axle cranes from Appleby for the LSWR, weighing 33 tons 17 cwt and with a maximum axle load of 13 ton 16 cwt at a cost respectively of £805 and £995 each. These likewise had fully latticed curved jibs supported on a superstructure formed of cast iron 'A' frame crab sides, behind which was a slim boiler and transverse water tank. Propping girders were provided at each end of the carriage, while at the front there was a support for the jib, such that, when in train formation, rather than resting the jib on the match wagon, the latter merely acted as a guard truck.

Although by 1896 the two cranes were stationed at Northam (Southampton) and Exmouth Jct, the former is previously likely to have been at Nine Elms until the arrival of its replacement in 1886. Both attended the Salisbury accident in July 1906, No. 3 still lettered 'Northam', despite presumably having been transferred to the new shed at Eastleigh three and a half years previously. Subsequently, as further new cranes were acquired, the earlier ones gravitated to less important depots. It is understood that No. 2's jib collapsed in Guildford yard while trying to lift an Eastern Section C class 0-6-0 weighing 43 tons 16cwt. Even one end would be nearly 22 tons!

Appleby Bros 10-Ton Cranes for LSWR		
Date deliv'd	1875	1880
Cost	£805	£995
LSWR No.	3, later 4	2
SR No.	33S	31S
Match wagon Nos:		
LSWR	63S	8809
SR	33SM	31SM
Allocation	Northam '96, Eastleigh 1/03, Salisbury *1/1/11*, Strawberry Hill *25/7/21*, Bournemouth '22-'23, Ashford (K) 1/12/24	Exmouth Jct '96-'05, Guildford *1/1/11-26/3/34*,
Disposal	Wdn 1925	Wdn 31/11/34

*Top - LSWR's 10-ton Appleby crane
No. 3 from Eastleigh, despite being
still labelled Northam, tackles the
debris following the accident at
Salisbury on 1 July 1905. (W
Vaughan-Jenkins collection,
courtesy Martin Welch)*

*Middle - LSWR's 10-ton Appleby
steam breakdown crane No. 4 has
come to grief on a turnout in the
yard of Strawberry Hill, its home
depot, on 25 June 1921. By this
date the rear end has received a
roof over the boiler.
(HC Casserley)*

*Bottom - On the same occasion, a
view from the jib end also showing
the 4-plank match wagon No. 63S.
Despite what is shown on the
diagram opposite, the jib rest is now
on the match wagon rather than at
the front of the crane carriage.
(HC Casserley)*

*Opposite page, Figure 7 - An
official Southern Railway diagram
for 10-ton Appleby steam
breakdown crane. The match
wagon shown presumably
represents No. 4's illustrated below.
(Author's collection)*

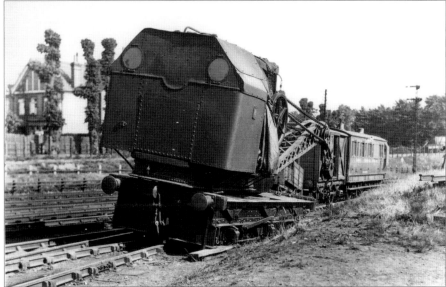

No. 2's second match wagon was formerly LSWR 10-ton 15ft 4in long open goods wagon No. 8809 of 1890 and, following withdrawal of the crane, it was renumbered 304SM before being condemned on 31 Nov. 1934. No. 4's match wagon was condemned in 1927.

Forrest 20-Ton Crane
for North British Railway

The first steam breakdown crane for a Scottish company appears to have been supplied by Forrest & Co of Port Dundas, Glasgow, to the North British Railway in 1882. The Locomotive Engineer, Dugald Drummond, a former apprentice of Forrest & Barr, ordered the largest crane of its day, having such "modern" features as a fabricated plate jib and crab sides, but no live race or powered travel. The crane mounted on three axles was capable of lifting 20 tons at 18 foot radius. It weighed 53 tons when standing alone, with a maximum axle load of 17 ton 3 cwt with the jib resting on the match wagon in train formation: but with the jib supported by the derricking chains the maximum axle load went up to 22 tons 18 cwt.'

Provision was made for three transverse propping girders below the carriage frame in the conventional manner with a single girder carried in each position. On extending each on one side a second could be taken from the match wagon to be inserted on the other side. More unusually in addition, and at the rear end only, there was a pair of longitudinal girders below the buffer beam (one presumes that these were internally joggled up over the rear axle), which could be drawn outwards and packed off the buffer beam of the attendant locomotive to enhance lifting capacity when working on

Forrest 20-Ton Crane for NBR							
Date delivered	Cost	Running No			Match wagon No	Allocation	Disposal
		Pre-grouping	Grouping	BR			
1882	£1,210	0	770539 971571	RS1051/18	770540 971572	Eastfield '11-10/22, Thornton '27-10/5/40, Bathgate Upper '40-1/11/47, Kipps 1/7/48-1/10/60, Dalry Rd '62	Wdn 26/9/64

The North British Railway's 20-ton steam breakdown crane supplied in 1882 by Forrest & Co of Glasgow, seen here ready for duty. (Locomotive Publishing Co, author's collection)

In the absence of sheer-legs, Forrest 20-ton crane LNER No.770539 lifts one end of an ex-NB 0-6-0 LNER Class J35 No. 9375 to enable the wheels to be withdrawn at Thornton. Note the pair of longitudinal draw beams poking out from under the buffer beam. (Real Photographs, author's collection)

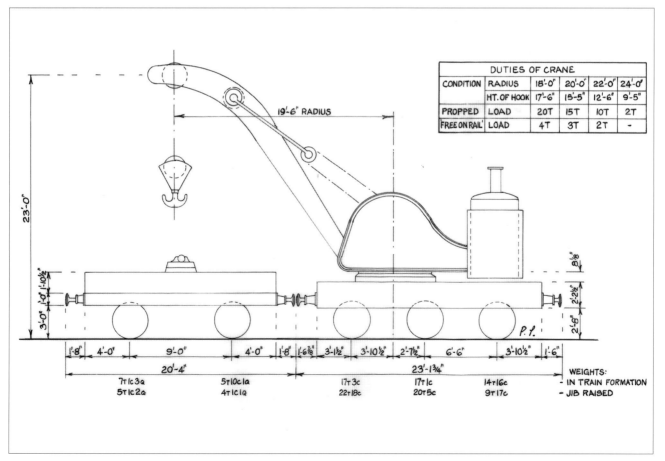

DUTIES OF CRANE					
CONDITION	RADIUS	18'-0"	20'-0"	22'-0"	24'-0"
	HT. OF HOOK	17'-6"	15'-5"	12'-6"	9'-5"
PROPPED	LOAD	20T	15T	10T	2T
FREE ON RAIL	LOAD	4T	3T	2T	–

Figure 8 - Tracing of LNER diagram for 20-Ton Forrest Crane for NBR. (Author)

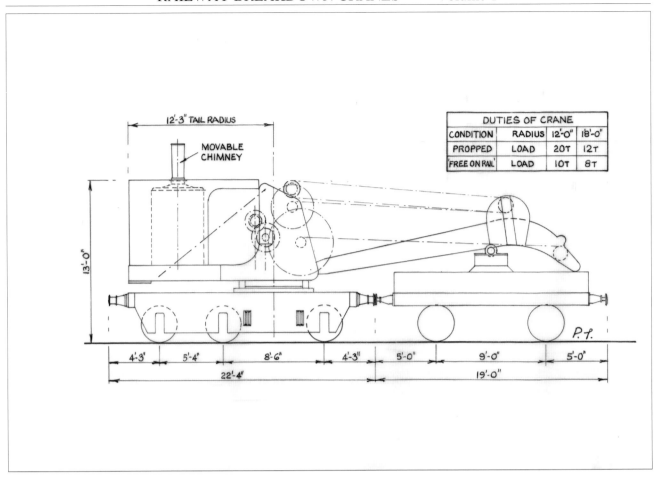

DUTIES OF CRANE			
CONDITION	RADIUS	12'-0"	18'-0"
PROPPED	LOAD	20T	12T
FREE ON RAIL	LOAD	10T	8T

Figure 9 - Tracing of GWR diagram for 20-ton Chaplin crane for Taff Vale Railway. (Author)

An engraving of the 20 ton steam crane supplied to the Taff Vale Railway by Messrs Alex. Chaplin & Co, Glasgow that appeared in 16 January 1885 issue of 'The Engineer'. (Author's collection)

single lines. This feature was to be developed and become a Drummond speciality.

Initially allocated to Eastfield, sometime later as newer cranes arrived on the scene, it had found its way in turn to Thornton, Bathgate, Kipps and Dalry Road from where, following its last overhaul in February 1960, it was withdrawn in September 1964. By 1940 it had been down-rated to 18 tons maximum capacity and it appears never to have had any protection for the driver provided.

Chaplin 20-Ton Crane
for Taff Vale Railway

Another Scottish company in the field at the time, Alexander Chaplin & Co Ltd of Glasgow, supplied a 6-wheel 20-ton crane to the Welsh railway company of the Taff Vale following an order in October 1884. Two sets of telescopic propping girders were provided centrally

about the centre of rotation of the superstructure upon the carriage and between the leading and middle axles. The jib was fabricated from wrought iron side plates with internal flange angles top and bottom between which there was a limited amount of transverse cross bracing. Much of the gearing and clutches were positioned outside the left hand crab side with two vertical shafts driving sets of gears on the right hand side. These were driven by a pair of 7 inch diameter by 12 inch vertical cylinders located inside the frames. This was one of the earliest self-propelled cranes, the final drive being by chains to two of the three axles. When propped, the crane was capable of lifting 20 tons at 12 feet radius and 12 tons at 18 feet, or 10 tons at 12 foot radius and 8 tons at 18 feet free on rail.

Initially it was stationed at Cathays in Cardiff from where it is likely to have been displaced in late 1911 to Caerphilly, when a much larger 36-ton crane was delivered from Cowans Sheldon. Sometime between May

Chaplin 20-Ton Crane for Taff Vale				
Date ordered - delivered	Works or Order No.	GW No	Allocation	Disposal
10/84 - c1885	2303	73	Cathays Cardiff '02, Caerphilly c'26	Wdn 30/7/35

Taff Vale Railway's 20-ton Chaplin steam breakdown crane at Carn Park attending to the results of what is thought to be a runaway of a goods train from Abercynon in 1904. (Robin Simmonds, courtesy Tony Miller)

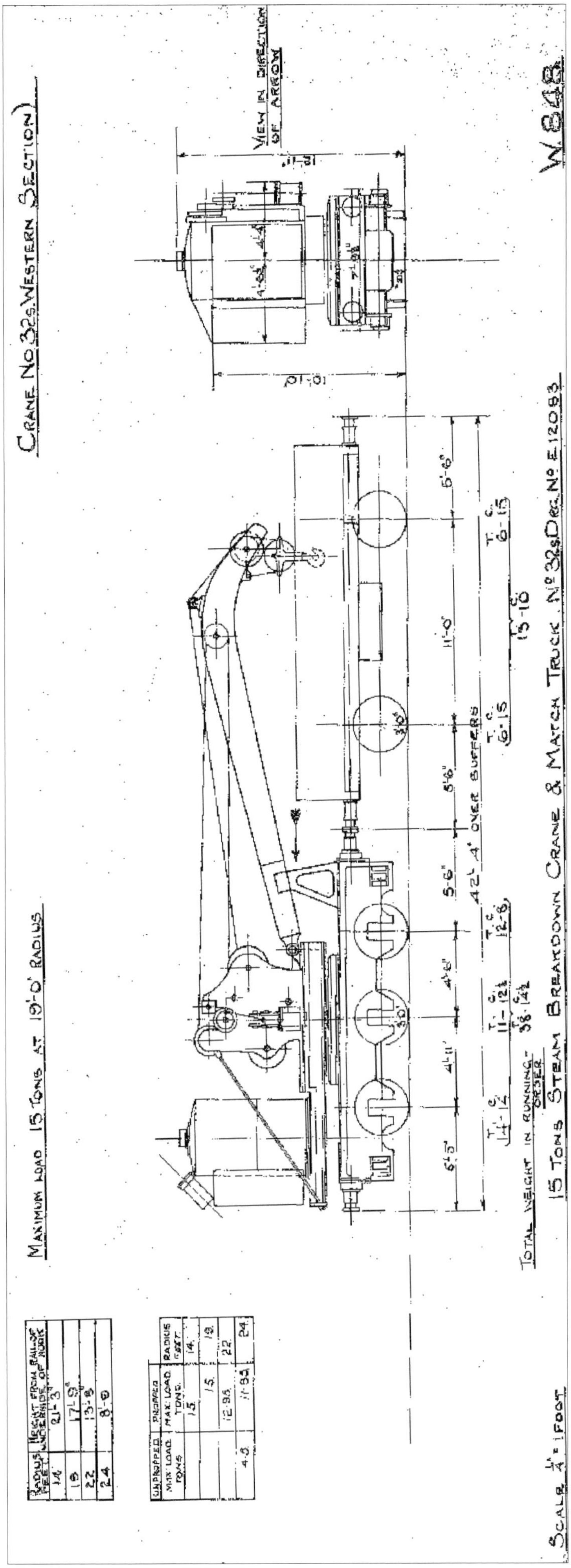

Left, Figure 10 - An official Southern Railway diagram for 15-ton Dunlop & Bell steam breakdown crane. (Author's collection)

1903 and July 1925 an enclosure was added around the boiler and a roof over the driver's position.

Dunlop & Bell 15-Ton Crane
for LSWR

Early among its contemporaries, for their next crane the LSWR went in 1885 to the firm of Dunlop & Bell, which provided a 15-ton crane on three axles, weighing in at 38 tons 14½ cwt with a maximum axle load of 14 tons 14 cwt. Cast iron crab sides were mounted on a fabricated wrought iron foundation to the superstructure, with boiler and water tank towards the rear. The cylinders were mounted vertically on the outside. The dead ends of a pair of derricking chains were fixed to the crab sides, passed round pulleys near the jib head and back to two more at the top rear of the crab sides, before passing down vertically to a winding drum at low level. The jib was built up from plate sides and lattice bracing top and bottom. Again propping girders were fitted at each end of the carriage and when in use the crane could lift its maximum load of 15 tons out to a radius of 19 feet.

It would appear that the crane stationed at Nine Elms was always numbered 1, causing the previous crane there to be renumbered. As we have seen, the 10-ton Appleby became No. 3, probably when the Dunlop crane arrived, and in due course this was displaced and renumbered 3, while the Appleby crane moved up one to 4. In this manner the crane found its way to Eastleigh, Salisbury, Feltham and finally Bournemouth, where it lasted until withdrawn on 27 April 1946.

At the front of the carriage there was a support for the jib while in train formation, so the

Dunlop & Bell 15-Ton Crane for LSWR	
Date delivered	1885
Cost	£1,095
LSWR No.	1, later 3
SR No.	32S
Match wagon Nos:	
LSWR	i) 70S (ii) 57450
SR	(i & ii) 32SM
Allocation	Nine Elms *c'95/6*, Eastleigh *1/1/11*, Salisbury *25/7/21*, Feltham *'22-'23*, Bournemouth Central 1/12/24
Disposal	Wdn 27/4/46

Right - While in the Southern Railway's ownership, the Dunlop & Bell, now No. 32S, was allocated to Bournemouth Central shed, paired with its replacement match wagon. Note the jib resting on a horse attached to the front of the carriage. (H Gordon Tidey, author's collection)

Above - *A side view of the LSWR's 15-ton Dunlop & Bell crane No. 1 at Nine Elms in 1890. Note the propping girders at each end drawn out and wedged up on a pile of timber blocks. The derricking barrel is to the left of the cylinders. The exhaust pipe is seen connected into the water tank, whereas in the view below it has been rerouted to discharge to atmosphere. (BR, author's collection)*

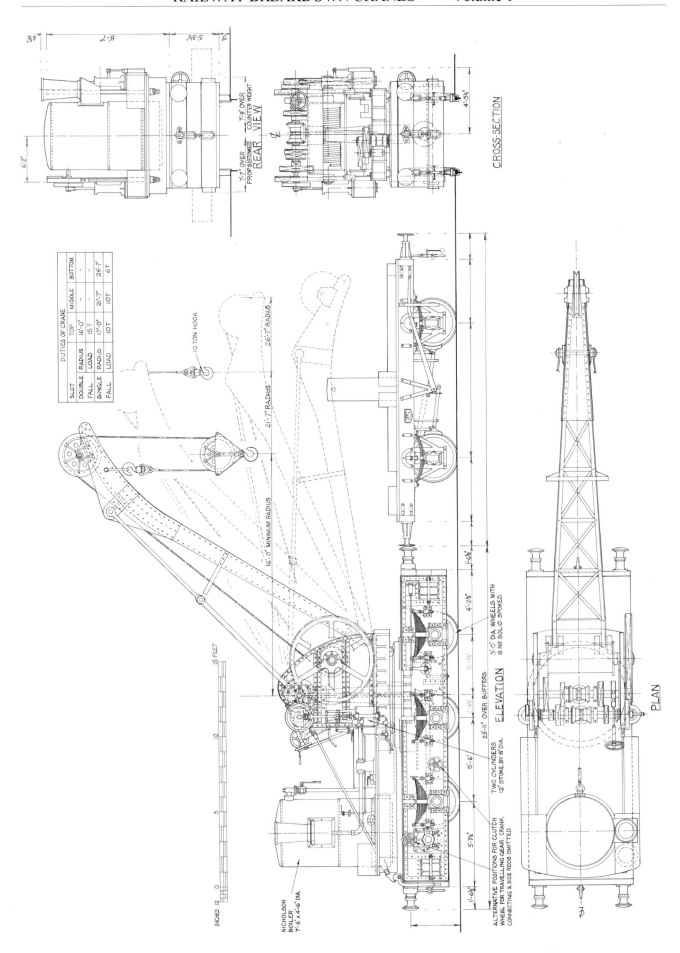

Figure 11 - *Drawing of GNR 15-ton Smith Rodley steam breakdown crane. (Peter Tatlow)*

match wagon acted as a guard truck, rather than supporting the jib. The 3-plank match wagon No. 70S built in 1888 was replaced on 11 November 1933 by former 5-plank batten truck No. 57450, itself withdrawn on 18 May 1946 shortly after the crane.

Smith (Rodley) 15-Ton Cranes
for Great Northern Railway

In 1892 a pair of 15-ton steam breakdown cranes were supplied by Thomas Smith of Rodley to the Great Northern Railway. The design of crane was unusual in three significant respects. Firstly it perpetuated the use of cotters inserted in slotted jib tie-rods to provide just three fixed radii of 16ft, 21ft 2in and 26ft 3in. This had been common among hand cranes, when the lifting block would have to be wound in against the underside of the jib to enable the jib to be raised, but was usually superseded on steam cranes by power-driven derricking gear with infinite adjustment. The second was the fitting of the Nicholson Patent boiler with a chimney attached to one side. It has been suggested that around 1915 these were exchanged for the more usual cross-tube type and No. 108 had such upon its withdrawal.

Finally, although from the outset self-propelled at slow speed while working on the site of operations, the adoption of a jack-shaft behind the rear axle driving a connecting rod and coupling rods is thought to be unique amongst breakdown cranes and other travelling cranes for use on main lines, as opposed to yard work only. This feature was presumably soon found to be unsatisfactory, resulting in the travelling gear being altered to the more conventional spur gears to probably two axles. Interestingly, the North Eastern Railway ordered two very similar cranes for engineering work in 1892, but these had spur gear drive from the outset.

As was not unusual at the time, the lifting tackle could be rigged either with a single fall for a load of up to 10 tons, while by adding a block and attaching the 10-ton hook to the underside of the jib, thus creating two falls, 15

tons could be lifted. At each end of the carriage a pair of telescopic propping girders, normally stowed within the carriage while travelling, could, at the site of operations, be extended and their ends firmly packed up off the ground to improve the crane's stability.

It is understood these two cranes were originally allocated to the Chief Engineer's Department and numbered 6 and 7, but were transferred to the Locomotive Engineer's in 1904, when they were renumbered 293A and 295A. LNER route availability was group 7, or 6 in an emergency at slow speed.

The structural elements of the crane were fabricated from rolled steel sections with a massive solid buffer beam. At the jib head the adoption of a large diameter pulley wheel mounted above the jib gave a direct run for the hoisting steel wire rope to the winding barrel, thereby avoiding the need for any intermediate pulley. The brakes were applied by turning a hand wheel on a longitudinal screw which then acted on the wheels of the front and centre axles.

The crane was capable of lifting 15 tons with two falls of the lifting rope at the minimum radius of 16 feet when fully propped, while 'free on rail' with a single fall it could lift 10 tons at a radius of 17 feet to a height of 20ft 9in. At a radius of 21ft 2in it could lift 10 tons when propped and at 26ft 2in 6 tons 'free on rail', to heights respectively of 17ft 6in and 10ft 10in.

Over the years the GN and its successors implemented various changes and enhancements. As already noted, the means of providing the travelling motion was altered from crank and side rods to spur gears within the frame. Visually this resulted in the repositioning of the clutch wheel from above the now redundant crank to lower down between the centre and rear axles. The Nicholson boiler was replaced by the more conventional vertical boiler. A rest for the tie rods was mounted on the jib. The side tanks may have been renewed and a roof over the driver's position added.

GN 15-Ton Smith Cranes						
Date delivered	Works	Running No			Allocation	Date wdn
		Pre-group	LNER '38 scheme	BR		
1892	4163	6, 295A	951502	108	Ardsley '04 to 11/47, Retford '48 to '68.	Wdn '68
1892	4164	7, 293A	941596	-	Kings Cross '04 to '17, Grimsby '26 to c'49/50.	Wdn c'50

An engraving that appeared in an unidentified contemporary technical publication of the GN 15 ton crane by Smith (Rodley) showing the jack shaft, connecting rod and coupling rods to provide the travelling motion. This was soon altered to internal drive. The adjustable tie rods in lieu of derricking tackle can also be seen. (Author's collection)

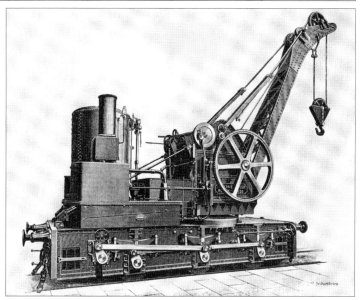

2. Early Cowans Sheldon Cranes

Cowans Sheldon 10/12-ton cranes for GER /
Cowans Sheldon 15-ton cranes /
Cowans Sheldon 15-ton cranes for CR /
Cowans Sheldon 15-ton crane for HR

Cowans Sheldon of Carlisle built their first railway recovery crane in 1866 and by the final decade of the nineteen century were dominating the market. The earliest crane of this type supplied to a British company is reported to be a 16-ton crane for the South Eastern Railway in 1881 to Works No. 1110. If so, it appears to have been withdrawn prior to the drawing up of the register of service stock by the Southern Railway soon after grouping.

Cowans Sheldon 10/12-Ton Cranes
for Great Eastern Railway

Over a period of six or seven years from 1892, Cowans Sheldon supplied three 10- and/or 12-ton cranes to the Great Eastern Railway. It is not clear whether these were initially ordered for use by the Civil Engineer, or that they subsequently were transferred to his department. They were mounted on three axles with positions for propping girders at the front and between the middle and trailing axles.

In several respects they anticipated many of the design features of the 15-ton standard cranes about to be described. The worm to the derricking motion, however, was outside the crab sides, rather than inside, while two chains were wound round the derricking barrel. The presence of a spur wheel above the central pillar suggests that drive to the travelling motion may have passed down its centre.

The early example (Works No. 1759) had a curved jib with five slots along the straight length of the sides, subsequently slightly greater depth was incorporated into the jib sides and the slots omitted, in some way reflecting parallel developments in the 15-ton cranes discussed below.

Cowans Sheldon 10/12-Ton Cranes for GER					
Date ordered	Works No	Running No			Allocation
		Pre-grp	LNER	BR	
1892	1759				
1896	1896		961006	271	Stratford, Leyton, Peterborough
1898/9?	2203	243	962600		Stratford Wks '38.

A pair of 10-ton travelling steam cranes was also supplied to the SECR in 1903 (Works Nos. 2626 & 2627) with swan-necked jibs, but these were always to have been employed on engineering work, rather than breakdown for which by then they would be considered under-powered, so are not considered further here.

Cowans Sheldon 15-Ton Cranes

Up until the mid-1880s, small cranes were usually mounted on two or three axles. The 15-ton cranes about to be discussed next, however, can be considered the forerunners of a standard design of crane supplied in reasonable numbers to many of the British, Irish and other overseas railways.

Crane Carriage

The crane carriage was mounted on two fixed axles towards the rear with outside bearings, while forward was a two-axle Adams bogie with inside journals. During the journey to the site of operations in train formation, all these axles were supported by conventional axle-boxes and leaf springs. Before raising the jib, however, the springing had to be rendered inoperative to make the crane solidly supported during its work. To achieve this, stout screws were lowered. Those over the fixed axles bore down on the top of the axle-boxes, the holes for which are apparent on the top of the carriage, while the screws on the underside of the framing over the bogie pressed down on the stub extensions of the axles. Obviously, on completion of its work, before commencing its return journey, the process had to be reversed.

To lift the maximum load, the crane had to be propped by means of three 12 by 6 inch rolled steel joists, one at the leading end, another in the middle under the central pillar and the last between the fixed axles. Before the crane could lift heavy loads, the propping girders would be unloaded from the match wagon, slid into the steel yokes attached to the underside of the carriage framing and finally tightened down on a pad of timber packing by driving home a pair of folding hardwood wedges. In addition rail clips mounted on the buffer beams would be unhooked and fastened over the rail head. In this condition the crane cannot travel along the track. It could, however, lift lesser loads without being propped, when it might travel at slow speed, using its own power if fitted with travelling gear, or otherwise relying on an attendant locomotive.

The original intention was that the three 14-foot long propping girders would normally have been carried in, or under, the match wagon. These, however, will have been heavy and unwieldy to manoeuvre into position, particularly in narrow cuttings or alongside a retaining wall. As a result, in due course a number of these cranes had these girders shortened to the width of the carriage and supplemented by a further set of three of similar

Opposite - *A former Great Eastern Railway 10- or 12-ton Cowans Sheldon crane at work carrying out permanent way renewals at Goodmayes West in 1939. (RE Vincent, Transport Treasury)*

length, so that they could be permanently accommodated within propping girder boxes added in place of the former yokes attached to the underside of the carriage, thereby achieving the telescopic arrangement usual on later designs of crane.

Crane Superstructure

The superstructure of the crane was mounted on a massive cast-steel foundation casting, including the slewing ring, forming the central part of the top of the carriage. The superstructure itself included an intricately cast-steel bed plate, fabricated steel crab sides and top casting. Through the bed plate the central pillar protruded and the moment induced by the superstructure supporting a load was transmitted by cast-steel wheels bearing on the foundation ring and collar at the top of the pillar.

At the rear end of the crab sides a vertical boiler was mounted with water tanks each side and coal bunker on the left hand side. The crane driver stood in front of the boiler from where he could attend to the fire and feed-water as required, while in front of him was a series of levers and hand wheels with which to operate the crane's motions. Inclined cylinders on the outside of the crab sides drove a disc crank wheel on each side and between which was a transverse crankshaft. By a series of clutches, gears and lay shafts, this shaft provided power for the motions of raising and lowering the jib; lifting or lowering a load; slewing the superstructure with respect to the carriage; and, if so equipped, propelling the crane along the track at slow speed. The hoisting motion and derricking motions were engaged by sliding spur pinion- or dog-clutches. The small adjustments of slewing and travelling motions, however, might require movement under power in either direction while concurrently carrying out another function, so one of a pair of opposing cone clutches were used as appropriate.

The mounting of the superstructure on the carriage was, typically for the day, fairly crude. Basically the moment induced by the load at the radius at which it was being lifted was resisted by a bearing at the top of the central pillar. This consisted of an inclined roller on a transverse member between the side plates bearing on an inverted cone section of the pillar and at the bottom by a single large roller, altered to two on later cranes, at the jib foot bearing on the chamfered edge of the horizontal roller path. There was also a single smaller roller at the rear to cope with backward moment of the boiler acting as a counter-weight while the crane was unloaded.

The Jib

The forward end of the superstructure supported a fabricated steel jib raised or lowered by the chains of the derricking tackle in four parts with one winding. Suspended from the end of the jib was a lifting hook and block. For heavier loads the hoisting chain in two parts passed round the block and was attached to the underside of the jib. For lighter loads, however, the speed of hoisting could be doubled by detaching this, removing the block and using its smaller hook at the end of the chain.

Additional Aids to Stability

As well as three sets of transverse propping girders, pairs of longitudinal draw beams at each end of the carriage and at the rear end of the superstructure were provided on the

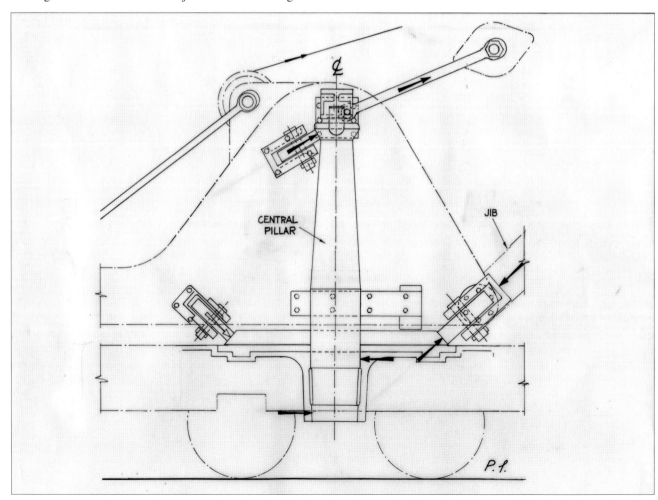

CENTRAL PILLAR

JIB

P.1.

Opposite page, Figure 12 - Transmission of forces through the superstructure of a Cowans Sheldon 15-ton steam breakdown crane. (Author)

Right - The top of the central pillar and its accommodation within the crosshead together with the anchoring of the bridle to the derricking tackle of the ex-GNR(I) 15-ton Cowans Sheldon steam crane now preserved at Whitehead by the RPSI. (Author)

CR and HR cranes about to be considered. When extended, those in the carriage could be blocked off the underside of the buffer beam of a locomotive, or its tender, coupled to the crane, to enable it to be moved under full load with the jib in line with the track. Also to improve stability when it was not possible to utilise the propping girders and travel with a substantial load, particularly when working on a single line, the beams at the rear of the superstructure could be drawn out and weighted down with any suitable heavy object for the same purpose. History does not relate whether, with any such extemporary counterweight in place, the crane was in danger of overturning backwards under no load!

The Crane's Motions

Derricking

A set of bevelled mitre gears redirect rotation of the crankshaft vertically upwards to supply rotation to a worm and worm wheel driving the derricking drum. The chain attached over this acts through sheaves to raise the jib from near horizontal when travelling, to an operating radius. Downward movement is constrained by the friction within the worm gear and the jib therefore has to be taken down in a controlled manner by the engine.

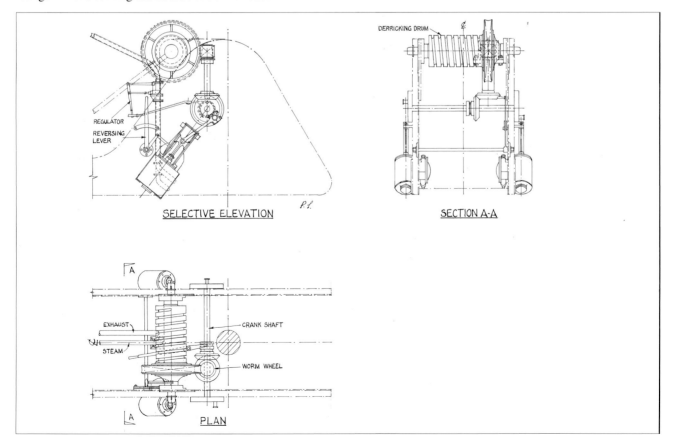

Figure 13 - The gearing for the derricking motion and engine. (Author)

Above - *The driver's view of some of his controls. In the centre right-hand of the picture are the steam supply and the exhaust steam pipes and below the regulator lever, with to the lower right the derricking lever. To the right-hand side can be seen the worm wheel and derricking drum, in this case arranged for steel wire rope instead of the earlier chain. (Author)*

Left - *To the left-hand side of the pillar viewed from the front, a set of mitre gears on the crank-shaft transmit the drive vertically upwards to the hidden worm of the derricking motion. Also on the crank-shaft is the sliding spur gear below, which, when moved to the left, engages with the larger spur wheel to provide the hoisting motion for the heavier lifts. Further to the left on the same shaft are the two eccentrics to the engine's valve gear. (Author)*

Hoisting

The gear train to hoist or lower the hook at the outer end of the jib had two speeds of operation, the clutch lever having three positions. When central, both sets are disengaged, but as the driver moves it to the right a secondary lever connected to the main lever engages a clutch on a pinion that provides direct drive off the crankshaft to the large gear wheel on the hoisting drum for lifting lighter loads. Alternatively for heavier loads by pushing to the left, the main lever engages a set of pinion and wheel gears reducing the speed of rotation of the crankshaft to a lay shaft below. Another pinion on this then drives the large gear wheel on the hoisting drum. The chain attached under this passes over a sheave at the jib head to raise the lifting hook. Downward movement is controlled by the engine in conjunction with a brake drum and band on the lay shaft.

Slewing

Each of the remaining two motions, slewing and travelling, required potentially equal effort from the crane's engine in either direction. The drive for both motions was, therefore, taken from the crankshaft to a lay shaft by a set of spur gears. On this was mounted a pair of opposing bevel gears acting on another bevel at the top of a vertical shaft below. Between the opposing bevels was a pair of cone friction clutches, which could engage one or the other by way of a screw-operated lever. Depending upon which cone was engaged would determine the direction of the motion.

Lower down the vertical shaft was a double-acting sliding dog-clutch. By raising the clutch, a single set of bevel gears drove a horizontal shaft which took the drive forward to another set of bevel gears and spur gears to reduce its speed of rotation and drive a spur pinion acting on the inside of an annular rack attached to the carriage. Experience showed that some means of braking needed to be provided and a band brake to the bevel wheel was added to some existing and later new cranes.

Travelling (if fitted)

Picking up on the two-way sliding dog-clutch described above, by lowering its lever, instead of engaging the slewing motion, the travelling gear was activated. A spur gear at the bottom of the vertical shaft drove the upper, larger diameter, gear of a double periphery spur 'idler' gear free to rotate around the central pillar of the crane. The lower gear of smaller diameter in turn drove another spur gear on top of the carriage and within the annular ring. It should be noted that, as the superstructure was rotated, the upper spur gear was free to pass over the lower one.

A further vertical shaft in the carriage, located to the rear of its centre line and the space occupied by the central propping girder when in position, drove a set of bevel gears to a cross shaft below the main frame and between the wheels. Between this and the inner fixed wheel axle a train of three spur gears transferred power to the axle. A clutch acting on the middle of the spur pinions allowed the gear train to be disconnected while the crane was being hauled in train formation by totally withdrawing this gear from between its two neighbours. Only one of the four axles of these cranes was powered. Whether equipped to propel itself or not, a hand brake operated from track level by means of a hand wheel was fitted and activated brake blocks on both wheels of the two fixed axles.

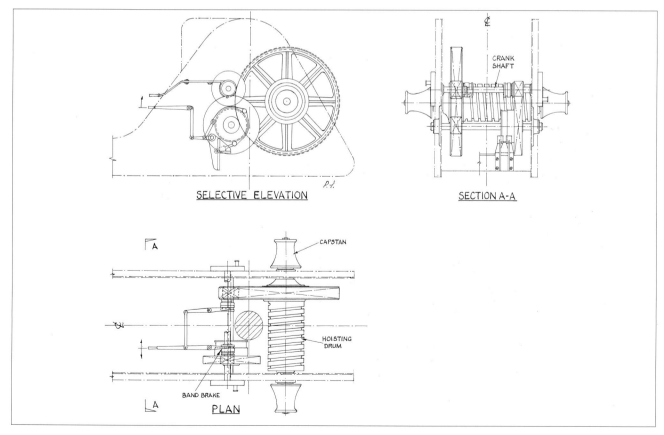

Figure 14 - The gearing for the hoisting motion. (Author)

43

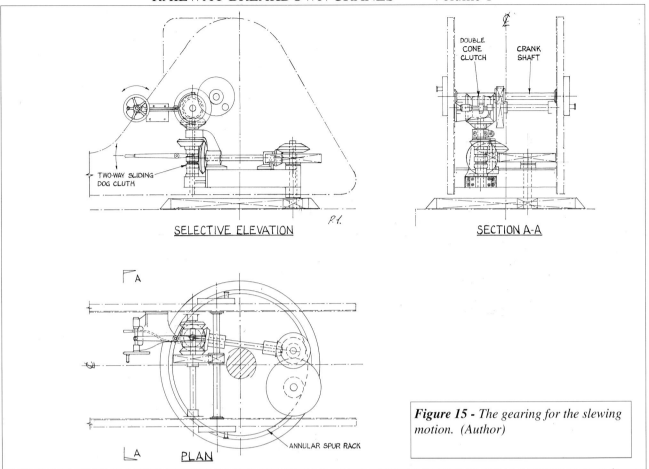

SELECTIVE ELEVATION

TWO-WAY SLIDING
DOG CLUTCH

P.1.

SECTION A-A

DOUBLE
CONE
CLUTCH

CRANK
SHAFT

A

PLAN

ANNULAR SPUR RACK

Figure 15 - The gearing for the slewing motion. (Author)

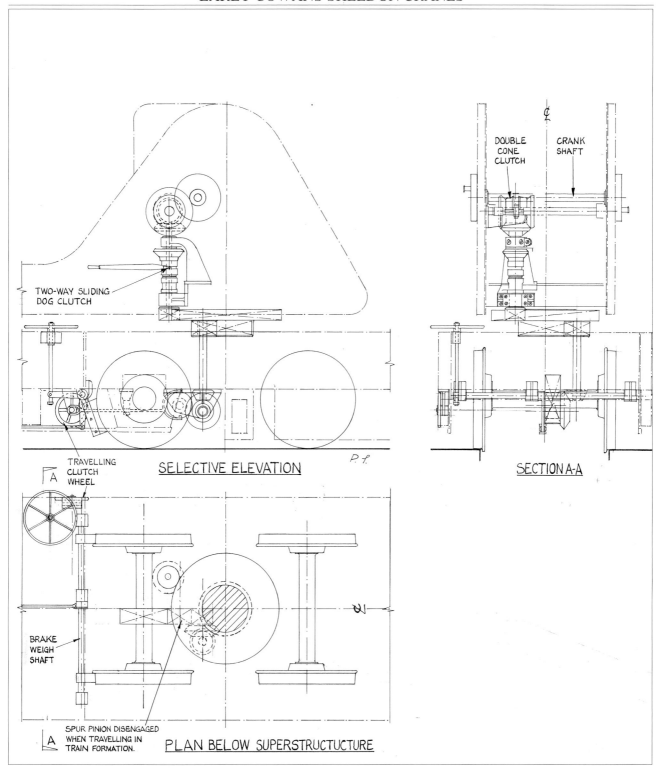

Figure 16 - *The gearing for the travelling motion. Note: the plan detail of the vertical component of the gear train within the superstructure is the same as that for the initial part of the slewing gear shown above. The hand brake wheel was peculiar to the Highland crane. (Author)*

Opposite bottom - *Another driver's view, showing at the top left the hoisting lever, below which is the wheel control to the double friction-cone clutches. Turning the wheel alters the position of the die on the threaded bar thereby engaging the cone clutch to one bevel gear or the other. Below this the bevel wheel for the slewing motion and the double-acting dog-clutch can be seen. Operating a lever to raise this engages the slewing motion, while, if fitted, downwards movement would engage the travelling motion. To the right-hand side behind the wheel is the steam supply pipe, the regulator handle, the exhaust steam pipe and hoist brake lever. Across the bottom of the picture run the weigh shaft for the reversing gear and the collector pipe for exhaust steam. (Author)*

Top - *On the right-hand side the pair of opposing mitre gears with the double cone clutch can be seen. Engaging one or the other activated the vertical shaft below for the slewing and in some cases travelling motions. Bridging this complex is the lever to engage the dog clutch to spur pinion for the lighter hoisting ratio and in front of which is the final spur pinion permanently meshed with the spur wheel on the hoisting drum. (Author)*

Left - *In the front of the superstructure the bevel gear at low level is the slewing drive, upon top of which is the band brake fitted to later cranes. To the right is the spur wheel on the hoisting drum, most cranes, however, had chains rather than steel wire rope. (Author)*

Opposite page, Figure 17 *- General arrangement drawing for the Great Southern & Western Railway of Ireland with the gear trains annotated and scheduled, viz: A-D hoisting; E-F lay shaft; G-K vertical shaft; L-P slew; Q-T derrick; and U-D1 travel. (Cowans Sheldon, author's collection)*

The above figures were derived from Cowans Sheldon's general arrangement drawing for the Highland crane of 1887 for no better reason than that, as well as the elevation and cross section usual on such drawings, it also had a plan of the superstructure and all of which tended to be more detailed than other drawings available. On the other hand, the photographs were taken of ex-Great Northern Railway (Ireland) 15-ton Cowans Sheldon crane now preserved at the Railway Preservation Society of Ireland's depot at Whitehead, while Figure 17 is the general arrangement drawing for the GS&W Railway of Ireland of 1899 included the schedule of gears.

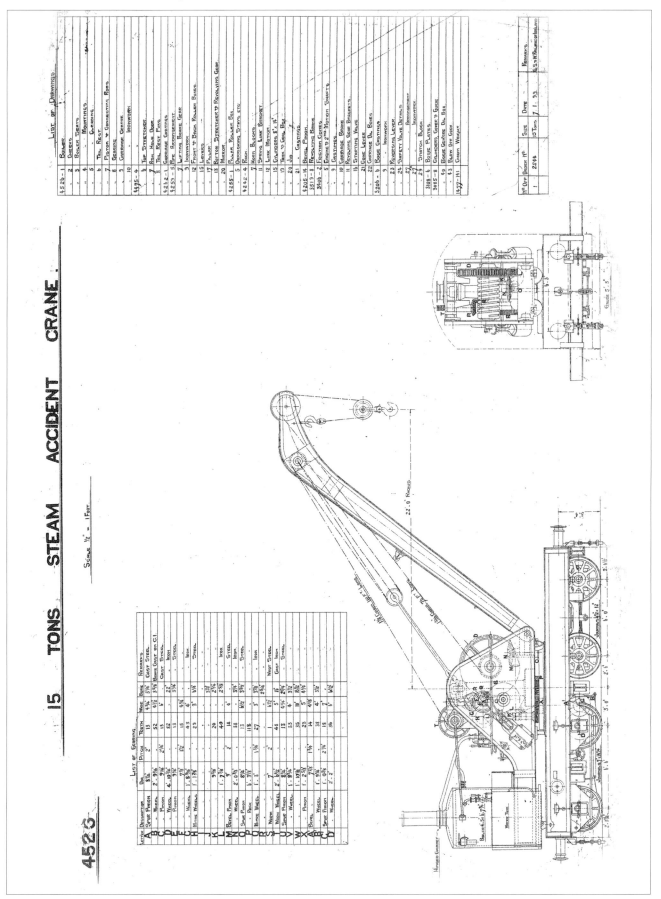

Development in design over the intervening years, however, means that these are not, of course, directly comparable, but the principles are clear. Several of the sizes quoted are clearly different and furthermore the final drive of the travel motion to the driven axle above has only two instead of three pinions in the set, nonetheless one of them will still be capable of being withdrawn.

Cowans Sheldon 15-Ton Cranes
for Caledonian Railway

By 1886 Dugald Drummond had transferred from the North British Railway to the neighbouring Caledonian Railway. Under his tenure two cranes were built for the Caledonian Railway by the well known crane makers, Cowans Sheldon of Carlisle. These were ordered on 5 February 1886 and delivered later that year as Works Nos. 1436 & 1437. Weighing in at 51½ tons, each could lift 15 tons to a radius of 20 feet and, when weighed, the maximum axle load was 14 tons 5 cwt. All plates, angles, shafts, pinions, pathway and pathway rollers were of steel, together with a steel boiler shell, firebox and tubes, while bearings were bushed in brass. These cranes were fitted with curved jibs with three oblong slots in the side plates. At the railway's insistence and against the maker's better judgement, 3 foot diameter wheels and Caledonian Railway standard 7 by 12 inch axle-boxes were fitted, instead of the 7 by 14 inch suggested. This is likely to have resulted in a propensity for hot axle-boxes to arise all too frequently to the discomfort of the locomotive running and operating departments.

As was to become the Caledonian Railway's pattern, both Nos. 1 and 2 were initially stationed at Motherwell, from where at the centre of the system they could be called out to wherever required. With the subsequent arrival of 20-ton Craven cranes in 1908, they were reallocated to Carlisle (Kingmoor) and Perth. Prior to about 1922, the boiler had been insulated with presumably a white asbestos cladding. Likewise, by the same time the propping girders were accommodated permanently on the crane within telescopic housings. This involved the front one projecting in front of the end of the crane, a vertical channel section at each side being attached to the front headstock. The General Arrangement drawing shows the safety valves on the boiler as the highest part of the crane, yet an LMS diagram of end views, prepared around 1939, indicates the hoisting drum gear wheel as the highest at 13ft 1in. This might suggest that the safety valves had been replaced by an alternative type to enable them to be repositioned. Even so the route availability will have been remained limited, as, away from the main lines, the Caledonian system was not known for its liberal loading gauge. The means of braking the crane carriage appears to have been by a hand-wheel on the left hand side only. By August 1931, the wheel of No. 1 had been changed to a revolving tee bar, and the driver and boiler received a corrugated iron roof, with the end and sides of the boiler area enshrouded in vertical flat plate.

Initially No. 2 at least was paired with a 6-wheel

Cowans Sheldon 15-ton crane Caledonian Railway No. 2 soon after delivery in 1886. Note the joggled extension beams projecting from the front of the carriage. The left hand bogie wheel is scotched, thereby questioning the effectiveness of the hand brakes on the right hand two axles without a locomotive in attendance! (Jim McIntosh collection)

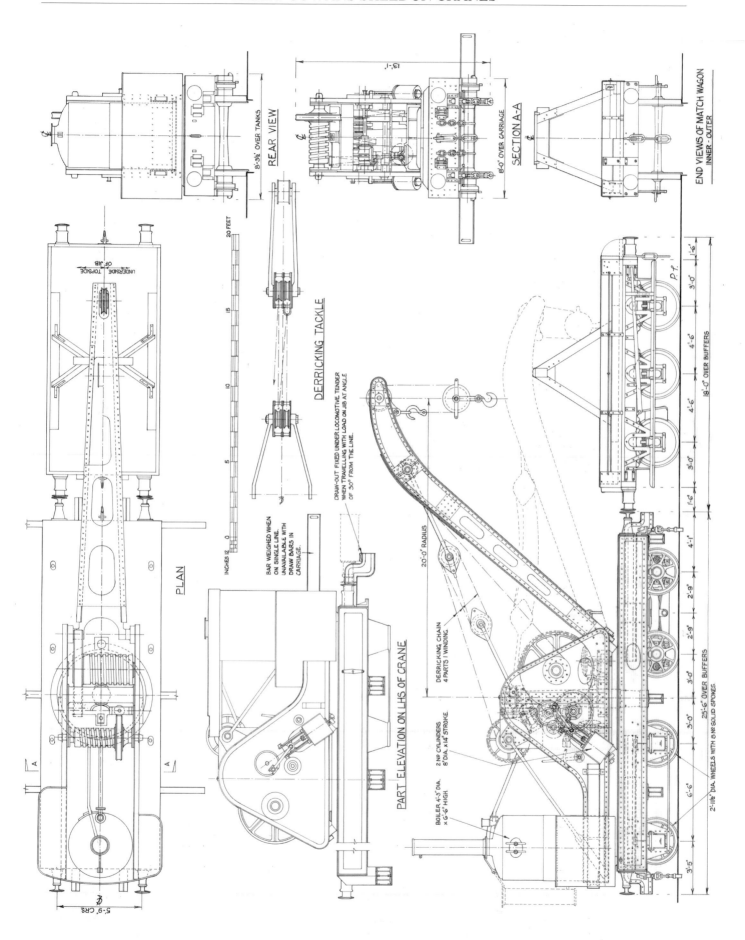

Figure 18 - *Caledonian 15-ton Cowans Sheldon steam breakdown cranes of 1886. (Author)*

CR No. 1 in Caledonian livery and paired with a 6-wheel 2-plank match wagon. Note that the propping girders have already been altered to the telescopic form. (AG Ellis collection)

By now No. 1 is in LMS lined colours, thought to be crimson lake locomotive livery, and coupled to its replacement ex-Midland Railway 3-plank fixed side match wagon. Adjacent to this is an ex-HR Peter Drummond style match-boarded side lavatory third No.18989. (WO Steel, author's collection)

Cowans Sheldon 15-Ton Cranes for CR						
Date ord'd - deliv'd	Works No	Running No			Match wagon No	Allocation	Disposal
		Pre-grp	MP/ Plant	LMS 5/41 & BR			
5/2/86 - 1886	1436	1	MP42	RS1029/15	(1) 208184, (2) 34319 post 8/31	Motherwell, Kingmoor '08-*8/35*, Birkenhead 2/37, Llandudno Jct '38, Springs Branch 27/4/42-'57	Wdn 7/59
5/2/86 - 1886	1437	2	724	RS1048/15	254809	Perth '08-*1/1/31*, Polmadie 10/32, Motherwell 11/39, Burton-on-Trent 2/43-'57	Scrapped 8/58

Above - The Highland Railway's single example of a 15-ton Cowans Sheldon steam crane supplied in 1887 and stationed at Inverness most of its life. This formed part of the Inverness breakdown train, including here a 6-wheeled riding van and packing wagon. Note the short post sticking up from the right-hand end of the van from which a pair of wires would be strung up to the lineside telegraph wires to enable contact to be established with the line's headquarters while on site. (WO Steel collection, courtesy RJ Essery)

Opposite page, Figure 19 - The unique version of a Cowans Sheldon 15-ton crane built for the Highland Railway in 1887. (Author)

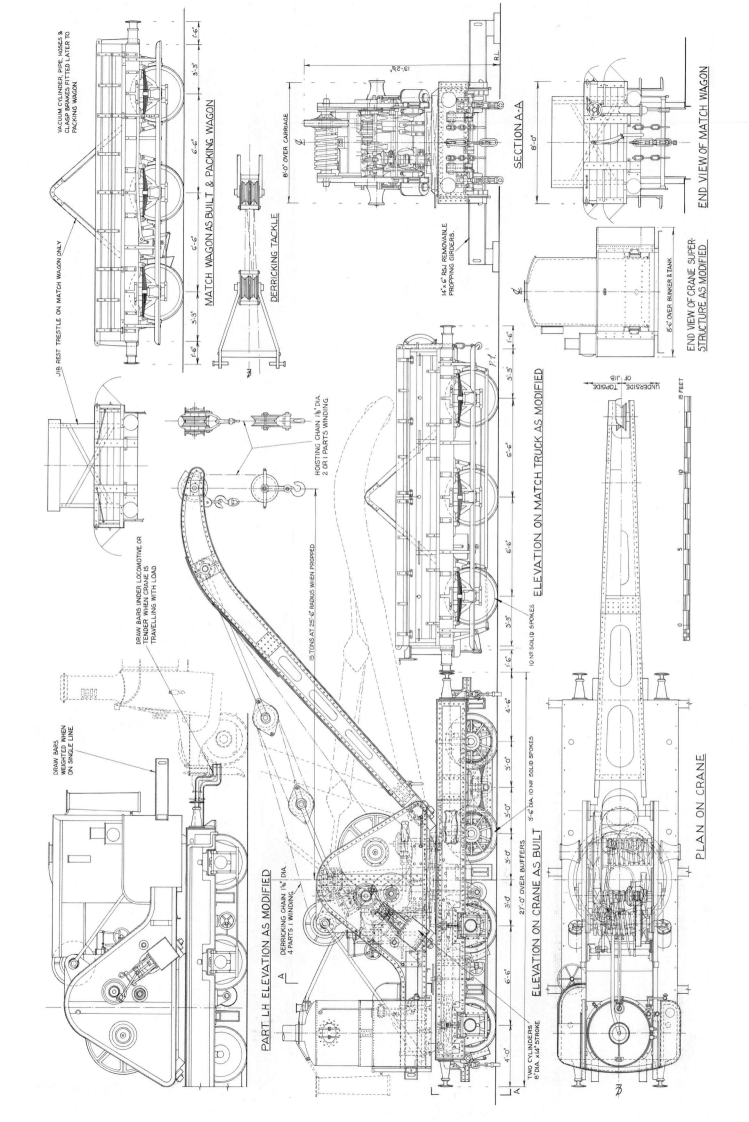

VACUUM CYLINDER, PIPE, HOSES & CLASP BRAKES FITTED LATER TO PACKING WAGON

1'-6" 3'-3" 6'-6" 6'-6" 3'-3" 1'-6"

MATCH WAGON AS BUILT & PACKING WAGON

JIB REST TRESTLE ON MATCH WAGON ONLY

DERRICKING TACKLE

8'-0" OVER CARRIAGE

13'-2¾"

R.L.

SECTION A-A

14" × 6" RSJ REMOVABLE PROPPING GIRDERS.

END VIEW OF MATCH WAGON

8'-0"

8'-6" OVER BUNKER & TANK

END VIEW OF CRANE SUPER-STRUCTURE AS MODIFIED

HOISTING CHAIN 1⅛" DIA. 2 OR 1 PARTS WINDING

p.l.

1'-6" 3'-3" 6'-6" 6'-6" 3'-3"

ELEVATION ON MATCH TRUCK AS MODIFIED

10 N° SOLID SPOKES

TOPSIDE OF JIB

UNDERSIDE OF JIB

0 5 10 15 FEET

15 FEET

PLAN ON CRANE

DRAW BARS UNDER LOCOMOTIVE OR TENDER WHEN CRANE IS TRAVELLING WITH LOAD

DRAW BARS WEIGHTED WHEN ON SINGLE LINE.

15 TONS AT 25'-6" RADIUS WHEN PROPPED

DERRICKING CHAIN 1⅛" DIA. 4 PARTS I WINDING

A

A

PART LH ELEVATION AS MODIFIED

1'-6" 4'-6" 3'-0" 3'-0" 3'-0" 3'-0"

27'-0" OVER BUFFERS

3'-6" DIA. 10 N° SOLID SPOKES

10 N° SOLID SPOKES

6'-6"

TWO CYLINDERS 8" DIA. × 14" STROKE

ELEVATION ON CRANE AS BUILT

4'-0"

Seen here in late pre-grouping days with the sides of the match truck raised and the boiler and driver's area enclosed in sheeting against the inclement weather of northern climes. The size of this crane should be compared with the Caledonian version, giving rise to an enhancement in radius at which the maximum load could be lifted. The draw beam in the superstructure can be seen between the cylinder and water tank, while those in the carriage are just visible at the left hand end of the crane. Vacuum brake pipe has been added. (Thomson, courtesy W Chalmers)

3-plank dumb-buffered wagon with outside W-irons, simple Scotch lever brake on one side acting on a wooden brake-block and a drop end remote from the crane. Prior to grouping, however, No. 1 was running with a 2-plank wagon with self-contained parallel buffers and the brake gear on the other side. Sometime after August 1931 and before June 1935, No. 1's was replaced by a recovered ex-Midland 4-wheeled 3-plank fixed-sided wagon and the jib rest reused.

These cranes had a pair of non-standard elliptical works plates, approximately 21 by 12 inches, attached per side, one on the carriage and the other on the crab side. Photographs of the cranes in Caledonian days show a lined livery, probably following locomotive practice, but whether goods black or less likely passenger blue is uncertain. The initials **CR** and the **No 1** or **No 2** were applied to the water-tank sides of the crane in block letters. **CR** was painted in white on the match-wagon sides, in earlier days accompanied by **STEAM CRANE RUNNER** and tare weight. Lining continued to appear on the crane after grouping, which in conjunction with a subtle change in tone of the main areas would appear to suggest the adoption of the LMS crimson lake livery, together with 'LMS' and 'No. 1' in serif style on the tank sides.

Cowans Sheldon 15-Ton Crane
for Highland Railway

On 1 September 1886 the Highland Railway also ordered a 15-ton crane from Cowans Sheldon and this was delivered the following year as Works No. 1485. Like the Caley cranes, it was of the 4-4-0 wheel arrangement, capable of traversing a minimum radius of 4 chains, but was substantially bigger. It had a curved jib with three slots in the sides with the flange angles carried around the end and a long vertical splice plate in the crab sides. On the other hand, uniquely amongst Cowans Sheldon cranes, the underside of the carriage girder-work was joggled over the fixed axles, thereby enabling adequately sized axle journals and 3 foot 6 inch diameter wheels to be accommodated. In addition the HR crane was fitted with a horizontal capstan on each side of the crab sides, the purpose of which was to be able to drag debris from the wreckage to within reach of the crane's hook.

The maximum axle load of the crane was 18 tons on the two fixed axles with 28 tons carried by the bogie, giving a total of 64 tons, and this no doubt accounts for its ability to lift its maximum load of 15 tons out to a radius of 25 feet 6 inches. This compares with a maximum total of about 55 tons for the subsequent standard 15-ton Cowans Sheldon cranes supplied to a large number of other railway companies during the 1890s and capable of lifting 15 tons at radii of only 20 or 22 feet. Indeed, subsequently, Cowans Sheldon were to develop their standard design at the beginning of the 20th century to 20 tons capacity by adopting similar axle spacings and loads to the HR's. In effect the Highland had a 20-ton crane 14 years ahead of its time. To put this in context, the Highland's largest locomotive at the time, Clyde Bogie 4-4-0 locomotives on the same number of axles and configuration weighed a mere 43 tons and no other HR engine, apart from the infamous 4-6-0 Rivers and even then on five axles, ever reached the same overall weight as the crane, the Clans being the nearest at 62 tons 4¾ cwt. Quite why the company's Engineer accepted this loading is not revealed, but perhaps it was seen as an infrequent slow moving load with, unlike a locomotive, no dynamic effects. Whilst the crane may have been stable enough to lift a load of 20 tons, and more under the emergency conditions that often arise during re-railing operations, this must have placed the winding gear under some strain.

According to Cowans' General Arrangement drawing No. 2089, even without adopting the restraining force of a locomotive acting on the extension girders, the crane was able to travel 'free on rail' with a load of 10 tons with the jib in line with the track and raised to a radius of not less than 18ft 4in. It could also operate with 10 tons over the side out to a radius of 16ft 2in without the use of rail clips or packing up the propping girders.

Over the years various alterations were made to the crane and match wagon. The six-wheel match truck and attendant 4-plank drop-side wagon for other equipment and packing timbers appear initially to have been similar, with just the jib rest added to the first. At some stage the match wagon was reconstructed with lockers along each side, surmounted by drop-sides two planks high. Steps were added to the ends of the headstocks and wagon ends, while foot holds were provided in the bottom corners of the outer locker doors. Approximately three-inch thick packing pieces were also added behind the buffers at the crane end, together with a screw coupling. Three link couplings continued elsewhere, which is surprising in view of the provision of the vacuum brake pipe hoses.

The match and packing wagons were originally provided with just a hand brake lever on each side operating a single brake block on the left hand wheel. On the match wagon this was later replaced by brake blocks acting on one side of all six wheels, which could be applied by either automatic vacuum or a hand wheel on a column, off what appears to be a redundant locomotive tender, at the crane end of the wagon. The packing wagon on the other hand kept the hand brake levers and had clasp brakes fitted to all wheels actuated by the vacuum brake cylinder.

Cowans Sheldon 15-Ton Crane for HR								
Purc'd by	Date ord'd - deliv'd	Works No	Running No			Match wagon No	Allocation	Disposal
			Pre-grp	MP/ Plant	LMS 5/41 &/or BR			
HR	1/9/86 - 1887	1485	1	1983/ MP45	RS1060/15	297231, or possibly 297233	Inverness '87, Hurlford 11/39, Belle Vue, Wick 9/43-*1/44*, Horwich Wks 3/44, Toton Sidings 17/8/44	Wdn 7/47. scrapped 15/10/47

The crane's boiler was at first fully exposed without any lagging. The oil reservoirs to the fixed axles on the carriage sides were lowered at some time, so that the feed pipes no longer obstructed access to the spring relieving screws. The driver's position on the crane was also enclosed as protection against the elements. Although a through pipe for vacuum brake was attached along the left hand side of the carriage, amazingly it appears that the hand brake, applied to both wheels of the fixed axles by means of the hand wheel on top of the carriage, was removed. All these alterations to both the crane and match wagon seem to have taken place sometime prior to 1914.

Not long after the crane had been put in service, it attended at the scene of the derailment at Dunachton between Kingussie and Kincraig on 2 August 1888. Perhaps over-confidence on the part of the then inexperienced crew in the crane's abilities led to it overturning and toppling down the embankment.

During Highland days the livery of the crane appears to have reflected the locomotive livery of green, with lining, if any, consistent with current locomotive practice. It is also likely that lined crimson lake was applied during the LMS period. The LMS initially gave it the number MP 45, while the Northern Division accorded

it the number 1983 in its Plant Register. From May 1941 it was renumbered RS1060/15. The six-wheel packing wagon, built at Lochgorm in 1875, was given the number 297232, which leads one to suppose that the match wagon may have been No. 297231, or possibly 297233.

The crane and breakdown train were kept in a purpose built corrugated-iron shed beside the Rose Street curve at Inverness opposite Lochgorm Works throughout the remainder of the Highland's independent existence and on until Nov. 1939, when the crane exchanged locations with the GSWR 15-ton Cowans Sheldon standard crane of 1893 from Hurlford. This came about because with the onset of war the railway authorities were looking at the inter-working of cranes with neighbouring companies should the need arise in the event of an emergency and, at 13 foot 6 inches tall, the Highland crane was barred from GNSR territory. After Inverness received a modern Cowans Sheldon 30-ton crane in July 1942, there is some suggestion that the HR crane went for a short while to Wick, but this may have been confused with the GSWR one. The HR crane did go to Horwich Works in March 1944 and was at Toton Sidings allocated to the Traffic Dept from 17 August 1944. It was withdrawn in July 1947 and cut up during the week ending 15 October 1947.

Saturday, September 2, 1939.

EW R.A.F. SPEED-BOAT

speed-boat for R.A.F. purposes has been launched at the Shore Street Harbour, Inverness. This picture shows the boat being lowered by cranes from the quayside.

3. Standard Cowans Sheldon 15-Ton Cranes

Standard 15-ton cranes - curved jib (Mk 1)
Standard 15-ton cranes - swan necked jib (Mk 2)

During the 1890s Cowans Sheldon had been highly successful selling a standard design of crane with 4-4-0 wheel arrangement capable of lifting 15 tons to a radius of 20 or 22 feet when propped. As can be seen from the tables below, a wide selection of companies invested in examples of this standard design and not necessarily the larger companies, a few of which were noticeable for their absence. The design was a development of earlier prototypes, as described above, supplied respectively to the Caledonian and Highland Railway in 1886 and 1887.

The carriage of these standard cranes remained consistent throughout their period of production and came with an option of with or without travelling gear. As originally conceived with the propping girders out of the crane and on the match truck, the total weight of the crane was approximately 55 tons with a maximum axle load of 14¾ tons. Of course, as with time the companies chose to arrange for the propping girders to be permanently mounted in the crane, these weights will have increased slightly. The axle journals were 7 by 14 inch for the fixed axles and 6½ by 12 inch for the bogie.

At first these cranes were fitted with a curved plate jib with four oblong slots in the side plates, altered from 1895 to a swan-necked shape without any slots and will hereafter be referred to respectively as Mark 1 and 2.

In both cases the jib seems to have been available in two lengths in the order of 24 and 26 feet between the bottom pin and top pulley. Cranes fitted with the shorter one could lift the load of 15 tons to a radius of 20 feet, whereas the longer one allowed the crane to hoist this load at 22 feet radius.

The travelling gear was offered as an option for both types, some companies preferring to rely on a locomotive coupled to the crane to manoeuvre the crane on site; not easy to achieve with precision. In later life, their allowable speed in train formation was limited by rather crude suspension and journals to 25 mph. Several companies modified the propping girders to provide for the girders being permanently carried within transverse boxes under the carriage. These are shown thus + in the tables below.

Standard Cowans Sheldon 15-Ton Cranes – Curved Jib (Mk 1)

The first tranche of the standard 15-ton crane was characterised by the curved jib with four slots in the sides of the lower straight section. The variation in jib length was accomplished by the use of a standard straight length spliced to a curved section of radius and length to suit.

Cowans Sheldon Standard 15-Ton Cranes – Mk 1 Curved Jib									
Purch'd by	Date Deliv'd	Works No.	Cost	Running No			Match wagon No.	Allocation	Disposal
				Pre-grp	Grp	LMS 5/41 &/or BR			
M&SL	1893	1847T		24+	951504	125	951663?	Gorton '93, Sheffield 2/09-10/5/40, Langwith *6/56*, Mexborough 2/59-*3/64*	Wdn c'65/6
MR	1893	1854N	£1,623	25, 245+	MP36	RS1023/15	114903	Leeds '93-7/23, Llandudno Jct *'35*, Birkenhead '38, Stoke '39-*57*, Llandudno *9/61*	Wdn 24/11/64
MR	1893	1855N	£1,623	26, 241	MP33	RS1022/15	114904	Saltley '93-*9/18*, Gloucester 11/31, Bath '42-*29/4/50.*	
MR	1893	1856N	£1,623	27, 242	-	-	114905	Derby, to WD '14-'18	
MR	1893	1857N	£1,623	28, 243	MP34	RS1036/15	114906	Wellingborough '93-*10/5/40*, Hellifield 31/3/43-1/7/47, Accrington 8/43, Hellifield 1/44-9/49	Scrapped 28/5/51
NER	1893	1858T	£1,575	CME 1	-	-		Gateshead/York? '93-'06, to WD '14	To WD
NER	1893	1859T	£1,750	CME 2	901627		901697?	York/Gateshead? '93-'06, Tweedmouth *1/9/21*, C&W Shildon *'48*	Wdn '55
GSWR	1893	1890N	£1,495	2, MP44 +	1549	RS1057/15	191479	Hurlford '93-*1/1/31*, Inverness 11/39, Wick *23/4/42-31/8/61*	Wdn 9/63 scrapped Inverness
NS	1895	1965N	£1,550		MP40	RS1027/15	4841, 6461	Stoke '95-*2/45?*, Shrewsbury, Birkenhead (Dock Rd) *10/5/40-24/11/43*, Llandudno 11/5/44-*'57*	Wdn 9/63

N = Not fitted for self-travelling.
T = Fitted with self-travelling gear.
+ = Propping girders permanently carried under the carriage.

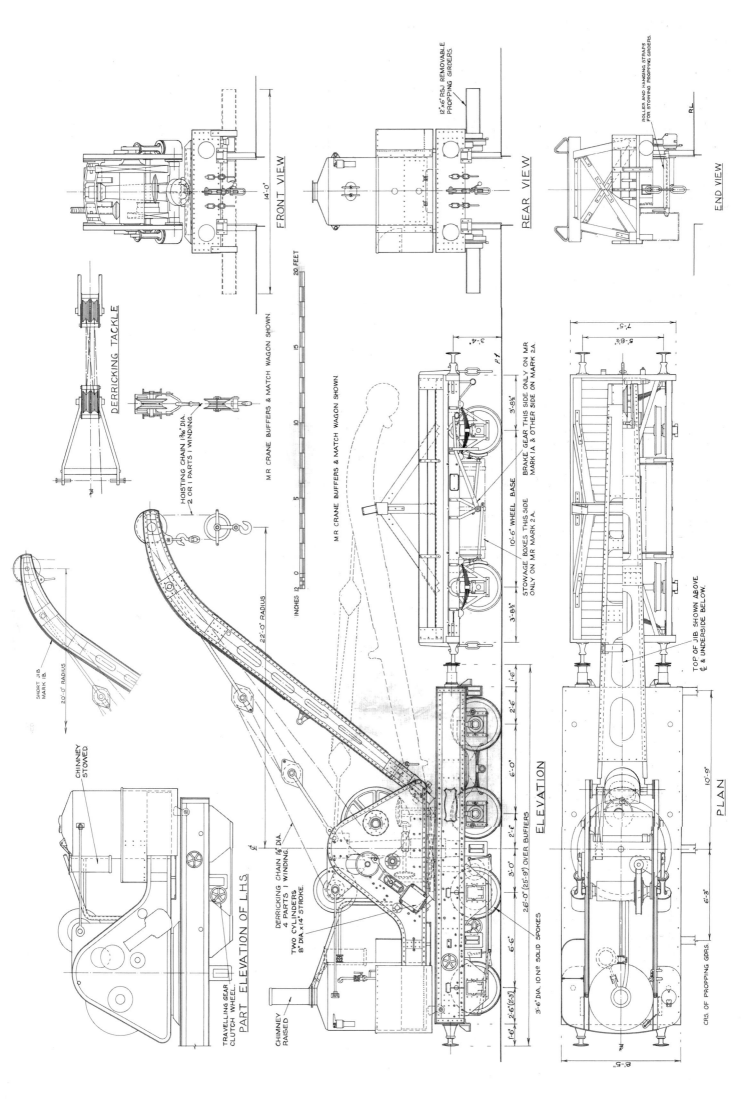

FRONT VIEW

REAR VIEW

END VIEW

DERRICKING TACKLE

HOISTING CHAIN 1⅜" DIA.
2 OR 1 PARTS 1 WINDING.

MR CRANE BUFFERS & MATCH WAGON SHOWN

20 FEET

15

10

5

INCHES 12   0

12"× 6" RSJ REMOVABLE
PROPPING GIRDERS.

ROLLER AND HANGING STRAPS
FOR STOWING PROPPING GIRDERS.

RL

7'-5"

5'-6½"

BRAKE GEAR THIS SIDE ONLY ON MR
MARK 1A & OTHER SIDE ON MARK 2A.

STOWAGE BOXES THIS SIDE
ONLY ON MR MARK 2A.

10'-6" WHEEL BASE

3'-8½"

3'-8½"

3'-4"

P.1

TOP OF JIB SHOWN ABOVE
℄ & UNDERSIDE BELOW.

PLAN

10'-9"

6'-3"

8'-5"

CRS. OF PROPPING GDRS.

PART ELEVATION OF L.H.S.

22'-0" RADIUS

MR CRANE BUFFERS & MATCH WAGON SHOWN

SHORT JIB
MARK 1B

20'-0" RADIUS

CHIMNEY
STOWED

TRAVELLING GEAR
CLUTCH WHEEL.

DERRICKING CHAIN 1⅜" DIA.
4 PARTS 1 WINDING.

TWO CYLINDERS
8" DIA.×14" STROKE.

CHIMNEY
RAISED

3'-6" DIA. 10 Nº SOLID SPOKES

℄

1'-6"   2'-6"(2'-3")   2'-6'-0" (25'-9") OVER BUFFERS   3'-0"   2'-6"   2'-6"   6'-0"   2'-6"   1'-6"

6'-6"

ELEVATION

Ex– Midland Railway 15-ton Cowans Sheldon crane No. 243, also plated MP 34 on the carriage and stationed at Wellingborough when photographed on 10 February 1939. It was subsequently renumbered RS 1036/15 in May 1941 and moved to Hellifield in 1943 and was scrapped on 5 May 1951. Note the lumber loaded on the 3-plank fixed-sided match wagon No. 114906. (BR, LMR author collection)

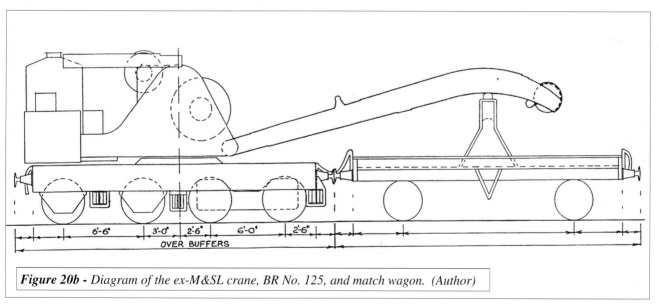

Figure 20b - *Diagram of the ex-M&SL crane, BR No. 125, and match wagon. (Author)*

Manchester, Sheffield & Lincolnshire Railway

The Manchester, Sheffield & Lincolnshire Railway, later the Great Central, was the recipient in 1893 of the first of the standard Mk. 1 cranes to be supplied to a British company. It was fitted with the longer variety of jib and travelling gear. As may be seen from the photograph of it later in life the telescopic arrangement of propping girders was applied to this crane. Less obvious is the vacuum brake pipe, and buffers mounted on hinged plates to enable them to be folded back and the crane to be positioned that little bit closer to the load to be lifted.

The match wagon was a typical GC product and it will be noted that the jib rest has been raised, thus increasing the purchase available as the derricking chains first start to raise the jib; the motion of derricking being the one that used the most steam from the boiler.

***Opposite page, Figure 20a** - Cowans Sheldon 15-ton Standard Mark 2 with swan neck jib paired with a Midland Railway match wagon. (Author)*

The Manchester, Sheffield and Lincolnshire Railway was the first British company to acquire what was to become the initial version of the standard Cowans Sheldon 15-ton crane with a curved jib. Note the four slots in the jib compared with only three on earlier 15-ton cranes. The steel match wagon is a typical product of Gorton for pairing with steam cranes of the period. This somewhat decrepit BR No. 125 was photographed at Doncaster on 10 October 1965, probably following withdrawal from Mexborough. The flaking asbestos boiler lagging would no doubt give a present day safety officer a fit! (RHG Simpson)

Midland Railway

As already noted, the Midland Railway was early in the field with the provision of steam breakdown cranes and continued its policy by ordering four Mark 1 cranes again with a relatively long jib, but without travelling gear, preferring instead to rely on an attendant locomotive to position the crane. Three-link couplings and parallel buffers were fitted from the outset, while the couplings may also have been replaced by the screw type.

The four match wagons were ordered on 22 March 1893 to Lot 321, Drg. No. 847. These were initially provided with hand brake on only the left-hand side. Some time after building, provision was made for stowing the propping girders under the wagons by the addition of a roller and straps suspended from the

underframe. Other modifications in service included the replacement of the lifting and derricking chains by steel wire ropes and the provision of telescopic propping girders.

No. 27 failed to reach the books of the LMS, it having been requisitioned by the War Department during World War 1. It was taken from Derby, where it had probably been 'the spare', in about 1914, and possibly went to the Sinai; the Egyptian State Railway had similar machines. It did not return to the MR, but after the war a pair of surplus WD Cowans Sheldon 15-ton steam cranes were advertised for auction at Richborough in Kent on 11 December 1919, for which this and possibly the NER crane, about to be referred to, are candidates.

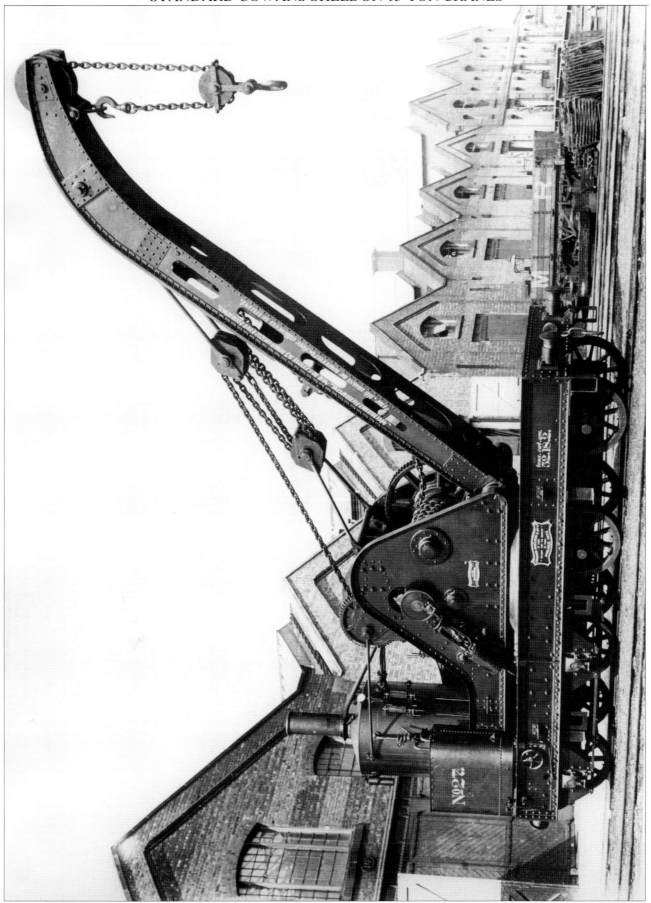

No. 27 is one of the four cranes bought by the Midland Railway in 1893. Photographed at Derby Works when new, various boiler fittings can be seen. Along the jib is written 'Midland Railway. Not to exceed 15 tons at 22 feet radius / The jib must be lowered before allowed to travel'. This crane was requisitioned by the War Department during World War 1 and failed to return to railway service. (BR, courtesy RJ Essery)

A close-up of No. 243 stationed at Wellingborough in what appears to be an all black livery. This crane is known to have been in a similar livery in early 1939. (HN Twells collection)

Former MR No. 25 became RS1023/15 under the LMS's renumbering scheme of May 1941, perpetuated by the London Midland Region, and after various postings found itself at Stoke when photographed there on 30 September 1961. By this time both its derricking and hoisting chains had been replaced by steel wire rope. (NEW Skinner)

Photographs suggest that as late as 1928 No. 26 from Saltley was still in locomotive red on the jib, crab side plates, water tanks and carriage sides.

North Eastern Railway

The North Eastern Railway appears to have been the first railway to adopt the shorter variety of jib for the two cranes it purchased in 1893. They were, nonetheless, provided with travelling gear. These were numbered CME 1 and CME 2 in the Chief Mechanical Engineer's list and initially allocated to Gateshead and York. What appears to be locomotive-style lining was applied to the tanks, crab sides and jib. One, however, was requisitioned during World War 1 and failed to return. The other lingered on until 1955.

At some stage one crane at least had a 2-plank fixed-sided match wagon. The crane initially stationed at Gateshead, however, was paired with a 4-wheel flat trolley wagon. No jib rest was provided at this time; instead the jib was held on the derricking tackle, and bridle gear fitted to restrain the lateral movement of the jib. At a fairly early stage the hoisting chain was also replaced by steel wire rope on this crane. When in 1912 the 15-ton crane at Gateshead was replaced by a 35-ton Craven crane, the match wagon appears to have been transferred to the new crane and again to the Cowans Sheldon crane in 1916.

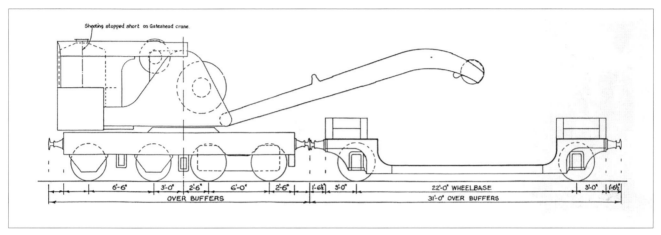

Figure 20c - Diagram of the NER crane with flat trolley match wagon. A more detailed version of the match wagon is shown on the drawing of the 35-ton Cowans Sheldon crane which follows - Figure 43. (Author)

The North Eastern Railway invested in two of Cowans Sheldon's 15-ton cranes in 1893, stationing them at the strategic locations of Gateshead and York from where they were well placed to attend the aftermath of the accident at Felling on 26 March 1907, this accident being a consequence of buckled rails. The crane from Gateshead is depicted in this view. Note the substitution of the hoisting chain by wire rope. (Author's collection)

Glasgow & South Western Railway

The final delivery in the year of 1893 was for a single example of the short jib pattern crane without travelling gear for the Glasgow & South Western Railway. GSWR crane No. 2 spent all its early years stationed at Hurlford. It only swapped places with the ex-Highland Railway 15-ton crane, as noted above, in November 1939. When Inverness received a modern Cowans Sheldon 30-ton crane No.RS1066/30 in July 1942, the GSWR crane then went to Wick where it remained until it was withdrawn and cut up in September 1963. Initially, no doubt, it was stationed at the far end of the Highland Section's Further North line to deal with any mishap to the important naval traffic to Thurso destined for Scapa Flow. Subsequently the nearby Dounreay nuclear research establishment may have been the reason for its continued presence, but the closure of Wick shed in 1962 spelt its end.

In 1914 a special 40ft long jib was provided by Cowans Sheldon to enable the crane to be used to lift boilers and to carry out other maintenance tasks on the many dockyard cranes owned by the company at Ayr, Troon and Irvine. This jib extension enabled the crane to lift 7½ tons at the height needed for the job.

So that the crane could work in the inhospitable weather conditions of those northern climes, the boiler and driver's position of the crane were almost totally enclosed. Telescopic propping girders together with vacuum brake pipe were also provided. In 1959 the crane was a grimy black with red buffer beams and white lettering.

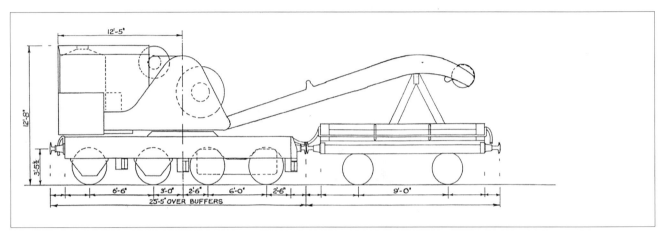

Figure 20d *- Diagram of the ex-GSW crane, LMS/BR No. RS1057/1, and match wagon. (Author)*

The Glasgow & South Western Railway was not slow to follow its neighbours in investing in a steam breakdown crane, Cowans Sheldon delivering one in 1893 to be based at Hurlford. Following an exchange with the Highland crane at Inverness in November 1939, it migrated north to Wick in 1942, where it was photographed as RS1057/15 on 20 September 1957. Equipped for use in Britain's northerly latitudes, most of the other usual modifications have also been applied, including the fitting of telescopic propping girders and through vacuum brake pipe. (J Templeton)

The final Mk 1 crane delivered to a British railway was to the North Staffordshire Railway in 1895. The crane is seen here at the head of the Stoke breakdown train with elaborate instructions painted on the back. (Author's collection)

North Staffordshire Railway

The North Staffordshire Railway was the last British railway to receive a Mark 1 crane with curved jib and this was in 1895. It was paired with a 2-plank match wagon with a jib rest of bent sections of old rail. This crane was unique in at sometime having outriggers fitted to provide additional support to the propping girders, following an incident when it overturned. These were hinged within the depth of the main members of the carriage to supplement the propping girders. The crane was later fitted with steel wire hoisting and derricking ropes.

This crane is understood to have been painted in North Staffordshire Railway locomotive red.

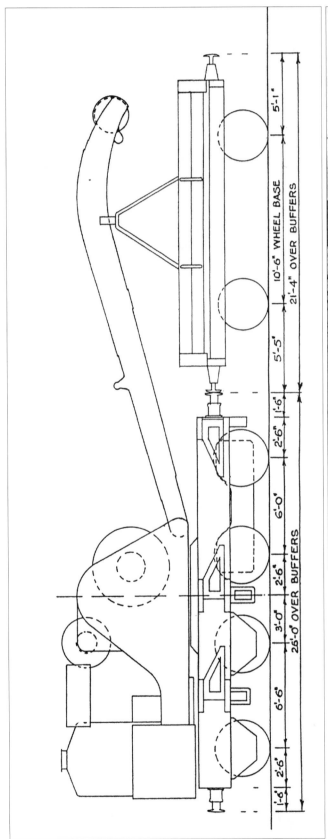

Left, Figure 20e - Diagram of the NSR crane and match wagon. (Author)

Above - Soon after delivery it toppled while recovering some derailed coal wagons at Diglake, as consequence of which it was uniquely fitted with hinged outriggers on each side of the carriage directly over each propping girder position. Whether this made any improvement in its stability is highly questionable! (Martin Welch collection)

Standard Cowans Sheldon 15-Ton Cranes
– Swan-neck Jib (Mk 2)

Whereas there had been nine Mark 1 curved jib cranes supplied to five different British railway companies within a period of three years, twenty of the Mark 2 swan necked type were subsequently purchased by nine companies over ten years, several coming back for repeat orders. Again, two lengths of jib were available – 26 feet and about 24ft 6in and with and without travelling gear. The variation in jib length of Mk 2 cranes was achieved by the use of a standard swan neck section spliced to a straight section of a length to suit.

Again after a while, most cranes seemed to have permanently carried shortened propping girders under the carriage, although a number of these stowed only a single beam and, one hopes, the second halves were available in the match wagon for insertion from the opposite side to prevent backward instability once the first was drawn out and propped up.

Cowans Sheldon Standard 15-Ton Cranes – Mk 2 Swan-necked Jib									
Purch'd by	Date Deliv'd	Works No	Cost	Running No			Match wagon No	Allocation	Disposal
				Pre-grp	Grp	LMS 5/41 &/or BR			
NB	1897	2117N			880044 981508+		880044 981509	St Margaret's, Thornton '14, Kitty-brewster *1926-1/11/47*	Wdn '51 scrapped Inveruie
NER	1897	2118T	£1,715	CME 3	901628+	(331)155	901705	York '97-'06, Sunderland S Dk *1/9/21-'38*, W Hartlepool *7/40-1/58*	Wdn '65
GC	1898	2119T			951505	104		Woodford 10/5/40, Hornsey *7/44-6/11/61*	Wdn c'63
GC	1898	2120T			951506	101		Ardsley *11/47-6/56*, Langwith Jct *10/60-post 4/64*, Lincoln	Wdn '66
GC	1898	2121T			951503	121	24693 on one!	Langwith Jct, Annesley, Mexbor-ough *10/5/40-6/56*	Scrapped '58
GC	1898	2122T			941594+	109		Colwick, Grantham *'47-6/11/61*	Scrapped '61
LBSC	1898	2181T	£1,626	16	315S	Ds315	315SM	Brighton, Ashford (K) *-26/3/34*, Ramsgate 5/46	Wdn 23/2/63
LBSC	1898	2182T	£1,626	17	316S+	Ds316	(1) 316SM (2) Ds22426	New Cross Gate-*26/3/34-44*, Stewart's Lane *25/8/50-1/5/63*	Wdn 9/3/63
MR	1899	2234N	£1,848	29, 244	MP31+	RS1037/15	114951	London (Kentish Town/Cricklewood?) *'99-10/27*, Nottingham *'27-'57*	Scrapped 26/1/64
MR	1899	2235N	£1,848	30, 240	MP41+	RS1028/15	116952	Durran Hill '99? *'01-'03*, Wakefield *'24-10/5/40*, Accrington *1/44-'57*, Hellifield 2/59	Scrapped 1/66
MR	1899	2236N	£1,848	31, 247	MP38	RS1025/15	116953	Bristol '99, Warrington, Edge Hill *2/37*, Bletchley *'42-10/60*	Wdn '61
MR	1899	2237N	£1,848	32, 246	MP35+	RS1021/15	116950	Belle Vue '99, Longsight *7/37-10/60*, Bolton Yd '60	5/65
GN	1899	2246N	£1,815	150A	961604+	-	(2) 961658	Peterborough *'04?*, Norwich *1/10/37*, Colchester *11/47*	C'60
GN	1899	2247N	£1,815	152A	941595	106		Doncaster *'04-'17*, Hornsey, Lincoln *10/5/40-'48*	Wdn '55
SER	1899	2250T	£1,910	L3	202S+	Ds202	(1) 4747 (2) 202SM, Ds3089	Ashford '00, Stewart's Lane *26/3/34-7/49*, Gillingham (K) *24/52-3/5/59*	Wdn 3/11/62
GW	1900	2406T			7	7	7	Oswestry *13/8/36-10/5/40*, Swindon '48, Oswestry *15/11/56*	Wdn '56
MR	1901	2421N	£1,961	33, 248	MP32	RS1030/15	117284	Grimesthorpe *'20*, Hasland *6/3/43-1/7/47*, Hellifield '57	Wdn 13/2/59
GW	1901	2448T			1 8 from '09	8	1, 8 from '09	Newton Abbot *13/8/36-15/11/56*, CCE's Dept 19/1/68 Swindon	Pre11/71
GW	1901	2449T			6	6+	6	Neath *13/8/36*, Swindon, Severn Jct '46, Neath *'55-11/11/57*	Wdn '65
LTSR	1906	2933T			MR 250	MP37+	RS1024/15	1855, 117654	Plaistow 8/06, Bescot *10/1/35-'56*	Wdn 11/63

N   =   Not fitted for self-travelling.
T   =   Fitted with self-travelling gear.
+   =   Propping girders permanently carried under the carriage.

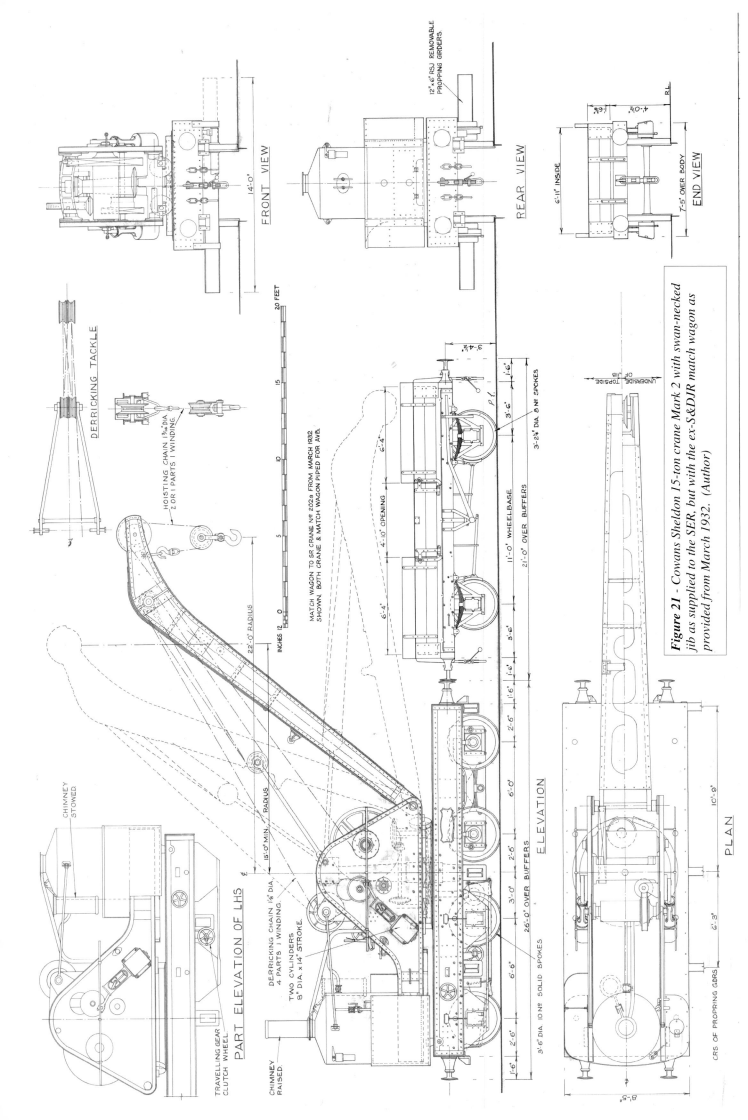

Figure 21 - *Cowans Sheldon 15-ton crane Mark 2 with swan-necked jib as supplied to the SER, but with the ex-S&DJR match wagon as provided from March 1932. (Author)*

North British Railway

As noted above, in 1882 the North British Railway acquired their first steam breakdown crane from the Scottish firm of Forrest & Co of Glasgow with a capacity of 20 tons. For their next crane they turned to the firm of Cowans Sheldon south of the Border country. This was the first Mark 2 15-ton crane and was fitted with the longer jib, but no travelling gear. It was paired with a 4-plank fixed-sided match wagon with a timber jib rest with a roller to accommodate longitudinal movement as slack in the coupling was taken up between the crane and match wagon. Although the 3-link coupling was in due course replaced by the screw type there is no evidence that automatic vacuum brakes pipes were fitted. The tapered buffers were later replaced by the parallel type. Unusually only a tarpaulin sheet was ever provided as shelter to the driver and to protect the machinery.

Early under the LNER's stewardship the disposition of cranes was rearranged; as a consequence of which this crane was transferred from Thornton to Kittybrewster for use on the Northern Scottish Area, previously only provided with a pair of 10-ton hand cranes. Under the LNER regime, the number 880044 was initially allocated. From 1938, however, the all system departmental numbering scheme was introduced when this crane became No. 981508 and the match wagon No. 981509. It was withdrawn in 1951, before a BR number could be applied.

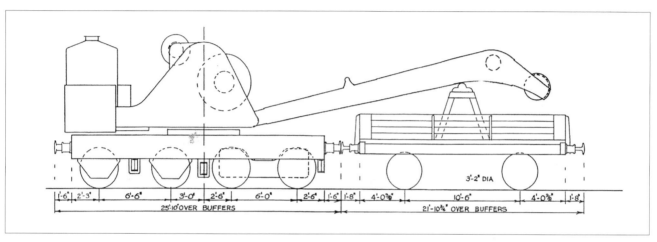

Figure 22a - Diagram of the NB crane, LNER No. 981508, and match wagon. (Author)

The first swan-necked 15-ton Cowans Sheldon crane to be acquired by a British company went to the North British in 1897. In 1928 the former NB 15-ton crane was moved to provide the first steam-powered breakdown crane to be stationed on ex-GNS territory. By now in LNER livery, No. 981508 is seen at Kittybrewster in 1949. (J Templeton)

Apart from the stowing of shortened propping girders on the crane, little appears to have been altered during its career. In particular, shelter for the driver was never more than a tarpaulin sheet over the tie rods between the crab sides and the boiler. On the other hand a ladder seen to be strapped to the side of the jib is unusual. It appears the crane had a hand in the removal of the bogie wheels of ex-GER 4-6-0 No. 8548 in the background. (JP Mullett)

North Eastern Railway

Presumably well satisfied with their two Mark 1 cranes, the North Eastern Railway purchased a single example of the Mark 2 with a short jib and travelling gear in 1897. The rearrangement of the propping girders into the telescopic mode was implemented, except that the front only had one girder. Presumably the second girder continued to be carried on the match wagon and installed on site. By March 1938 the lift of 15 tons when propped had been reduced to a maximum of 19 feet, with 10 tons at 26 feet and 5 tons at 28 feet.

Initially a 2-plank dropside wagon was attached as a match truck. Subsequently, by 1938, this had been replaced by an LNER 12-ton all steel plate wagon to diagram 65. In both cases no jib rest was provided.

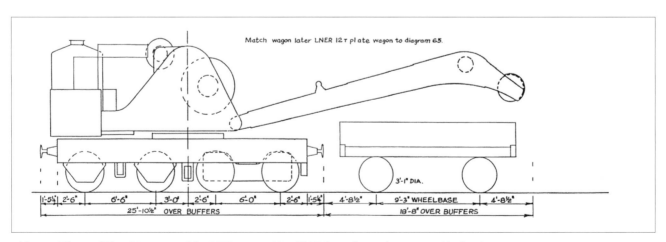

Match wagon later LNER 12 т plate wagon to diagram 65.

3'-1" DIA.

1'-5¼" 2'-6"   6'-6"   3'-0" 2'-6"   6'-0"   2'-6" 1'-5¼"   4'-8½"   9'-3" WHEELBASE   4'-8½"
25'-10½" OVER BUFFERS   18'-8" OVER BUFFERS

***Above, Figure 22b** - Diagram of the NER crane, No. CME 3, and match wagon. (Author)*

***Opposite page** - In addition to the two Mk 1 cranes the NER purchased from Cowans Sheldon in 1893, they added a third, four years later. During the inter-war period this was stationed at Sunderland and by 1938 had acquired a replacement match wagon in the form of an LNER 12-ton standard all steel plate wagon without a jib rest, while wire ropes have been installed in place of the original lifting chains. (N Wilkinson)*

From 1897 cranes flowed from Cowans Sheldon's works at Carlisle thick and fast. The GC took delivery of four the next year as part of the great equipping for the opening of the London extension. Neasden's 15-ton Cowans Sheldon crane poses behind GC 0-6-2T No. 772, when fairly new, although a corrugated-iron canopy has been added over the driver's position. (LGRP, author's collection)

Great Central Railway

The Great Central Railway, which the M&SL had become on 1 August 1897 with the imminent opening of the extension to London, took delivery the next year of four Mark 2 cranes with short jib and travelling gear. Match wagons to the same design as that paired with the solitary Mark 1 were provided for the new cranes. Again it appears the height of the jib rest was raised to improve the facility with which the jib could be raised, the jib of the Neasden crane seems even to have had an additional block under the jib to raise it by a further 6 inches or so.

On 4 December 1925, 15-ton steam cranes were allocated to Colwick GC (ex-Annersley) No. 1053, Mexborough 877, Neasden 1215, Sheffield 531 and Woodford 1189. For the record, as well as the 20-ton Craven at Gorton (see below), there were concurrently 15-ton Craven hand cranes at Langwith (ex-Immingham) 980, Leicester (ex-Grimsby) 1003, Retford 1012, Staveley 1043 and Wrexham 500. Further 10-ton hand cranes (T Larmuth) were at Barnsley 362, Lincoln (ex-Leicester) 1174 and Immingham (ex-Langwith) 1093, a Cowans Sheldon, while the 10-ton crane once at Lincoln had moved to Lowestoft (GE). Unfortunately the relationship of the GC numbers to subsequent ones has yet to be established. By circa 1938 the crane, then at Grantham, had shortened single propping girders permanently carried in the stowed position on the crane. A crude corrugated-iron sheet shelter was provided for the driver and to enclose the boiler, and vacuum brake pipe fitted.

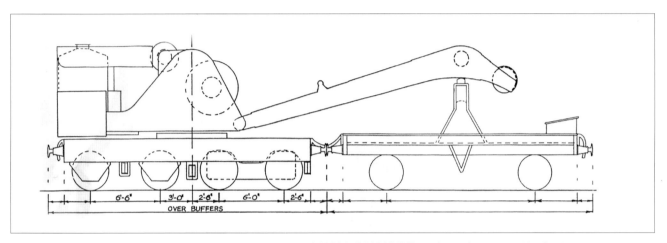

Figure 22c - Diagram of the ex-GCR crane, LNER Nos. 941594, 951503/5/6, and match wagon. (Author)

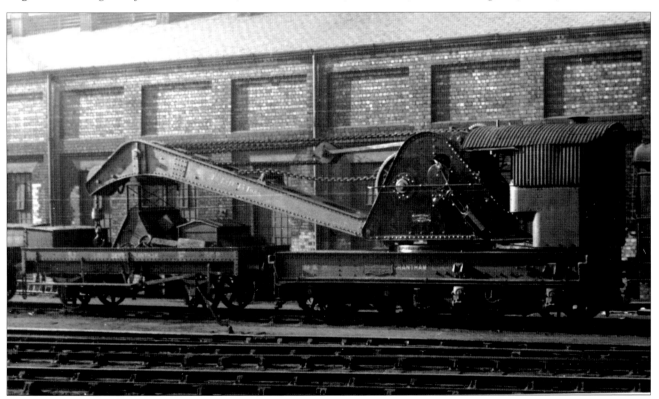

Under reallocations carried out by the LNER, one of the GC's cranes found its way to Grantham where it was photographed circa 1937. It is paired with a sturdily built match wagon with extended jib rest. On the crane the cover to the driver has been extended over the boiler and the sides enclosed with corrugated iron. The propping girders have been permanently stowed on the crane and vacuum brake pipe added. (GY Hemingway, courtesy HMRS)

London, Brighton & South Coast Railway

The London, Brighton & South Coast Railway was the first southern company to acquire this design of breakdown crane, although, as recorded above, the LSWR already had three from other sources. Two Cowans Sheldon 15-ton cranes with long jibs and travelling gear were supplied in 1898. Initially allocated to New Cross Gate and Brighton, the first moved to Stewart's Lane while the second had migrated to Ashford (Kent) by 1934 and on to Ramsgate by July 1937, the two being withdrawn in early 1963.

Both were originally paired with 3-plank fixed-sided match wagons with timber jib rests. Crane and match wagon, SR Nos. 316S and 316SM, were fitted with vacuum pipe in September 1933, as was No. 317S at some similar time. In due course rudimentary shelters were added for the driver's comfort. In 1953 No. Ds316, as it had become under British Railways, received a replacement match wagon No. Ds22426, which bears a strong resemblance to the underframe of an ex-LBSC 20-ton goods brake van with self-contained buffers.

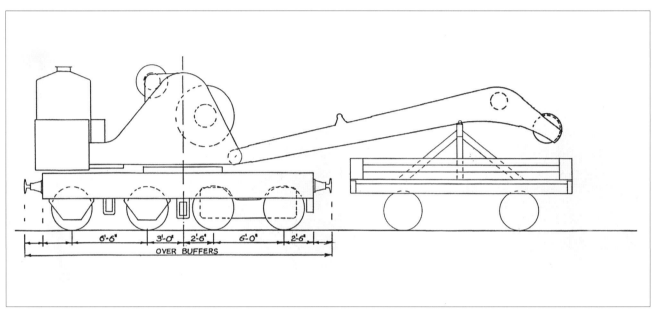

Figure 22d - *Diagram of the LBSC crane, Nos. 16 and 17, and match wagon. (Author)*

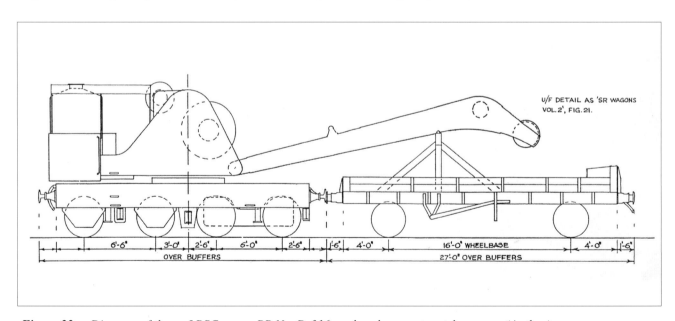

Figure 22e - *Diagram of the ex-LBSC crane, BR No. Ds316, and replacement match wagon. (Author)*

Opposite bottom - *In 1953 No. Ds316 (ex-LBSC No. 17) acquired a replacement match wagon, which appears to have been derived from the underframe of an ex-LBSC 20-ton goods brake van, probably with the original trestle type jib rest transferred. As may be seen in this view at Stewart's Lane, a sheet metal shelter and vacuum brake pipe have been fitted and again shortened single propping girders mounted in the crane, presumably the complimentary other halves were in the match wagon. (Author's collection)*

Also supplied in 1898 were two long jib cranes for the LBSC with travelling gear. The derailment of Stroudley 0-4-2T No. 239 Patcham *on a goods train at Cocking in September 1904 provided a fine sight for the photographer as 15-ton Cowans Sheldon steam cranes Nos. 16 and 17 set about recovery. Note the forward two propping girders on the front crane in position, but the third lying on the embankment. Observe also the tarpaulin stretched between the tie bars. The paintwork of the nearer crane, No. 17 from New Cross, glistens in the light, while the headstock can be seen to be lined out in a panel. (RC Riley collection)*

Midland Railway

In 1898 the Midland Railway came back to Cowans Sheldon with an order for four more cranes, construction continuing into 1899, and a fifth added in 1901. As before, long jibs and parallel buffers, but no travelling gear, were provided. Four match wagons were ordered on 5 May 1899 and built to Lot 463 to Drg No. 847/A, followed by another authorised on 17 January 1902 to Lot 504. These were similar to the 1893 batch, except that the brake gear was now on the right-hand side with provision from the outset for stowing the propping girders beneath the underframe.

By the grouping of the railways in 1923, the Midland Railway had fitted cabs to both types of crane. To achieve this, there appeared to be a curved iron roof plate between the crab sides and the boiler supported by iron bars off the tie bars between the boiler and crab, while tarpaulin side sheets were fitted to the support bars. Differences in these features between various cranes leads one to suspect that the roofs may have been fitted locally. Some ex-MR cranes had their chains replaced by wire ropes and/or propping girders permanently fitted to the carriages as telescopic. With time, vacuum pipes were also added.

Ex-MR 15-ton Cowans Sheldon steam crane No. 246 allocated to Manchester (Belle Vue) circa 1920. Apart from the addition of a roof, this crane remains in largely original condition. With the rationalisation of motive power facilities on the LMS, this crane was transferred from the Midland shed to the ex-LNWR one at Longsight by the mid to late thirties. (Real Photographs, author's collection)

By 1942 No. RS1025/15 had migrated from Bristol to Bletchley via Warrington and Edge Hill. It is seen still on duty at Bletchley around 1959, from where it was withdrawn in 1961. (MS Welch)

Great Northern Railway

The Engineer's Department of the Great Northern Railway had acquired two 15-ton steam cranes from Smith of Rodley in 1892 and the Locomotive Department soon realised these were useful items of plant. As a consequence Cowans Sheldon supplied two of their cranes in 1899 with long jibs and without travelling gear. These were stationed at the strategic locations of Peterborough and Doncaster. The former was displaced in 1914 and sent to Colwick and after grouping it was transferred to ex

-Great Eastern Railway territory when it went to Norwich and later Colchester, being broken up at Stratford in 1960.

Initially these cranes were coupled to former GN plate wagons without jib rests, but at some time LNER No. 961604 acquired an ex-GE twin-bolster wagon No. 961658 as its mate and which was equipped with a jib rest fabricated from angle section. The propping girders had by this time been shortened and permanently carried on the crane, whilst a sheet metal roof had been provided over the driver's position.

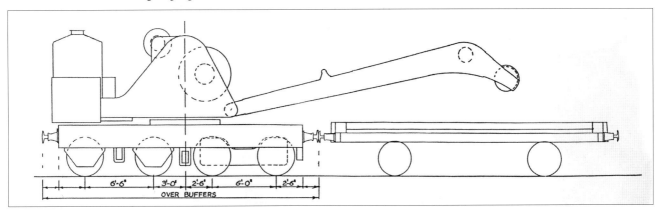

Figure 22f - *Diagram of the GNR cranes, Nos. 150A and 152A, and match wagon. (Author)*

The Great Northern Railway's 15-ton Cowans Sheldon steam crane assists in the erection of the steelwork to Crescent Bridge, Peterborough circa 1913. Note that at that time the boiler and driver's position were exposed to the elements and the crane's speed was limited to 20 mph. There are signs of lining round the water tank. (Brian White collection)

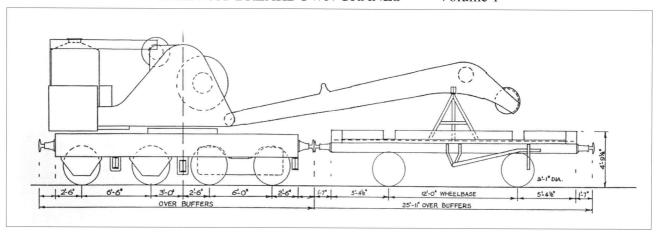

Figure 22g - *Diagram of the ex-GNR crane, LNER No. 961604, and later match wagon. (Author)*

Ex-GNR 15-ton Cowans Sheldon steam crane, as LNER No. 961604 and match wagon No. 961658, at Stratford North shed in 1959, having been transferred to the GE Section between the wars and at the time formally allocated to Colchester. (Denis Seabrook & Leo Gibbs collection, courtesy of HMRS)

South Eastern Railway

No doubt spurred on by its neighbour the LBSC, the South Eastern Railway ordered a 15-ton crane from Cowans Sheldon in 1899, likewise with a long jib and travelling gear. Following testing in February 1900, upon delivery this crane was stationed at Ashford (Kent). Under early Southern Railway rearrangements it was sent to Battersea, later known as Stewart's Lane, circa 1927 and Gillingham (Kent) around 1950.

According to the SR's register of service vehicles ex-SER No. L3 (SR 202S)'s first match wagon was a former SER 6-ton 12'-6" x 7'-8" ballast truck No. 4747. This, however, was barely long enough to extend under the full length of the jib and it seems a cut-out had to be made in the remote end of the wagon to accommodate this. Whatever, the first No. 202SM was withdrawn on 5 March 1932 and replaced by ex-Somerset & Dorset 10-ton 18'-0" x 7'-5" x 5'-6⅞" 2-plank open goods wagon No. 423 of 1912 to diagram 1309 and also accorded the number 202SM, later Ds3089. Of Midland Railway design, a third plank was added to the fixed part of the sides, but not the ends or doors, and at some stage a timber jib rest was fitted.

Since at least 1925 the cylinder, motion and flywheel have been encased and a sheet metal roof added, while later a through vacuum brake pipe was fitted to the crane and match wagon. The propping girders were also permanently carried on the crane. It would appear the crane was perhaps painted black with the number '202S' on the buffer beam one-third from the top between the left -hand buffer and draw gear. The match wagon No. 202SM was in a medium tone, presumably either brown or red oxide, with the letters SR the height of the middle plank. Under BR's ownership the crane and match wagon were painted a lighter tone, such as light grey, while the match wagon was given its own numbers Ds3089.

Former SER 15-ton Cowans Sheldon crane as SR No. 202S at Stewart's Lane sometime after March 1933 when paired with its second match wagon, an ex-S&D 2-plank open goods wagon. Note that the connecting rod and flywheel have been encased and a crude shelter erected over the driver's position and the boiler. (Author's collection)

By 23 May 1959, when this picture was taken, No. Ds202, as it had become under BR's ownership while the match wagon was now No. Ds3089, had been moved to Gillingham (Kent). Further protection for the driver's position has been provided in the form of makeshift vertical sheeting and a curtain. Note the various hooks hung around the wagon side and the two steps and grab iron on the far corner. (RC Riley)

Great Western Railway

It was the 20th century before the Great Western acquired any steam-driven breakdown cranes. They made a tentative start in 1900 with one 15-ton crane from Cowans Sheldon, in due course duly numbered No. 1. Presumably finding this satisfactory, they ordered two more the following year, later Nos. 6 and 7. No. 1 was renumbered No. 8, probably about 1909 to make way for a more modern and higher capacity 36-ton replacement, and it is possible Nos. 6 and 7 had previously been 2 and 3 as other cranes acquired these numbers in 1908 and 1912.

The three 15-ton cranes supplied to the GW had the shorter version of the jib and travelling gear. From early on the company seems to have added a combined enclosure to the boiler and cover for the driver in a style not un-reminiscent of an up-turned coal scuttle. Cranes Nos. 1 and 6 had 22ft 6in long match wagons to diagram L4 built in 1901/2, yet crane No. 8 had a 19ft 6in long one to diagram L15 built in 1913/4. What it was paired with prior to this is unclear. GW crane match wagons took the same number as the crane.

Early allocations of such GW cranes are elusive, but important works and sheds such as Old Oak Common, Swindon and Wolverhampton are likely. It is apparent that over a period more than one crane stationed at Old Oak Common was numbered 1 and the displaced crane promptly renumbered. By 13 August 1936, the earliest date for which a complete list has come to light, Nos. 6 to 8 were respectively at Neath, Oswestry and Newton Abbot.

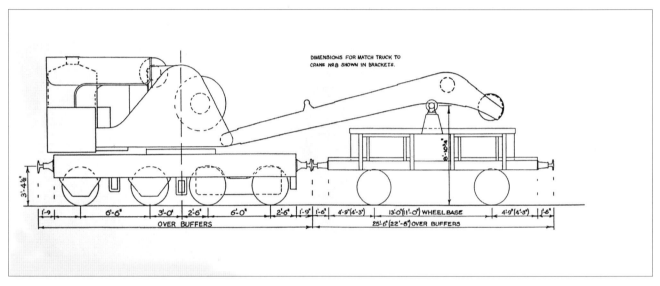

Figure 22h - Diagram of the GWR cranes, Nos. 1 (later 8), 6 and 7, and match wagon to diagrams L4 (and L5). A more detailed version of L5 is shown on the drawing of the 20-ton crane which follows. Details of L4 will be similar, if a little more stretched out. (Author)

Better late than never, it was the 20th century before the Great Western Railway purchased a single example of Cowans Sheldon's products and then quickly ordered two more. Illustrated here is No. 1, later renumbered 8, with its jib lowered on the match wagon, of the same number, and ready to be despatched in train formation to the site of operations. (British Railways, author's collection)

No. 1 with its jib raised in July 1902. Built with travelling gear and a short jib, the boiler and driver's position were provided, probably by Swindon, with a workman-like protection from the elements. The left-hand side of this and all subsequent cranes of this type have a large star-shaped casting on the crab side for the lower cross shaft. This may have been to aid withdrawal of the shaft for maintenance without the need to dismantle the crab sides. (British Railways, author's collection)

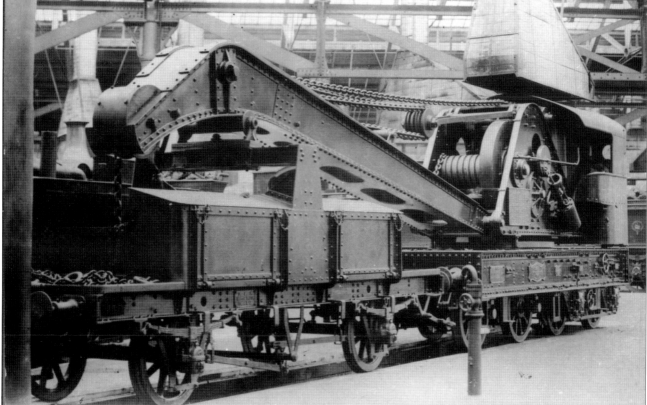

No. 7 from the 1901 batch showing the purpose-built match wagon. This view was reputedly taken at Old Oak Common in about 1910, either while the crane was standing in for the Stothert & Pitt 36-ton crane delivered in May the previous year, or taken earlier. (LGRP, author's collection)

GW 15-ton crane and match wagon No. DW 6 at Neath in BR days. Note the fitting of double telescopic propping girders. (JS Brownlie, courtesy C Capewell)

In 1906 the LT&SR was the last company to acquire a 15-ton crane of this design and by then lattice bracing had been adopted for the transverse members of the jib. It is seen here behind that company's 4-4-2T No. 23 Laindon *with the Plaistow breakdown train. As well as the 15-ton Cowans Sheldon steam breakdown crane soon after delivery complete with match wagon No. 1855; these are followed by packing wagon No. 3; equipment wagon No. 1854; and two 4-wheeled tool vans Nos. 2 and 1. (WO Steel collection, courtesy RJ Essery)*

London, Tilbury & Southend Railway

The last 15-ton standard Cowans Sheldon crane to be supplied to a British company was to the London, Tilbury & Southend Railway as late as 1906. This was of the longer jib pattern and was provided with travelling gear. There were, however, a couple of differences of detail in the jib. Firstly, the top and bottom slotted plates of the jib were replaced by lattice bracing, while the rivet spacing in the flange angles was increased over the length of the main shank of the jib. On the carriage the brake and clutch wheels were of disc form, rather than spoked, parallel buffers were fitted and propping girders seem to have been stowed on the crane from the outset. Reputed

to be a strong crane, it was claimed it could lift 20 tons at short radius.

The match wagon shows a marked resemblance to the Midland Railway's design, although it was to be another six years before that company officially took over the LT&SR. The wagon, however, had a different style of brake lever and two steps. After being displaced from Plaistow in early in 1931, the crane spent the rest of its life at Bescot.

The LTSR crane was painted unlined loco green and lettered LT&SR/armorial device/LOCO DEP^T on the bunker/tank sides, whilst the match wagon was lettered L.T.S.R./LOCO DEP^T + 1855.

The LT&SR's 15 ton Cowans Sheldon crane with its chimney raised in the upright working position and when new in that company's livery of unlined green etc. (R J Essery collection)

The LT&SR's 15-ton crane some time into its life. The absence of ownership initials suggests this may be following the take-over by the Midland Railway, but before being repainted. (RJ Essery collection)

Furness Railway's hybrid 15-ton breakdown crane based on a hand crane photographed at Barrow on 10 February 1939. This was, nonetheless, fitted with cylinders which relied on steam supplied by an attendant locomotive specially equipped for the purpose. Note the steel wire rope, side platforms extended and canopy over the machinery. (London Midland Region, author's collection)

4. Further Cowans Sheldon Cranes

Cowan Sheldon 15-ton steam-driven hand crane for Furness Railway
Standard 20-ton cranes
Standard 25/30–ton cranes

The small Furness Railway economised by acquiring a 15-ton hand crane from Cowans Sheldon to which 7 inch diameter by 10 inch cylinders were added, but omitting the boiler and instead relying on steam to drive them provided via a flexible pipe from an attendant locomotive. Nonetheless, in addition fold down side platforms, for men to stand on, and squared ends to the winding gear provided, suggest that it might also still be operable by hand as well.

Mounted on three axles, this crane, unlike steam cranes, had a moveable weight box, which was capable of being moved along the projection of the crab sides towards the rear of the crane. The purpose of this was to be able to optimise the axle loads while in train formation when positioned towards the centre and to maximise the counter-weight by being moved to the rear before commencing work. Facilities for two sets of propping beams were fitted and in later years at least these were stowed in place.

The 20 foot long curved head jib had no derricking gear, instead having just two radii of 18 and 21 feet fixed by inserting a pair of cotter pins in the appropriate slots in each adjustable bridle. When propped it could lift 15 and 12 tons respectively together with 7½ tons and 6 tons while free on rail. By LMS days it had a steel wire hoisting rope; and by

then through vacuum pipe and screw couplings were fitted, while sheeting round the driver's position and a roof had been added. The crane was paired with a 3-plank fixed-sided wagon, which had the inner end cut short.

It was based at and remained at Barrow all its life. At one stage a Furness 2-4-0 locomotive No. 44 was fitted out with a steam pipe from the dome leading forward to the front buffer beam from where a connection could be made to the crane positioned ahead.

Furness Railway 2-4-0 No. 44 was one of a pair of engines supplied by Sharp, Stewart in 1882 and these were the final engines of a group of nineteen of this wheel arrangement. The design was a standard Sharp, Stewart one and similar engines were supplied to other British railways, particularly the Cambrian. The engine was placed on the duplicate list as No. 44A in 1920. Late in its life it was used as a steam generator for the Barrow breakdown crane and survived in this form until 1925. It had been allocated the LMS Number 10002, which it never carried. What replaced it following withdrawal has not come to light, but it must have involved fitting a take-off from the boiler for the steam to be supplied to the crane.

Cowans Sheldon 15-Ton Crane for FR						
Works No	Cost	Running No		Match wagon No	Allocation	Disposal
		MP	5/41			
2654N	£1,800	39	RS1026/15	293579	Barrow 10/2/39-'57	Wdn 10/61

Furness Railway 2-4-0 No. 44 coupled to the FR's 15-ton hand crane and fitted with piping and flexible connection to provide steam to the crane's cylinders. (Cumbria Railway Association)

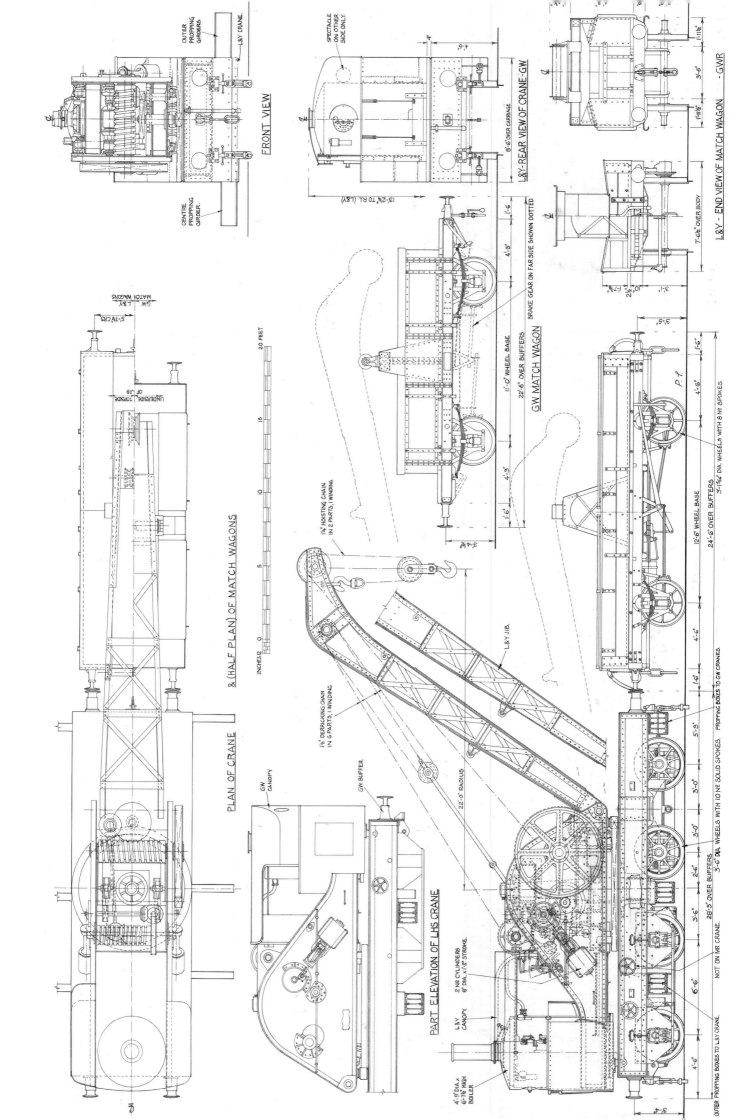

FRONT VIEW

OUTER PROPPING GIRDERS.

L&Y CRANE.

CENTRE PROPPING GIRDER.

SPECTACLE ON OTHER SIDE ONLY

L&Y-REAR VIEW OF CRANE-GW

8'-6" OVER CARRIAGE

13'-2⅝" TO R.L (L&Y)

L&Y - END VIEW OF MATCH WAGON - GVR

7'-6½" OVER BODY

10'-0½"

3'-1"

2'-1⅞"

1'-7⅞"

GW MATCH WAGON

BRAKE GEAR ON FAR SIDE SHOWN DOTTED

22'-6" OVER BUFFERS

11'-0" WHEEL BASE

4'-3"   4'-3"

1'-6"   1'-6"

4'-3½"

1¼" HOISTING CHAIN IN 2 PARTS, 1 WINDING

1⅛" DERRICKING CHAIN IN 6 PARTS, 1 WINDING.

L&Y JIB.

22'-0" RADIUS

5'-7⅝" CRS

GW MATCH WAGONS
L&Y

UNDERSIDE   TOPSIDE OF JIB

PLAN OF CRANE

& (HALF PLAN) OF MATCH WAGONS

INCHES 12   0   5   10   15   20 FEET

PART ELEVATION OF LHS CRANE

GW CANOPY

GW BUFFER.

L&Y CANOPY

2 N° CYLINDERS 8" DIA. x 12" STROKE.

4'-9" DIA. x 6'-7¼" HIGH BOILER.

P.t

3'-5"

1'-6"   4'-6"   1'-6"

24'-6" OVER BUFFERS

12'-6" WHEEL BASE

3'-1⅝₆" DIA. WHEELS WITH 8 N° SPOKES.

PROPPING BOXES TO GW CRANES.

3'-6" DIA. WHEELS WITH 10 N° SOLID SPOKES.

28'-3" OVER BUFFERS

4'-6"   3'-4"   6'-6"   3'-6"   2'-6"   3'-0"   3'-0"

3'-4"

OUTER PROPPING BOXES TO L&Y CRANE.

NOT ON MR CRANE.

Purch'd by	Date deliv'd	Works No	Cost	Running No			Match wagon No	Allocation	Disposal
				Pre-grp	1st grpg	2nd grpg			
L&Y	1902	2545T	£2,280	2231	MP28	RS1062/20, W Reg 25	(1)30456, 160456, 167388 (2) Dw25	Newton Heath '02, Plaistow 3/31-*10/5/40*, Gloucester 8/42-*11/9/70*, to WR '52	Scrapped '71
GW	1903	2614T			4		4	Bristol *13/8/36-10/5/40*, Neath *10/42-15/11/56*, Swindon *mid '65*	Wdn '65
GW	1903	2615T			5		5	Old Oak Common *2/07*, Swindon Wks *13/8/36-10/60*	Wdn '65
MR	1904	2617N	£2,525		1569	RS1058/20		Derby Wks	Wdn '69

Table heading: Cowans Sheldon 20-Ton Cranes

Standard Cowans Sheldon 20-Ton Cranes

By the beginning of the 20th century something with slightly greater lifting capacity was being called for by the railway companies. The standard 15-ton design was enhanced by an increase in the length of the carriage, by inserting 6 inches in the wheel-base between the inner axle of the fixed and the centre line of the pillar, while the tail radius was also increased by a little over one foot. A cross-braced lattice jib was adopted in lieu of the plate form previously employed, while telescopic propping girders were provided from the outset. This enabled 20 tons to be lifted out to a radius of 22 feet, although the GW seems at some stage to have limited its cranes to 20 feet. Much of the large intricate castings of the 15-ton crane, particularly of the bedplate, were replaced by fabricated steelwork, while the slewing rack was placed outside the roller path.

The crane weighed 67¾ tons and with the jib resting on the match wagon the maximum axle load in train formation was 17¾ tons. The amended design led to more even axle loads with the result that the journals were now made 7 by 14 inch all round.

Whilst it was the Lancashire & Yorkshire Railway's first venture into steam-powered breakdown cranes, the other two, the GW and MR, had both been purchasers of the 15-ton standard crane, albeit rather late in the case of the former. As the first of the batch, the underside of the propping girder boxes to the outer girders of the L&Y crane were different from those of the GW, in that the corner angles were below the boxes whereas the GW ones were formed by rolled steel channel sections on their sides. The jib of the L&Y crane also had a longer length of plate at the jib head and slightly shorter bracing panels. The L&Y had replaced its chains on the lifting and derricking tackle by steel wire rope by 1917, the GWR later following suit with at least one crane.

Above - The L&Y 20-ton Cowans Sheldon crane in June 1935 after its move to Plaistow on the LT&SR and coupled to that company's tool vans. The main spur wheel driving the hoisting drum has moved outside the crab sides, which themselves show an increase in size. (W Potter, author's collection)

Opposite page, Figure 23 - Cowans Sheldon 20-ton steam breakdown crane as supplied to the L&Y, GW and MR between 1902 and 1904. The first two also have their respective match trucks shown.

Lancashire & Yorkshire Railway

The Lancashire and Yorkshire Railway's first purchase of a steam breakdown crane was the new 20-ton enhanced version of Cowans Sheldon's product, the first supplied to a British railway. Based at first at Newton Heath, it was displaced from there in March 1931 with the arrival of a much larger 36-ton crane from Craven Bros. The 20-ton crane was then transferred south to Plaistow (LT&SR), where it remained until again displaced in August 1942 by a modern 30-ton crane by Ransomes & Rapier. Its final destination was Gloucester, which with regional boundary adjustments ten years later ironically fell into Western hands, when it was renumbered 25.

The match wagon, or safety wagon as they termed it, was built by the L&Y on a 21ft 6in underframe in 1902 at a cost of £92-8-2d. It was originally equipped with grease axle-boxes, but by 1931 these had been exchanged for the oil-lubricated variety. This wagon was numbered with the rest of their goods stock as 30456, which became 160456 under the LMS's ownership. Sometime between June 1935 and early 1939, however, what appears to be the same wagon had become No. 167388. Following the crane's transfer to the Western Region, at some time it was exchanged for a GW example.

Great Western Railway

On 23 June 1903 the GW ordered a couple of 20-ton cranes from Cowans, which were delivered before the year was out as Works Order Nos. 2614 and 2415 and these

were numbered 4 and 5. No evidence has come to light to suggest either was allocated to Old Oak Common prior to the arrival there of the 36 tonner to be described below, hence their numbers follow on to the existing three 15-ton cranes the company already possessed. Two match wagons 19ft 6in over headstocks to diagram L5 were built at Swindon to Lot 445 in 1903.

To enable No. 5 to carry out work at a high level at Swindon, it was temporarily fitted with a long jib. To reach the hook at a much greater height the hoisting tackle was re-rigged with steel wire rope instead of chains, yet retained the latter for the derricking gear, albeit with longer tie rods. Later the derricking chains would also be changed for wire rope.

Midland Railway

Little is known about the 20-ton crane the Midland Railway acquired in 1904 which appears to have been for use at Derby Locomotive Works and during its time seems not to have ventured far. It was probably not employed on breakdown work and hence appears not to have featured in the LMS MP numbering scheme, instead having the plant No. 1569, nonetheless received the number RS1058/20 in May 1941. A match wagon was ordered on 2 Sept 1903 to be built by Derby Works to Lot 566 and drawing 508/03.

Opposite top - No. 5, the second of the GW's two 20-ton cranes acquired in 1903, with the usual GW- style cab and married to one of its typical GW purpose-built all-steel match wagons. *(Photomatic)*

Above - Under Western Region management the former L&Y crane was renumbered 25 and its match wagon exchanged for a GW-built example, as seen here at Gloucester on 9 September 1970 with hazard stripes on the water tanks. (Author)

Above - *No. 5 again, but fitted with a 10-ton long jib very much in the style of a Ransomes & Rapier, photographed in the process of erecting structural steelwork for the extension to Swindon A Shop on 23 April 1917. Work on this started just before WW1 and continued as and when possible during the war. Fancy climbing those tall ladders? (BR, author's collection)*

A close up of No. 4's side towards the end of its life showing details of the carriage and superstructure with the usual GW cast iron notice plates attached to the tank. (Author's collection)

Standard Cowans Sheldon 25/30-Ton Cranes

As the first decade of the 20th century progressed, Cowans Sheldon developed their concept of the standard crane even further. Another 12 inches were added to the axle spacings of the previous 20-ton version between the centre and rear axle centres. This permitted the centre propping girder yokes to be moved forward of the centre of rotation thereby simplifying the accommodation of the travelling gear train. The leading edges of the propping girder boxes were provided with rollers to ease the withdrawal and return of the girders. The larger crane, according to which official diagram is consulted, resulted in increased axle loads of between nearly 16 and 19 tons, which in turn led to journal size of 8 by 15 inches.

The adoption of steel wire ropes from the outset enabled a revised hoisting gear arrangement to be substituted with a smaller final pinion wheel on the left-hand side, instead of the right. A similar lattice jib, but more lightly constructed with four cross-braced side panels, was designed to lift 30 tons at its minimum radius of 17 feet and 25 tons out to a radius of 22 feet. In the case of the former LNWR crane, supplied as 25-ton capacity at 22 feet radius, under the auspices of the LMS this was up-rated to 30 tons at minimum radius around 1938/9.

At some time prior to 1938, vertical stiffeners were added in the web of the carriage sides over each of the three propping girders of the L&Y crane. The presence of these, at least over the central and rear girders, on the general arrangement drawing for the LNWR crane suggest these may have been fitted from the outset.

Cowans Sheldon 25/30-Ton Cranes									
Purch'd by	Date delv'd	Works No	Cost	Running No			Match wagon No	Allocation	Disposal
				Pre-grp	MP	5/41			
L&Y	1906	2954	£4,750	2265	16	RS1019/30 126	32314, 162314	Sandhills '07, Wakefield 1/12-'20 (requisitioned 12/16), Leeds '25, Grimesthorpe '31-*6/11/61*, to ER 1/2/58, Lincoln c'62	Wdn 10/11/69
LNWR	1908	2987	£2,585		21	RS1020/30	284235	Rugby '08, Saltley 11/31-*10/60*, Bletchley 4/61-*5/64*, stored 4/67	Preserved – see text

Opposite page, Figure 24 - *Drawing of the 25/30-ton Cowans Sheldon steam supplied to the L&Y in 1906 and LNWR in 1908. (Author)*

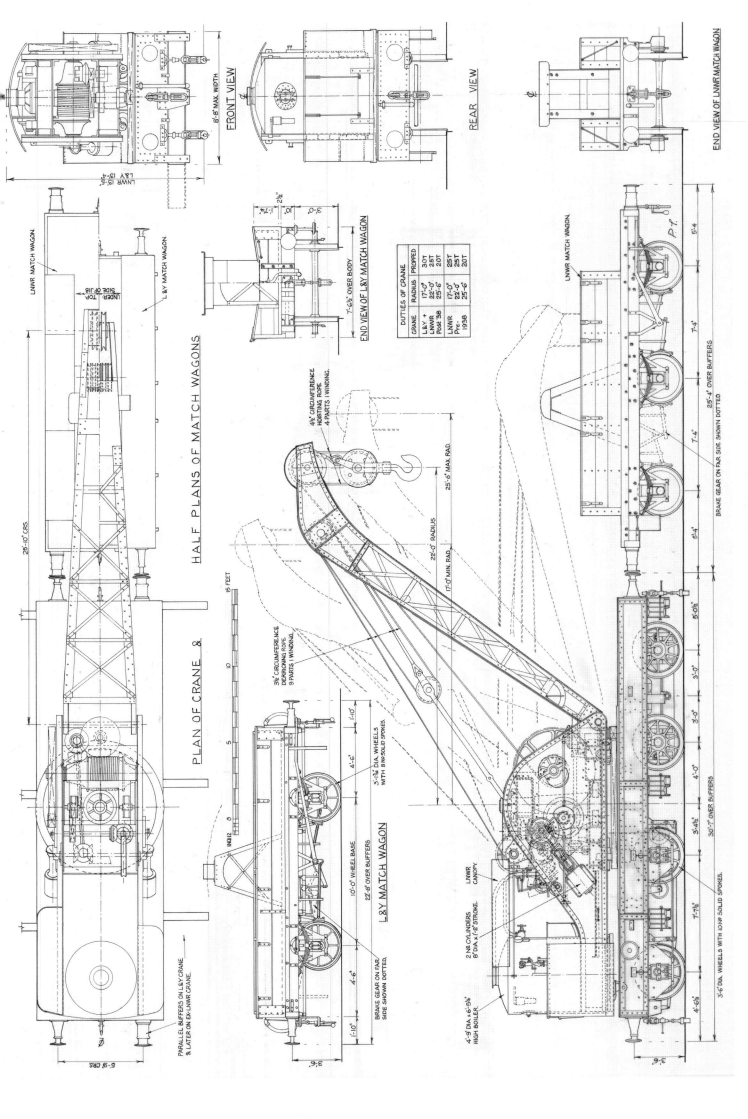

FRONT VIEW

REAR VIEW

END VIEW OF LNWR MATCH WAGON

L&Y 13'-4"
LNWR 13'-5"
8'-8" MAX. WIDTH

LNWR MATCH WAGON.

UNDER TOP SIDE OF JIB

L&Y MATCH WAGON.

25'-10" CRS.

HALF PLANS OF MATCH WAGONS

PLAN OF CRANE &

PARALLEL EL BUFFERS ON L&Y CRANE.
& LATER ON EX-LNWR CRANE.

5'-9" CRS.

END VIEW OF L&Y MATCH WAGON

2½"
10"
1'-7¼"
3'-0"

7'-6½" OVER BODY

DUTIES OF CRANE		
CRANE	RADIUS	PROPPED
L&Y + LNWR Post '38	17'-0" 22'-0" 25'-6"	30T 25T 20T
LNWR Pre- 1938	17'-0" 22'-0" 25'-6"	25T 25T 20T

4½" CIRCUMFERENCE
HOISTING ROPE.
4 PARTS 1 WINDING.

3½" CIRCUMFERENCE
DERRICKING ROPE.
9 PARTS 1 WINDING.

25'-6" MAX. RAD.

22'-0" RADIUS

17'-0" MIN. RAD.

LNWR MATCH WAGON.

BRAKE GEAR ON FAR SIDE SHOWN DOTTED.

P.†.

5'-4"

7'-4"

7'-4"

5'-4"

25'-4" OVER BUFFERS

5'-0½"

3'-0"

3'-0"

4'-0"

3'-4½"

30'-7" OVER BUFFERS

7'-7½"

4'-6½"

3'-6" DIA. WHEELS WITH 10 N° SOLID SPOKES.

15 FEET
10
5
0
1234

3'-1¾" DIA. WHEELS
WITH 8 N° SOLID SPOKES.

4'-6"

1'-0"

L&Y MATCH WAGON

10'-0" WHEELBASE

22'-6" OVER BUFFERS

4'-6"

1'-0"

3'-6"

BRAKE GEAR ON FAR SIDE SHOWN DOTTED.

LNWR CANOPY.

2 N° CYLINDERS
8" DIA x 1'-2" STROKE.

4'-9" DIA x 6'-5¾"
HIGH BOILER.

Lancashire & Yorkshire Railway

The first crane of 30 tons capacity was supplied to the Lancashire and Yorkshire Railway in 1906. This was numbered 2265 and allocated to Sandhills in Liverpool, moving in December 1912 to Wakefield. Exactly four years later the LYR temporarily lost this crane when it was requisitioned from there for war service. It later returned to the LYR at Wakefield. Under LMS management it first became No. MP16 at Leeds and in May 1941 RS1019/30, by when it was at Sheffield Grimesthorpe shed. The match wagon No. 32314, later becoming LMS No. 162314, was built by the L&Y railway company in 1907 with oil-lubricated axle-boxes at a cost of £93-3-8. Like its predecessor for the 20-ton crane, it had automatic vacuum brake from the outset and the crane piped for this type of brake.

On 1 January 1958, Grimesthorpe shed, with its crane, was transferred to the Eastern Region. They renumbered the crane 126 and circa 1962 it was transferred to Lincoln. Whilst there it received a full overhaul and was paired with a 4-wheel match wagon No. DM 339990 30ft 4½in long over the buffers. All, except below the crane carriage and the match wagon solebars which were black, was painted bright red, relieved only by a white jib head and lettering together with the black buffer heads. It was finally withdrawn from Lincoln on 11 November 1969.

Left - The Lancashire & Yorkshire 30-ton steam crane at the time of its completion by Cowans Sheldon in 1906, possibly in photographic grey. This clearly shows its heritage as a scaled up version of the 20-ton crane supplied to the railway four years earlier. The match wagon was provided by the L&Y. (Author's collection)

Opposite page - On the same occasion the crane with the jib raised. Note the steel wire rope hoisting and derricking tackle, corrugated iron roof and four instead of three lattice panels in the jib sides. Also, as yet, no vertical stiffeners have been added above the propping girders, which will require the repositioning or discarding of the works plate. (Author's collection)

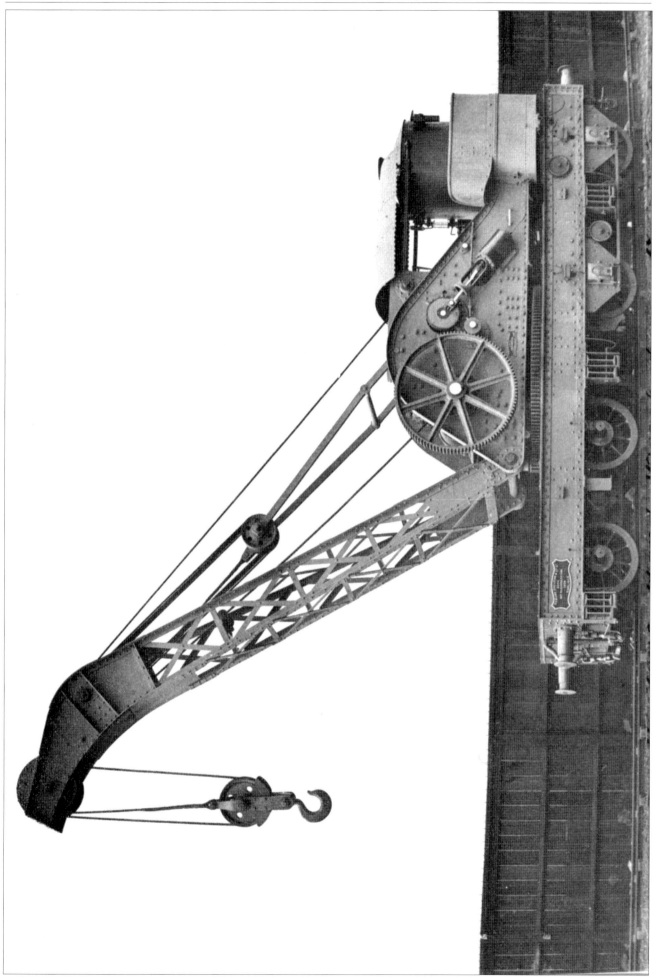

London & North Western Railway

By early 1907 it had become clear to the LNWR that its attempt to construct its own steam breakdown crane was failing to produce a satisfactory product, to be described below. With Francis Webb now retired, it was necessary for the Locomotive Department to swallow its pride and purchase a crane from a recognised outside builder. They seemed to have gone in quick succession to a couple of these, the first being Cowans Sheldon, with whom an order was placed on 23 May 1907 for a crane similar to the L&Y's a year earlier, but actually rated as capable of lifting 25 ton at a radius of 22 feet. In 1938/9, however, its ability to lift a load greater than 25 tons at minimum radius of 17 feet was formally recognised when it was upgraded to 30 tons. At first listed as number MP 21 by the LMS, like its companions it was renumbered in May 1941, becoming RS1020/30 which it retained until the end.

Stationed from the outset at Rugby, it was only displaced from there in 1931 with the acquisition by the LMS of a 36-ton crane. By November that year it had found its way to Saltley where it stayed until late 1960 or early 1961, when a further cascading of cranes occurred and it spent its last days at Bletchley until withdrawn and stored with a view to preservation. At sometime tall gusset plates were added to the sides of the propping girder boxes to provide lateral restraint, together with vertical angles on the lending end headstock.

LNWR breakdown cranes are believed to have been painted dead black.

This crane was claimed for the National Collection direct from BR for preservation and stored in the old Pullman car works at Preston Park until 1978, after which it was despatched to Carnforth. For reasons now obscure, it is understood that the unusual LNWR match truck was one of the reasons it was claimed in the first place and this was restored from a ruinous state at Carnforth in 1993. There had been some suggestion that, if both this crane and the Cravens crane already on site at NRM were restored, then demonstrations of railway cranes working together could be effected.

Following the closure of Carnforth as a visitor centre in April 1998, the crane was transferred to the Churnet Valley Railway (CVR), a registered museum and where a number of loans had been placed. In 2004 it was decided that having two steam breakdown cranes in the National Collection was an unsustainable luxury. The artefact was, therefore, de-accessioned and offered to the Churnet Valley Railway on condition it was maintained in fair condition and made accessible to the public if they showed an interest in it.

There had been a programme to restore the crane, however in recent years it had on several occasions been the victim of scrap metal thieves and its condition seriously deteriorated. Seeing no way forward, the CVR Company allegedly first made offers to others, but, on receiving no positive response to their limited enquiries, the decision was sadly taken to scrap the last of the once so numerous earlier generation Cowans Sheldon cranes. As a consequence it was regrettably sold for scrap in April 2011. However, following consultation with the NRM, it demise was put in abeyance while a buyer was sought. It is reported to have been delivered to the Crewe Heritage Centre during October 2011.

Ex-LNWR 25-ton steam crane supplied by Cowans Sheldon in 1908 and up-rated by the LMS circa 1939 to 30 tons and numbered RS 1020/30. Notice the vertical stiffeners above the right hand propping girders. It is seen here at Bletchley around 1962. (MS Welch)

RS1020/30 on 6 June 1979, then in the National Collection, on loan to Steamtown at Carnforth, who restored the crane to working order, showing the 6-wheeled match wagon. (MS Welch)

Again at Carnforth RS1020/30 with the jib raised on 22 March 1981. (MS Welch)

5. Early Competition

Jessop & Appleby 20-ton crane
Craven Bros 20 & 25 ton cranes
Stothert & Pitt 20-ton cranes for LSWR

Jessop & Appleby 20-Ton Crane

Cowans Sheldon having monopolised the British market in steam breakdown cranes for nearly two decades, others began to move in on the lucrative field during the first decade of the 20th century. By the time of the building of the 20-ton crane for the Alexandra (Newport & South Wales) Docks Railway in 1904, the firms of Appleby and Jessop had joined forces. Little material on this crane has come to the author's attention, but following the amalgamation of 1923 the Great Western Railway prepared diagrams of this and other acquisitions. From the

diagram for this crane, reproduced below, it can be seen that it was a typical product of the period with inclined cylinders within an extensive shrouding of the rear half of the superstructure. The superstructure was mounted on a live ring and the carriage was carried on four axles, the rear two being in the form of a bogie. At about 32 feet the length of the jib was greater than previously the norm on British breakdown cranes, but this was soon to be exceeded. It was plate sided and supported by steel wire ropes, as was the hoisting tackle.

It seems to have spent its entire career in South Wales until withdrawn in 1956.

Jessop & Appleby 20-Ton Crane for A(N&SW)DR			
Date delivered	*Running No*	*Allocation*	*Disposal*
1904	74	Cathays, Newport Pill, Ebbw Jct *13/8/36-15/11/56*	Wdn '56

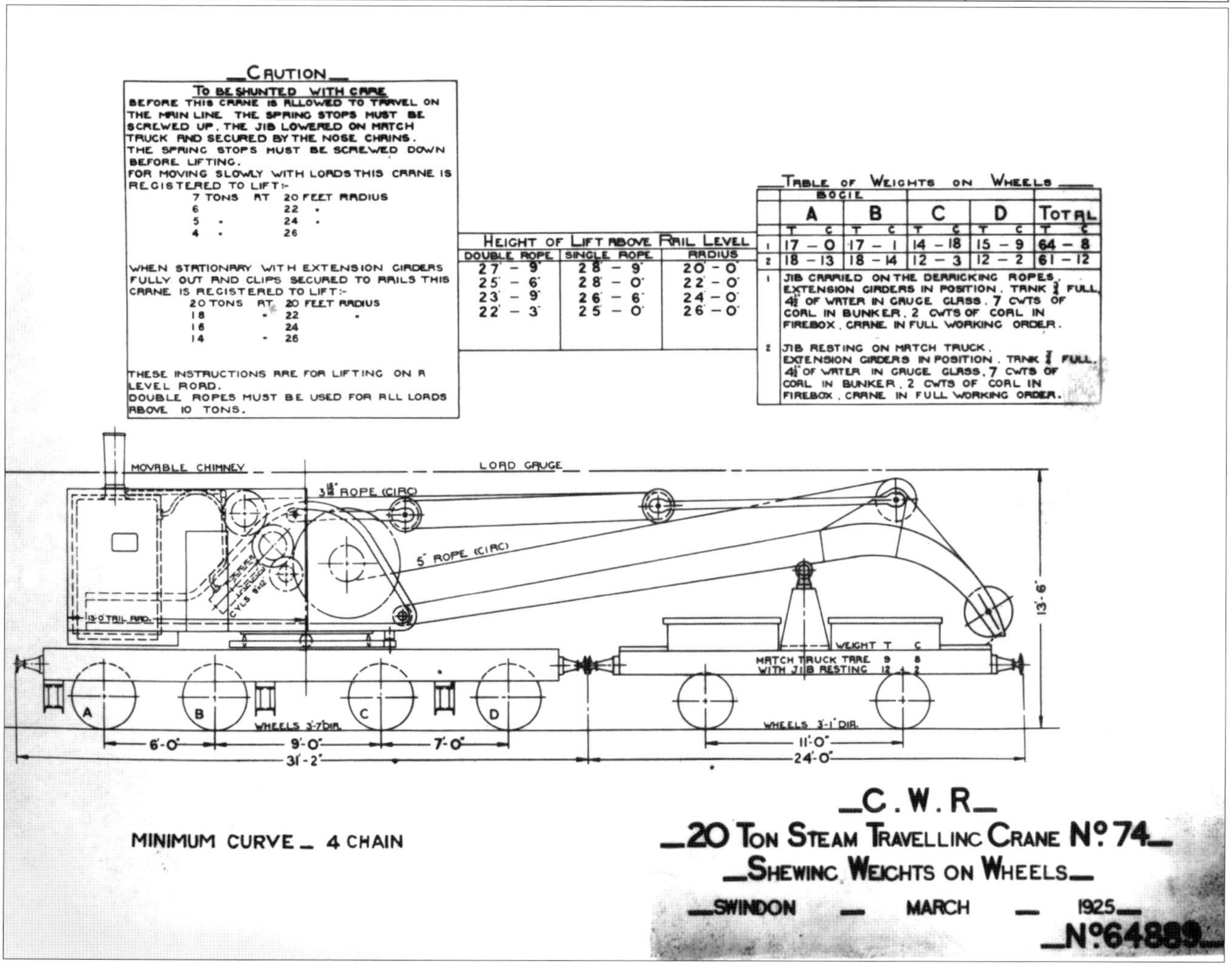

Figure 25 - The GW's diagram for the Jessop & Appleby 20-ton steam crane supplied to the Alexandra (Newport & South Wales) Docks Railway in 1904. (Author's collection)

Purch'd by	Date ord'd - deliv'd	Order No	Cost	Running No			Match wagon No		Allocation	Disposal
				Pre-group	Grp'ing	LMS 5/41/ BR	Pre-Gr'p	Group		
CR	5/06 - 1907	C8117	£1,499	3	1243	RS1052/20, RS1052/18¾	(1) 4746	(2/3?) 349271	Motherwell '07-1/1/31, Polmadie *2/2/39-10/5/40*, Motherwell *7/10/43-1/10/60*, Perth '62-'66, Polmadie *3/8/68-7/2/74*, Motherwell *4/75-9/6/76*	Scrapped 23/8/76
CR	5/06 - 1907	C8117	£1,499	4	1244	RS1053/20, RS1053/18	(1) 32511	(2) 320632 (3) DM 320632	Motherwell '07-1/1/31, Perth '31 *-10/5/40*, Carstairs *30/10/43-1/44*, Kittybrewster 10/50-*7/9/52*, Ferryhill *14/9/53-1/10/60*, Carstairs '62, Eastfield '63-*28/6/70*	Sold for scrap 1/73
GC	6/06 - 1907	C8138	£2,055		951501	105	13582		Gorton 9/08-*10/5/40*, Neasden *16/9/42*, Darnall *7/44-3/64*, Wath *post 4/64*, Shirebrook '70	Wdn '69

Craven Bros 20- & 25-ton Cranes

The Manchester firm of Craven Bros in Reddish entered the field in 1906 when it received in May that year an order for two 20-ton cranes from the Caledonian Railway, to be followed a month later by a single example for the Great Central Railway and three 25-ton cranes for the North Eastern Railway. All these were strongly built, with a reputation for riding smoothly in train formation at a good turn of speed, as well as being capable of moving quickly under their own steam at the site of operations.

The steel carriage was formed of two girders built of plates and rolled steel sections, braced by cross beams. Upon this was fitted a forged steel centre post of large diameter, surrounded by a steel roller path and circular steel spur rack in halves for slewing. Of 2-4-2 wheel arrangement with radial axles at each end and fixed axles between, the spacing of the latter was slightly increased on the NER 25-ton cranes. The drive for self propelling was to the inner axles and capable of propelling the crane at 4 mph, while hand wheels on the sides of the carriage applied the brakes on all four wheels of these two axles.

The revolving superstructure was constructed on two heavy steel beams carried on a heavy steel centre fitted with rollers running on the steel path on the carriage and vertical rollers which bore on the centre post. The driver stood on a platform between the machinery in the crab and the boiler to his rear, from where he could conveniently operate the controls of the crane and attend to the boiler. The 8 inch by 14 inch cylinders were mounted horizontally on the crab sides driving a transverse crankshaft from which all four motions were powered.

The hoisting gear had two speeds and lowering of a load was controlled by the engine and a powerful brake on the second motion shaft. The derricking motion was achieved by a worm gear, the angle of which was self-locking so that it was impossible to run without being powered, driving on the derricking barrel. The slewing motion was worked by a bevel and spur gear driving pinion gearing into the slewing rack and fitted with a brake to control the slew. The self-propelling motion was taken from the second drive shaft by a bevel gear driving

into an intermediate wheel concentric with the centre post. All gears, axles and shafts were of steel with gun-metal bearings. While the crane was not working, the weight of the tail to the superstructure on the centre post could be relieved by heavy duty cams from the carriage.

They had swan-necked steel lattice jibs fabricated from rolled sections and plate. Although all batches had steel wire rope for the derricking tackle, instead of chains, hoisting was still by chain on the 20-ton cranes, with wire rope only on the 25-ton version. Derricking tackle of steel wire rope was in double winding each of seven parts.

On the 20-ton cranes the hoisting chain was attached and wound on to a grooved barrel, from where it passed over a pulley at the head of the jib, under the pulley in the lifting block and back up to a hook attached to the underside of the jib. Thus arranged the crane could lift its full load, but by removing the block the hook could lift half the load at twice the speed.

Caledonian Railway 20-ton Cranes

Twenty years after acquiring their two early examples of 15-ton cranes, Nos. 1 and 2, from Cowans Sheldon, the Caledonian Railway invested in a pair of 20-ton cranes, this time from Craven Bros. The new cranes were numbered 3 and 4 and displaced Nos. 1 and 2 from Motherwell which went for duty elsewhere. Like their predecessors on the CR, these cranes had longitudinal draw-beams at each end of the carriage, which as before could be used to induce greater counterweight by wedging off the underside of an engine or tender underframe. In this case, however, the draw-beams were made of cast steel, rather than being fabricated of steel sections.

When delivered these cranes were paired with 4-plank open wagons, viz: Nos. 4746 and 37511, with the timber trestle jib rest much nearer the outer axle and the jib projecting over the end of the wagon. This arrangement was clearly unsatisfactory and may have been temporary. To remedy this, two 26ft 5¼in long by 7 foot wide 15-ton 6-wheel rail wagons were commandeered in their place. Interestingly these wagons were of two alternative wheel arrangements. Crane No. 3 was paired with one which had the Bissel truck arrangement to the

Opposite page, Figure 26 - Craven 20-ton crane, as supplied to the Caledonian and Great Central railways in 1907. (Author)

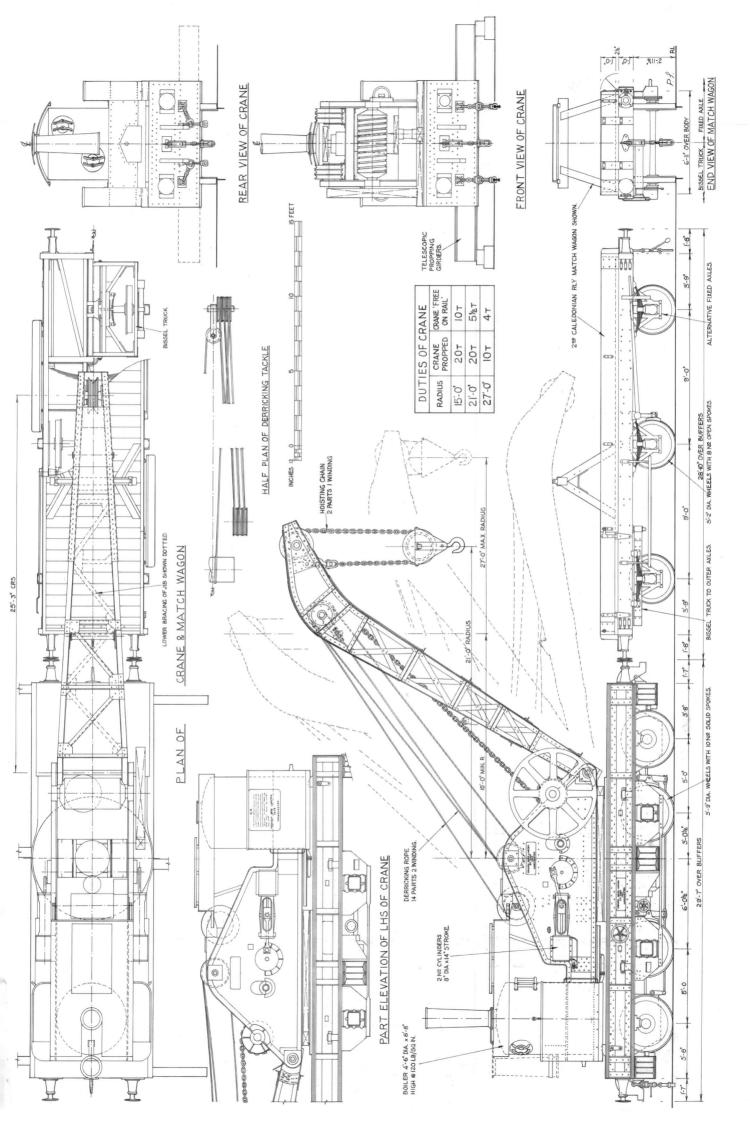

REAR VIEW OF CRANE

FRONT VIEW OF CRANE

TELESCOPIC PROPPING GIRDERS.

2ⁿᵈ CALEDONIAN RLY MATCH WAGON SHOWN.

END VIEW OF MATCH WAGON

BISSEL TRUCK. FIXED AXLE.
6'-11" OVER BODY

BISSEL TRUCK.

PLAN OF CRANE & MATCH WAGON

LOWER BRACING OF JIB SHOWN DOTTED.

25'-3" CRS

HALF PLAN OF DERRICKING TACKLE

15 FEET

INCHES 12   0   5   10

HOISTING CHAIN 2 PARTS 1 WINDING

DUTIES OF CRANE

RADIUS	CRANE PROPPED	CRANE 'FREE ON RAIL'
15'-0"	20T	10T
21'-0"	20T	5½T
27'-0"	10T	4T

27'-0" MAX. RADIUS

21'-0" RADIUS

15'-0" MIN. R.

PART ELEVATION OF LHS OF CRANE

DERRICKING ROPE 14 PARTS 2 WINDING.

2 Nº CYLINDERS 8" DIA. x14" STROKE.

BOILER 4'-6" DIA. x 6'-8"
HIGH @ 120 LB/SQ.IN.

2ⁿᵈ CALEDONIAN RLY MATCH WAGON SHOWN.

ALTERNATIVE FIXED AXLES.

28'-10" OVER BUFFERS

3'-2" DIA. WHEELS WITH 8 Nº OPEN SPOKES.

BISSEL TRUCK TO OUTER AXLES.

3'-9" DIA. WHEELS WITH 10 Nº SOLID SPOKES.

29'-7" OVER BUFFERS

1'-8"   3'-9"   9'-0"   9'-0"   3'-9"   1'-8"   1'-7"   3'-8"   5'-0"   3'-0½"   6'-0½"   5'-0"   5'-8"   1'-7"

2'-0" 2'-0" 2'-11¾" R.L.

outer axles, while No. 320632 with crane No. 4 had all fixed axles albeit with a degree of side play to the centre axle.

In due course both were replaced. By the early 1960s, if not earlier, a 6-wheel steel underframe was utilised for RS1053/18, the number DM 320632 being perpetuated by the replacement. No. RS1052/18's was substituted by No. DM 349271, a long wheelbase 4-wheel vehicle with a pressed steel underframe. This was branded **CRANE RUNNER MOTIVE POWER - for R.S.1052/18¾ POLMADIE**, some time prior to the withdrawal of the crane in 1976.

With the delivery of a modern 36-ton crane to Motherwell by the LMS in 1931, these two cranes were cascaded to Polmadie and Perth, only to be displaced again by the arrival of up-to-date 30-ton cranes in the early '40s, one returning to Motherwell, the other going on to Carstairs. Nationalisation in 1948 resulted in a fresh assessment of their location and further moves, until they ended up as relief cranes prior to their withdrawal. By the 1960s increasing concern as to the load to be safely transmitted by chains and the consequent need to anneal them at regular intervals led to the steady down-rating of both cranes, to either 18 or to 18¾ tons.

Left - *Ex-CR 20-ton Craven cranes Nos. 3 and 4 in the breakdown train at Motherwell prior to 1931 awaiting the call of duty. Both cranes appear to be attired in the LMS crimson lake livery with coach insignia. (Real Photographs, author's collection)*

Opposite bottom - With nationalisation No. RS1053/20, formerly CR No. 4 was transferred to Kittybrewster in place of the ex-NB 15-ton Cowans Sheldon crane, which was duly withdrawn. Freshly painted in BR livery, it is still paired with its ex-CR 6-wheeled match wagon No. DM 320632. (J Templeton)

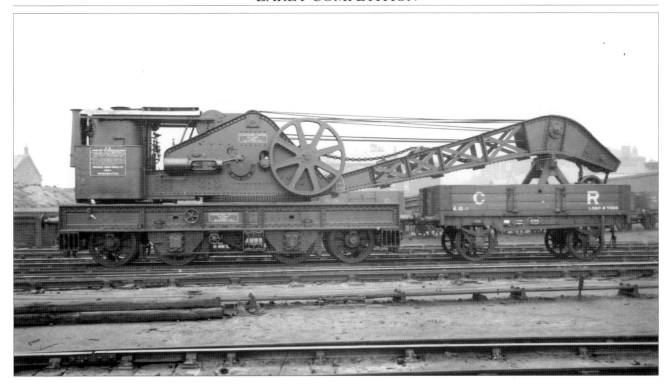

Above - One of the Caledonian Railway's 20 ton cranes as supplied by Craven Bros of Manchester in 1907 seen here coupled to a 4-wheel 3-plank open wagon No 4746. This shows the tip of the jib projecting slightly beyond the end of the wagon. (Jim MacIntosh collection)

This page, top - No. RS053/18 on 28 June 1970, by now at Eastfield, with its capacity reduced to 18 tons and coupled to its third match wagon, a 6-wheeled steel underframe. (Author)

This page, right - The rear view of No. RS1053/18, amongst other things showing the cast-steel draw beams each side of the draw hook. (Author)

Great Central Railway 20-ton Crane

Shortly after the Caledonian Railway, the Great Central also ordered a 20-ton crane from Cravens to supplement the five 15-ton Cowans Sheldon cranes they already possessed. It likewise had draw beams in the carriage. By 1945 at least one side tank and coal bunker had been increased in height to provide for a greater feed water and coal capacity. By then it also had been fitted with hinged buffers.

It was stationed at the company's locomotive headquarters at Gorton, where it remained until temporarily displaced in 1940 by a new 45-ton crane. The latter and a similar crane at Kings Cross, were, however, sent to Iraq in early 1942 resulting in a further upheaval until replacement cranes were supplied in 1943, No 942501 going to Neasden during the interval. Nonetheless, it eventually went across the Pennines to Darnall, Sheffield, only to move on to Shirebrook shortly before withdrawal.

Ex-GC Robinson 4-6-0 LNER class B8 No. 5442 sets off with the Gorton breakdown train including the GC's 20-ton Craven Bros steam crane. (Real Photos, author's collection)

On 7 October 1945 the ex-GCR 20-ton Craven crane assists in the erection of a steel gantry for the support of overhead signal and catenary required in connection with the LNER's Manchester, Sheffield to Wath electrification scheme. Note the taller water tank at the rear of the crane's superstructure. (BR, ER, author's collection)

North Eastern Railway 25-Ton Craven Bros Cranes

The NER were at first going also to acquire the same design, but to meet their requirements for a 25-ton capacity crane, the dimension between the inner fixed axles and that of the pony truck was increased from 5 foot to 5ft 11½in at both ends. These cranes used a pair of steel wire ropes attached to and wound round the hoisting barrel with two opposing lines of grooves. From here the ropes passed over a pair of pulleys at the head of the jib, under two more pulleys in the lifting block and back up to a smaller block with a hook attached to the underside of the jib. Arranged thus the crane could lift its full load, but by removing the larger block the hook on the smaller one could lift half the load at twice the speed. These cranes were fitted with four warwick shackles on each side of the carriage, see page 211. (Operation of cranes).

The match wagons to all three cranes are thought initially to have been of the 4-wheel type. However, No. 153's second No. 3150/901695 was a 6-wheel steel under-framed wagon, possibly recovered from the 35-ton Craven crane from Gateshead requisitioned by the WD in 1914, see below. Its third match wagon No. DE320952, acquired in BR days, reverted to the 4-wheel type having been built at Stratford in 1926. BR No. 331153 has been preserved in the National Collection at York.

			Craven Bros 25-Ton Cranes for NER					
Date ord'd - Deliv'd	Order No	Cost	Running No			Match wagon No		Allocation	Disposal
			Pre-group	Group 'ing	BR	Pre-group	Grp'g- BR		
6/06 - 1907	C8153	£2,498	CME12	901637	152	(1) 048657 (2) 46731	(2) 901701	Darlington '07-'32, Sunderland S Dk '7/40-1/10/60, Holbeck 9/1/61, Dairycoates 7/61	Wdn 13/4/64
6/06 - 1907	C8153	£2,498	CME13	901638	(331) 153	(1) 04864 (2) 3150	(2) 901695 (3) DE320952	York '07, Middlesbrough 1/9/21-'58, Thornaby '58-22/11/63, Sunderland '65, Wakefield 11/65, Dairycoates 5/66, Shirebrook '68-3/70, Doncaster OOU 7/10/72	Wdn 3/71, NRM
6/06 - 1907	C8153	£2,498	CME14	901639	157		901711	Gateshead '07, Dairycoates c'13-1/10/60	Scrapped '62

A maker's photograph of the 25-ton steam crane, with the jib raised, as supplied by Craven Bros to the NER in 1907. This crane is fitted with steel wire ropes to both the derricking and hoisting tackle. (Herbert Morris, author's collection)

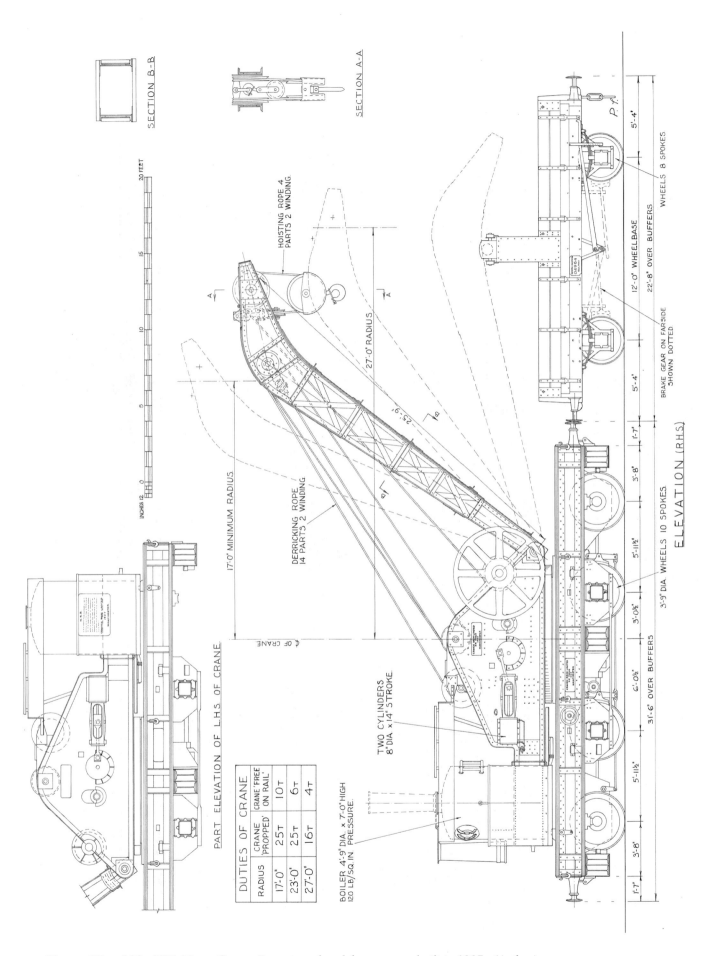

SECTION B-B

SECTION A-A

PART ELEVATION OF L.H.S. OF CRANE

20 FEET

HOISTING ROPE 4
PARTS 2 WINDING

27'-0" RADIUS

17'-0" MINIMUM RADIUS

DERRICKING ROPE
14 PARTS 2 WINDING

25'-9"

₵ OF CRANE

TWO CYLINDERS
8"DIA × 14" STROKE.

BOILER 4'-9" DIA. × 7'-0" HIGH
120 LB/SQ.IN. PRESSURE.

DUTIES OF CRANE		
RADIUS	CRANE 'PROPPED'	CRANE 'FREE ON RAIL'
17'-0"	25т	10т
23'-0"	25т	6т
27'-0"	16т	4т

ELEVATION (R.H.S.)

5'-4"

WHEELS 8 SPOKES

12'-0" WHEELBASE

22'-8" OVER BUFFERS

BRAKE GEAR ON FARSIDE
SHOWN DOTTED

5'-4"

1'-7"

3'-8"

5'-11½"

3'-9" DIA. WHEELS 10 SPOKES.

3'-0½"

6'-0½"

31'-6" OVER BUFFERS

5'-11½"

3'-8"

1'-7"

P.7

Figures 27 and 28 - *NER 25-ton Craven Bros steam breakdown cranes built in 1907. (Author)*

106

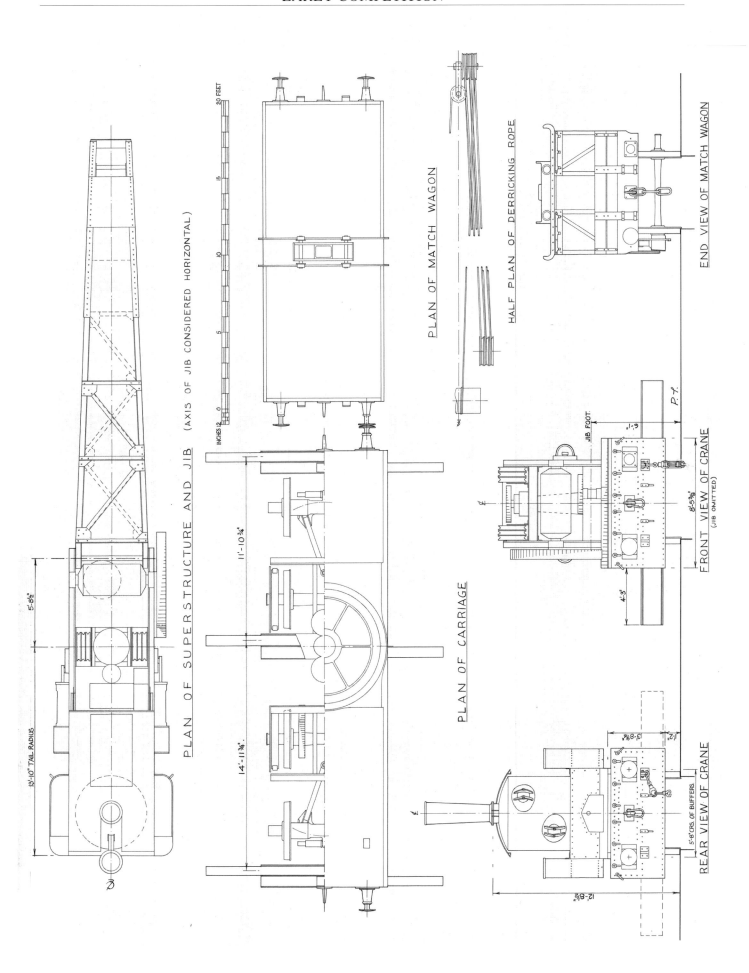

PLAN OF SUPERSTRUCTURE AND JIB (AXIS OF JIB CONSIDERED HORIZONTAL)

PLAN OF MATCH WAGON

HALF PLAN OF DERRICKING ROPE

END VIEW OF MATCH WAGON

PLAN OF CARRIAGE

FRONT VIEW OF CRANE (JIB OMITTED)

REAR VIEW OF CRANE

13'-10" TAIL RADIUS

5'-8½"

11'-10¾"

14'-11¾"

20 FEET

INCHES 12   0   5   10   15

JIB FOOT.

8'-5⅝"

4'-3"

1'-9"

5'-6" CRS. OF BUFFERS

13'-8⅜"

12'-6⅞"

On the same occasion, with the match truck No. 04864 in place indicating that the crane was the one allocated to York. Note the 4-wheel match wagon provided by the railway, but in this case it was later changed for a 6-wheeled one. (Herbert Morris, author's collection)

In contrast with the formal views above, a number of Hull's breakdown gang pose beside the crane with a girder hanging above them. The solitary man on the right-hand end may be the lookout man. (Author's collection)

No. 153, allocated to Middlesbrough, in BR days coupled to a 6-wheel match wagon No. DE 901695. (Photomatic)

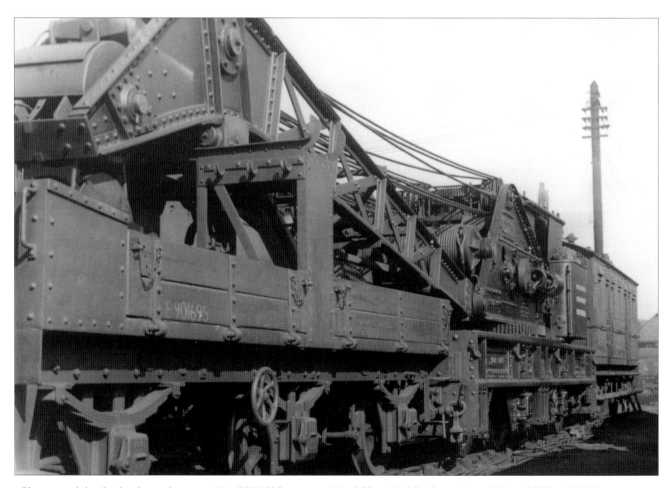

Close up of the 6-wheel match wagon No. E901695 to crane No. 153 at Middlesbrough on 1 June 1952. (RK Blencowe collection)

Stothert & Pitt 20-Ton Cranes
or LSWR

The serious accident at Salisbury on 1 July 1906, when the Up Boat Train from Plymouth to Waterloo failed to reduce speed through the station and derailed on the curve at the London end with catastrophic results, taxed the LSWR Company's existing one 15-ton and two 10-ton cranes in their attempt to clear the line of debris. It would seem that, as a consequence, a pair of 20-ton cranes was soon acquired from Stothert & Pitt of Bath, who, although long established as a company making cranes, were relatively new to the breakdown crane business.

With the reverse wheel arrangement to the standard Cowans Sheldon 15 to 30 ton cranes, as a 0-4-4 the fixed wheels had outside bearings supported by springs outside the carriage sides, while the bogie had inside bearings with axles extended onto which the blocking screws would bear while in working condition. The crane had a fully latticed jib and adopted steel wire ropes instead of chains from the outset. They were unusual in being fitted with vertical cylinders and an early example of protective sheeting to the external hoisting drum spur wheel. Initially provided with a canopy over the driver's position, whose controls were positioned outside the left hand crab side, and boiler, in due course both were fully enclosed with windows in the front and side for the driver and a circular window in the end.

In 1913, a 20-ton crane of similar design was ordered (BB517) by the War Department for service at Shoeburyness. This, however, differed from the 20-ton cranes supplied to the LSWR four years previous in a few dimensions, not least in maximum height and width which would have precluded it operating on the British network.

Date delivered	Works or Order No	Cost	Running No			Match wagon No			Allocation	Disposal
			Pre-group	Group 'ing	BR	Pre-group	Group ing	BR		
1908	T89	£1,785	1	30S	Ds30	885	30SM	Ds??	Nine Elms '08-*1/1/11*, Eastleigh *25/7/21-10/5/40*, Bournemouth 4/46	Wdn 8/6/63
1909	T89	£1,814	5	34S	Ds34	895	34SM	Ds3082	Exmouth Jct '09-*10/5/40*, Feltham 4/46-*5/3/63*	Wdn 17/5/63, cut up Cashmore

Stothert & Pitt 20-Ton Cranes for LSWR

The LSWR's 20-ton steam crane No. 1 allocated to Nine Elms, supplied by Stothert & Pitt in 1908. The superstructure is swung through 180 degrees from its normal travelling position. Note the driver standing beside his controls outside the left-hand crab side. (Real Photographs, author's collection)

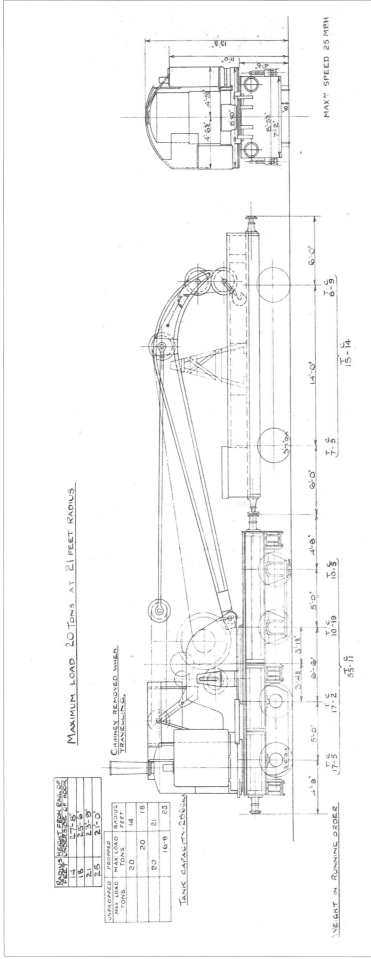

The two new LSWR 20 ton Stothert & Pitt cranes started life at the company's principal depots of Nine Elms and Exmouth Jct, the former crane being displaced to Eastleigh following the arrival of larger 36 ton cranes at the end of the First World War. With the assembling of the Allied invasion forces and associated heavy equipment over the whole of southern England during 1943/4 in preparation for D-Day, Exmouth Jct's crane was somewhat outclassed in the event of a derailment or accident, but it was to be November next year before it was replaced there by a 45 ton Ransomes & Rapier crane. So, after the cessation of hostilities, both 20 ton cranes were moved again to Bournemouth and Feltham respectively from where they were withdrawn in 1963.

Left, Figure 29 - The official SR diagram for the ex-LSWR 20-ton Stothert and Pitt cranes of 1908/9. (Author's collection)

Opposite page - By 1946, when this photograph was taken by Stephen Townroe on the quadrupled section at Wallers Ash between Micheldever and Winchester, No. 1 had become SR No. 30S. Ex-LSWR 4-6-0 S15 class No. 502 had over-run the end of the Up loop causing some of the wagons of its train to derail obstructing all four lines. The Stothert & Pitt crane cleared the other lines, seen here recovering an LMS 12-ton van which appears to have gone down the embankment, to enable traffic to resume, while the engine was lifted by a larger crane later. Note the enclosure of the cab and boiler, which with side window is of American style. (SC Townroe, author's collection)

In contrast SR No. 34S at Feltham on 16 May 1948 has fully radiused corners to the corners of its enclosure. Note the cast number plate on the cab side. (JH Aston)

Broadside view of No. Ds 34 at Feltham on 5 March 1963, shortly before its withdrawal. Note the vertical cylinder immediately in front of the cab. (TM Abbott)

6. Railway Built Cranes

GER-12 ton Hand Cranes Converted to steam power
LNWR 20-ton cranes
GER 20- ton cranes

GER 12-Ton Hand Crane Converted to Steam Power

Around 1885 he Great Eastern Railway had built three 12-ton hand 'accident' cranes at their Stratford Works, as shown in Figure 1. The first two appear to have had timber underframes, albeit strengthened by ½ inch flitch plates: while the third, later in life at least, had a wrought-iron or steel carriage. In 1895, however, these three cranes were converted to steam power by means of replacing the counter weight by a boiler and adding a pair of vertical cylinders to drive the hoisting gear. The diagram shows the provision of derricking tackle, but the size of the blocks suggest that this was sufficient only to raise the jib and one suspects that this would have to be fixed in a limited number of predetermined positions by inserting a cotter in the manner previously employed as a hand crane.

Thereafter these cranes survived until at least 1926, but had by then been transferred to the Engineer's Permanent Way Department. From November 1918 two cranes were down-rated to 10 ton capacity and subsequently one to only 8 tons.

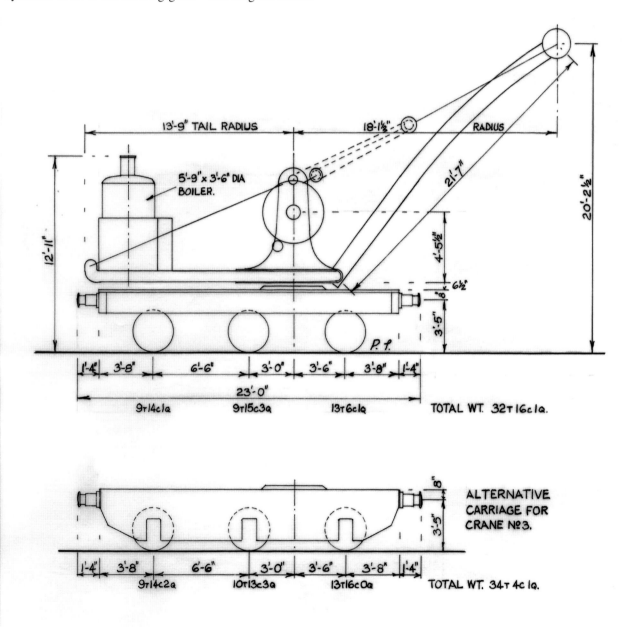

Figure 30 - *A tracing of the diagram for GER 12-ton hand cranes converted to steam power. (Author)*

115

Built by	Date delivered	Order No	Running No		Allocation & remarks
			Pre-grp	LNER	
GER	1885	U16	1A		Stratford No. 2 set '10, Cambridge, Down-rated to 10T 11/18 & later to 8T
GER	1885	U16	2A	SB19	Ipswich '10, Norwich, Peterboro' E 7/26, Down-rated to 10T 11/18
GER	c1885	?	3A		Stratford No. 1 set '10, Kings Lynn

GER 12-Ton Cranes Converted to Steam Power appears as the table heading:

GER 12-Ton Cranes Converted to Steam Power

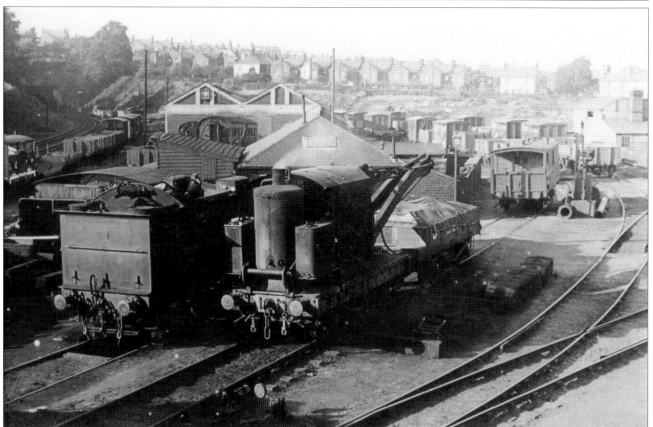

LNWR 20-Ton Crane

Late in the evening of 11 June 1897 a serious accident occurred on the single line near Welshampton on the Cambrian Railways, when a crowded Sunday school outing returning from Barmouth on the Welsh coast to Royton in Lancashire derailed with the loss of eleven lives. The Cambrian sent its modern 15-ton hand crane from Oswestry to the scene and sought the assistance of the LNWR who despatched a more ancient 10-ton crane, but standard for the line at the time, from Crewe North shed. It is reported that much to the latter's embarrassment its crane was unable to lift its share of a carriage to be re-railed. The resulting report back to Mr. FW Webb, the Chief Mechanical Engineer, led to thoughts of obtaining a steam crane.

Webb, however, was not prepared to purchase from the trade plant he considered able to be produced in house and instead, without any experience of designing and building such a machine, he initiated plans for the production of a breakdown crane at Crewe. As a result of a lot of 'trial and error', a 20-ton machine mounted on 8 wheels eventually emerged from Crewe Works in 1905. Nonetheless, this crane is reported to have had a poor reputation and perhaps it was not always available in times of need.

It exhibited none of the usual features of any of the known commercial builders. Among the novel aspects of its construction were: inside bearings to spoked wheels and six part with three winding steel wire ropes for the derricking gear. To secure the hoisting gear, a ratchet wheel and pawl were installed, while wooden brake blocks were capable of being applied to the wheels of two of the axles. More typical of common practice was the swan-necked jib with three longitudinal slots, a vertical boiler supplying steam to inclined cylinders mounted on plate crab sides. The four part with two winding hoisting ropes passing under a large block and terminating in a smaller block secured under the jib was a feature also adopted by Craven Bros. It was fitted with a horizontal capstan as an

Above - *Confident as ever that Crewe could produce anything the LNWR needed, Francis Webb embarked on the design and construction of a breakdown crane. After a protracted period this 20-ton machine appeared with both predictable and some more unusual features. In this view taken at Crewe Works near No. 8 erecting shop, it can bee seen that the gears to the final drive of the hoisting drum were of the double helical type rather than the more usual straight cut. While on the other hand inside bearings were provided to four axles and the derricking tackle had six parts of which three were winding. (Ted Talbot collection)*

Opposite top - *A converted GER 12-ton hand crane at Ipswich on 24 September 1911 clearly showing the boiler, coal bunker and water tank added at the rear of the superstructure. A wisp of smoke suggests the crane is ready should the call to duty come. (HF Hilton collection, courtesy HMRS)*

Opposite bottom - *A distant view of the rear of a converted 12-ton hand crane dealing with the results of a collision at an unidentified location circa 1910. (HF Hilton collection, courtesy HMRS)*

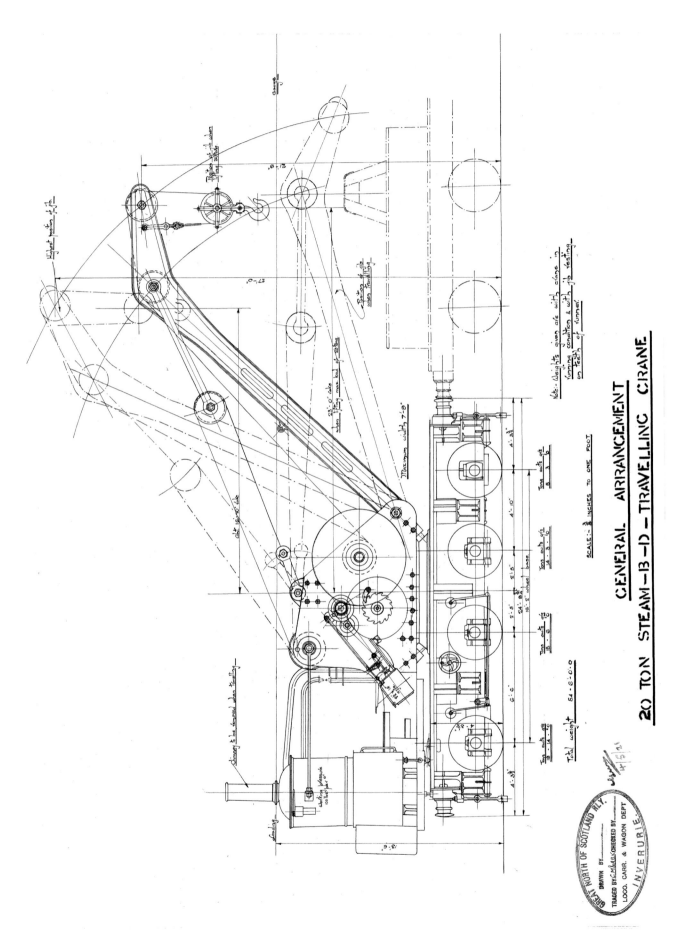

extension of the winding barrel shaft outside the right-hand crab side, but was not capable of propelling itself along the line unaided.

LNWR 20-Ton Crane		
Date delivered	Allocation	Disposal
1905	Crewe N 9/08, Willesden '10	Sold to WD '16

It was capable of lifting 20 tons from a minimum radius of about 16ft 10in out to 23 feet radius when propped.

At the accident at Shrewsbury on 15 Oct 1907, when presumably it was unavailable, and failure to clear the line by the drastic expedient of dragging the wreckage clear by hawser attached to as many as eight engines resulted in the cable breaking, the LNWR was forced, much to its chagrin, to borrow a crane from the GWR at Stafford Road Works, Wolverhampton. With the Locomotive Department now under the direction of George Whale, a 25-ton crane from Cowans Sheldon was, however, already on order, soon to be followed by a 36-ton long jib crane from Ransomes & Rapier.

The latter displaced the home-built product at Crewe, which was transferred to Willesden. This was badly strained while re-railing 4-4-0 No. 1417 *Landrail* at Euston shortly before the 1914-1918 war. It was sold outright from Willesden depot in 1916 to the War Department and not returned to the LNWR, the company being well rid of it. It was advertised for sale in 'Surplus' of May 1921 and stated as lying at Richborough, Kent. A diagram of the crane, reproduced opposite, found in the records of Inverurie Works dated 4 May 1921 suggests the Great North of Scotland Railway might have been considering a bargain. If so, they thought better of it. In 1926 the same machine was again advertised for disposal by TW Ward and stated as being at Preston. It had probably been used at the Morecombe Bay ship scrap yard of Wards, which closed about that time.

Opposite page, Figure 30A - *Diagram of LNWR 20-ton steam breakdown crane built at Crewe during the early years of the 1900s. (Courtesy Great North of Scotland Railway Association)*

Above - *Following a "Railway smash" at Rugeley (Trent Valley) on 12 November 1905, the LNWR 20-ton steam crane clears the debris, on what may have been its first outing. Note the steel wire ropes to both the derricking and hoisting tackle, together with the horizontal capstan. (Courtesy of Mrs Margaret Neal)*

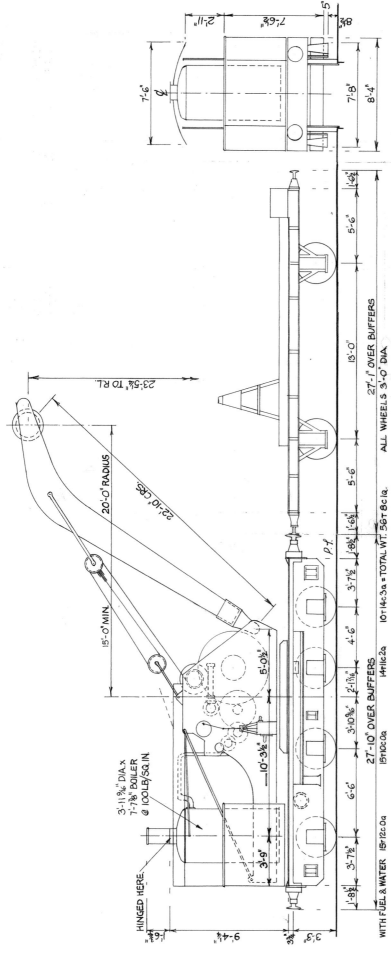

Figure 31 - Diagram of the two 20-ton steam cranes designed and built by Great Eastern Railway at Stratford. (Author)

GER 20--Ton Cranes

Clearly satisfied with their work in converting the 12-ton hand cranes to be steam-powered, the GER felt competent to undertake the design and construction of a larger crane of 20-ton capacity. In this they were a great deal more successful than the LNWR. Indeed the two cranes they built in 1908 continued in service as long as many others from the specialist makers and really only met their end with the demise of steam and the general clear out of much old plant.

The crane was carried on a four-axle carriage of shallow construction, thereby affording greater depth for the superstructure than other contemporary designs. A short plate-sided jib of 22ft 10in length was supported by twin winding steel wire ropes. A double purchase snatch-block was provided for loads of up to 20 tons, which could be lifted out to a radius of 20 feet. On the other hand, re-rigged with a single rope, a lift of up to 12 tons was allowed. Twin transverse telescopic propping girders with narrow flanges were provided within the carriage towards each end, together with a single one in the centre with a wider flange. Adjacent to each a jack was carried ready for use under the girder ends once extended.

It possessed hydraulic controls and a uni-directional constantly rotating steam engine driven at a fixed cut-off by vertical cylinders. Fluid for the hydraulic functions was pressurised by steam reciprocating pump to charge accumulators positioned beside the boiler. The pressure within these reacted against cast iron counter-balance weights within the cylinders. For control, small hydraulic jacks operated the friction clutches to provide the motions of lift, derrick, slew and travel, together with a powered capstan on the right hand side with which to haul wreckage to within reach.

A 24 foot long 4-wheeled steel under-framed match wagon was provided for each crane and although the jib was rested on the wagon while in train formation, short chains from the lower end of the jib were hooked up to the front end of the crane's carriage, presumably as some form of restraint.

When first built, the two were stationed at Stratford. One was requisitioned by the War Department during WW1 and sent to France, sometime stationed at Borre, and in due course it was returned. Later one emigrated first to Ipswich, followed by March before returning to Stratford, while the other also went to Ipswich towards the end of its life. By early BR days the lifting capacities of the two cranes were reduced: No. 132 to 17 tons at 18 foot radius; while No. 134's was reduced to 20 tons at 18 ft 6in and 10¾ tons at 25 feet, both when propped and its maximum load 'free on rail' reduced to 10¼ tons at 19 feet and 6½ tons at 25 feet. Nonetheless, their short jibs may have proved handy under the overhead wires of the electrification schemes then being implemented.

GER 20-Ton Cranes					
Date delivered	Running No			Allocation	Disposal
	1st	2nd	BR		
1907/8	4A	961602	134	Stratford '10, Ipswich, March 1/11/47-6/11/61, Stratford post 4/64	Wdn '64
1909	5A	961603	132	Stratford '10, Ipswich 1/11/47- post 4/64	Wdn '67

Ex-GER 20-ton steam breakdown crane in LNER livery. The jacks are carried beside the propping girders. (Lens of Sutton, author's collection)

Ipswich's crane No. 132 and match wagon in British Railways black livery at Stratford on 18 July 1957. Note the tarpaulin curtains around the driver's position and the boiler.
(H Watson, Stephenson Locomotive Society collection)

20-ton crane No. 134 from March in use at Liverpool Street removing parts of a redundant turntable using a single rope.
(P Caley)

7. Long Jib Cranes

Ransomes & Rapier 36-ton cranes for GW
Stothert & Pitt 36-ton crane for GW
Ransomes & Rapier 36-ton crane for LNWR
Wilson 12-ton crane for GW

Having started late in the adoption of steam-powered breakdown cranes, the Great Western Railway accepted the benefit they offered and went on to anticipate the need for both much greater capacity and also larger reach. In particular the former was needed to be able to handle the larger members of Churchward's new range of standard locomotives. By drawing up a comprehensive performance specification for 36- and 12-ton capacity cranes with jibs of sufficient length to be able to lift an item of rolling stock over a locomotive or other obstruction on the ground at more than minimum radius, they stole a march on other railways and left the crane makers not involved in their production floundering for a while.

Fulfilling the requirements of the new specification for the 36-ton version was challenging and, in order to allow comparative testing of more than one design, two cranes were ordered by the GWR in early 1908 from different makers. On 11 February 1908 one was ordered from Ransomes & Rapier and the other was to be built by Stothert & Pitt of Bath. The Stothert & Pitt crane was delivered in 1909 and became GWR Crane No. 1, while, to free up this number, the original No. 1 crane, a 15-ton Cowans Sheldon machine, was renumbered 8. The Ransomes & Rapier crane was considered superior to the Stothert & Pitt one, and the next crane the GWR ordered was another Ransomes and Rapier 36-ton unit, identical to No. 2, which entered service in 1912 and became No. 3.

Both of types could lift their maximum load at a radius of 20 feet, or reach out to lift 16 (15 in the case of the Stothert & Pitt) tons at a maximum radius of 40 feet when propped or from 14 (12) to 4½ (3½) tons respectively when free on rail. Steel wire ropes were employed for derricking and lifting, while to fall within the loading gauge while in train formation, the chimney was hinged. Mounted on five axles, with a 4-wheel bogie to the rear, the cranes were capable of negotiating a 5 chain curve. The wheels, springs, axles, axle-boxes, draw gear, buffers, brake blocks etc were supplied by the railway company.

The similarity in layout and certain technical features of both designs is apparent. For instance, both had live slewing rings. Clutches were provided so that the travelling gear could be entirely disengaged while the crane was hauled as part of a train. Screw jacks were fitted at the end of the propping girders, thus ensuring that the load was reliably transmitted to the packing, rather than depending on hardwood folding wedges. On the other hand, the difference in the jibs of the two designs and for coping with the moveable counter-weight should be noted, suggesting that the makers had some conceptual and detailed design to undertake.

In service, as well as the match wagon, a second support wagon, known as a weight tender was associated with the crane and was used for transporting the kentledge (removable tail-weight), together with lifting tackle etc. Originally, this wagon was used also to transport the supporting girders and jacks for the crane. These wagons were built at Swindon to diagrams L11 and L10 respectively.

When the cranes were delivered, not only were they the largest-capacity breakdown cranes ever constructed for a British railway, it was also was the first time that all the features of what was until recently considered a 'modern' steam crane had been brought together in a single unit, and this established a format which was followed, with only very minor changes, right up until the end of steam crane manufacture in the 1960s.

Ransomes & Rapier 36-Ton Cranes
for GWR

Figure 32 is a plot of curves for load against outreach achieved by Rapiers' new crane, together with Stothert & Pitt's, compared with other earlier and contemporary designs. From these, it can be seen that both new 36-ton cranes represent a considerable advance in performance. All the same, to achieve a wide route availability for a crane weighing, in the case of the Rapier example, 91½ tons in working order, there was a penalty to pay to keep within a maximum axle load of 14 tons and, hence, be acceptable to the civil engineers of the time. In this case the counterweight of the crane was capable of being detached from the tail of the superstructure and lowered on to the rear of the crane carriage, from where it was lifted subsequently by the crane using a special bridle and stowed on the special weight wagon. Likewise, initially the propping girders were removed and also placed in the weight truck. By this means the intention was to reduce the load imposed by the crane on the track while travelling in train formation to 70 tons. The weight actually measured was reduced to only 72½ tons, while the lack of even distribution of the axle loads resulted in a couple exceeding 16 tons. On each occasion the crane was used, however, this considerable exercise had to be

Opposite page - *The GW's two new super-power 36-ton cranes beside Swindon Works on 28 October 1910 lifting its only example of a Pacific 4-6-2, No. 111* The Great Bear, *weighing in at 97 tons 5 cwt in working order, but still over 90 tons perhaps if empty! On the left is the product of Stothert & Pitt of Bath delivered in May 1909 and on the right, Ransomes & Rapier's supplied the previous year. (BR, WR, author's collection)*

performed to make the crane ready for work and, on completion, packed away prior to moving off site. While the removal of the counterweight and propping girders afforded the crane the necessary route availability, at a quoted 25 minutes this was a time consuming and laborious process.

Figure 33 shows the procedure for attaching the counterweight to the tail of the crane. The crane arrived in travelling condition with the counter-weight stowed in the weight truck, or in the case of some other companies in the match wagon. The jib was then raised and the superstructure slewed round over the weight truck to enable chains to be attached to the counterweight in preparation for it to be lifted. As the jib could not be derricked to tight enough radius to enable it to lower the counter-weight directly to the position required, once the weight was lifted the jib was derricked into its minimum radius and further light chains from the jib coupled up to the weight. As the weight was then lowered, these acted as a 'choker' to draw it in as it descended on to the rear end of the crane's carriage. With the weight in the allotted position, the superstructure was again slewed round so that its tail was over the weight, which could then be raised up by screw jacks at its corners and bolted

to the underside of the tail. It was necessary for all of this complex operation to be carried out clear of over-bridges, station canopies, retaining walls and over-head wires, although in an emergency the crane jib would have made short work of any telegraph wires. The propping girders would too have to be taken out of the weight wagon and inserted into the propping boxes to make the crane ready for its work.

Whilst the adoption of this elaborate procedure will undoubtedly have permitted the cranes to work safely down the many lines on the GWR's system, one has to wonder whether it was worth all the effort. Much of this might have been saved, if concessions were made by allowing the propping girders and/or counter-weights normally to remain in their working position and only remove and place them in the weight wagon on the few anticipated occasions when it was necessary to traverse a severely restricted line. As it was, by 1931 sanction had been obtained to leave the propping girders in position, when the weight of the crane increased to 78 tons 4 cwt and the maximum axle load to 18 tons 6 cwt. Nonetheless, the counter-weight was still placed on the weight wagon.

It is perhaps surprising too, knowing that

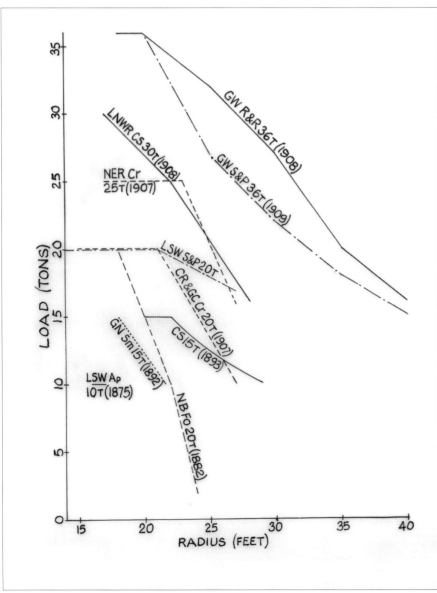

Figure 32 - A plot of load against radius of a selection of earlier cranes compared with the new GW 36-ton cranes of 1908/9. This also clearly demonstrates that, although the Stothert & Pitt example achieved the same maximum load, the Ransomes & Rapier crane had superior performance at increased radius. (Author)

Opposite page, Figure 33 - *Diagrams showing the procedure necessary to reposition the counter-weight from the weight truck or match wagon and attach it on the underside of the rear of the superstructure. (Author)*

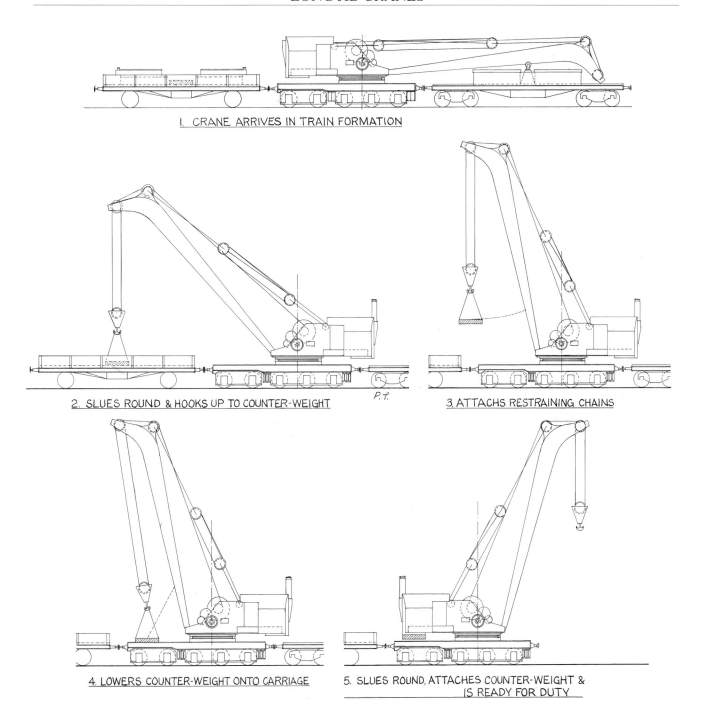

1. CRANE ARRIVES IN TRAIN FORMATION

2. SLUES ROUND & HOOKS UP TO COUNTER-WEIGHT

3. ATTACHS RESTRAINING CHAINS

4. LOWERS COUNTER-WEIGHT ONTO CARRIAGE

5. SLUES ROUND, ATTACHES COUNTER-WEIGHT &
IS READY FOR DUTY

Ransomes & Rapier's Wilfred Strokes' initial training had been in the New Works Office of the GW, that his, by then patented, relieving bogie system was not adopted as a simpler means of achieving necessary weight distribution. An application for a patent had been submitted in 1904 and accepted a year later. It was first applied to an order for overseas in 1906, yet not taken up in Great Britain until the Midland Railway ordered an example for a 36-ton crane on 22 April 1914. As it was though, although the GW inherited a further couple of high capacity cranes from its constituents at grouping in 1923, it did not acquire any more breakdown cranes until 1939, when it joined with two other companies to purchase jointly a dozen 45-ton cranes, which employed the relieving bogie system as will be revealed in Volume

2 of this work.

The carriage followed locomotive practice, the crane being carried on five sets of axles, having a total wheel-base of 21ft 6in. Alterations in red ink on the abstract of the order for the GW crane suggest that the spacings for the fixed axles were originally intended to be 5 feet and these were increased to 5ft 3in before construction took place. The three forward axles formed a fixed wheelbase of 10ft 6in, whilst the two rear axles were carried in a bogie fitted with spring centralizing gear. The axle-boxes were of the locomotive oiled pad type outside the frames and slid in cast steel horn-guides, and carried their load through suitable suspension gear and laminated-bearing springs. As part of the crane's preparation for lifting, wedges were inserted over each

Opposite page - In 1912 the GW acquired a second 36-ton crane from Ransomes & Rapier, thereby confirming their preference for the product from Ipswich. Here Nos. 2 and 3 were photographed together on 22 July 1925 lifting the brand new No. 4088 Dartmouth Castle, *a load when full of 79 tons 17 cwt. Note the light chains hanging from the underside of the jib about a quarter of the way up used during the installation and removal of the counter-weight. The smokebox and chimney of the Turner boiler are also apparent on the left hand crane. To undertake this special lift, the propping girders are doubled up. (BR, WR, author's collection)*

Above - The weight truck No. Dw 2A associated with GW Ransomes & Rapier 36-ton crane No. 2 at Swindon Works on 23 August 1971. (Author)

axle-box to take the strain off the springs and improve stability. In addition, these could be used to adjust the crane's level when working on gradients or curves. When it was being propelled under its own power, two of the centre axles were driven from the engine through a train of spur, bevel and worm gears, the final pinions of which drove onto the axle spur wheels. These were arranged to slide out of gear when the crane was in train formation. Two of the fixed axles had their wheels fitted with screw-on brakes, operated by hand wheels located on both sides of the carriage.

On top of the crane carriage, near the centre, was a live-roller race about 8ft 6in in diameter on which the crane revolved. Teeth cut on the outside of the race meshed with a gear on the underside of the crane frame to impart a slewing motion. The crane was prevented from lifting off the carriage by a hollow spindle, 10 inch diameter with a thrust bearing at its upper end, while a vertical shaft which drove the travelling gear by means of bevels passed through the centre of this spindle.

The carriage was fitted at each end with standard buffers and draw gear of the locomotive type, and a vacuum train pipe with rubber hose and couplings was provided for use when the crane was marshalled within a train. The crane was propped by means of two sets of

telescopic girders fitted under the carriage at each end of the fixed axles, one end of each girder being fitted with a screw jack and cast steel footstep. Both Ransomes & Rapier cranes were supplied with eight rather than just four propping girders, so that each girder box could take a girder fitted from each side. Originally all eight had to be carried in the weight tender and the crane was not allowed to run with any girders in the girder boxes. Subsequently it would appear that the four extra girders were mislaid.

The superstructure was mounted on a live ring of conical rollers. The frames of this were of double mild steel plates and sections, and had fitted to them the bearings for the hoist and derrick motions, the engines and valve gear. The frames were mounted on a cast-steel foundation, which revolved about a mild steel centre pin, and incorporated with it the main bearing for the slewing gear; the remainder of the slewing gear was fitted to the top of this casting.

This casting incorporated:-

a) Half the slewing spear-shaft bearings (other half in a cap bolted to bed casting)
b) The jib-foot pivots
c) All the crankshaft bearings

129

d) Most of the other motion bearings

e) The machined seats for the crab side plates
(a pair of plates per side)

f) The upper slewing roller path

g) The top bearings for the central spear-shaft
(travelling gears)

h) Machined seats for the four channel section
girders which support the cab, boiler and tail-
weights

The casting was quite short at the rear and relied on backstays running from the drumhead to the tail bars.

The engine cylinders, 9 inch diameter by 14 inch stroke, were lagged and finished off with planished steel sheet. Steam from the boiler was admitted by link motion reversing gear. A coal bunker of large capacity was situated on one side of the boiler, whilst on the other side was a large water tank. The boiler, bunker and tank were carried by the tail of the superstructure, on the underside of which were equipped the locking sockets to engage with the locking cams on the carriage, thereby holding the super-structure in its correct position when the jib was lowered on to its match-truck for running in a train. A steel shelter, equipped with an adjustable hatch in the roof and two look-out windows at the rear was fitted over the boiler, tank and brake and as much of the machinery as practicable. The driver's platform, situated immediately behind the gear and under the adjustable part of the shelter roof, was so placed that an almost uninterrupted view of the load being handled could be obtained.

All the motions of the crane were worked direct from the crankshaft, the hoisting, travelling and derricking operations being manipulated through claw or dog clutches, and the slewing gear through a double cone friction clutch. This latter arrangement enabled the crane to be revolved in either direction without reversing the engines. The hoisting and slewing motions were provided with powerful foot-applied brakes, whilst the derrick motion was fitted with a screw-actuated brake. A screw-applied mechanism was also provided, and worked in conjunction with the hoist brake foot lever, enabling the driver to brake the load either by foot or hand at will. The whole of the gear was of steel, the teeth being cut from solid machined blanks, except the main slewing rack and pinion, and the main travelling spurs situated on the axles together with their adjacent pinions, in which case the form of the tooth was of special design.

The load was lifted on four parts of steel wire rope with one part winding, and the derrick motion was operated through ten parts of steel wire rope winding on two parts. The jib was of the swan-neck pattern, enabling the rams-horn hook to be lifted 38ft 3in above rail level at a radius of 20 feet and 22ft 6in above rail level at 40 feet radius. The lifts from below rail level ranged from about 10 feet to 26 feet respectively. The minimum radius of the crane was 18 feet and the maximum working radius 40 feet. An automatic radius needle was fitted in close proximity to the driver which pointed at the safe load when on level track.

The placing of an order in November 1911 with Ransomes & Rapier for a second crane suggests that their product was a better solution and preferred over Stothert & Pitt's offering. Despite the changes in design of 36-ton

cranes supplied by then to the LNWR and about to be to others discussed below, the construction of the carriages to GW Nos. 2 and 3 was the same.

Although the order form would suggest that a Hopwood Boiler had originally been intended, this was crossed out and Turner smoke tube boiler inserted in red ink. As built, both cranes Nos. 2 and 3 were fitted with 4ft 8in diameter by 7ft 2in high vertical boilers, working at a pressure of 80lb per sq inch, manufactured by ER & F Turner of Ipswich, see page 19 (Boilers). Evidence of this can be seen to this day on No. 2, in the form of the plated-over inverted-keyhole-shaped opening at the rear of the shelter.

Not long after the delivery of No. 3, the GWR appears to have concluded that there were drawbacks to the Turner boilers, since in 1917 at least one had been replaced by an alternative type. Turners had by that time ceased to produce boilers, being fully occupied in war work. But instead of the more usual cross-tube boiler, this was a simple vertical fire-tube (VFT) boiler of the dry head type, with a cylindrical firebox connected by a number of vertical fire-tubes to a horizontal upper tube-plate, in effect a simplified version of the rail-motor boilers. One such boiler that has survived with No. 2 is of this later type.

Nonetheless, at least one, and possibly both, Turner boilers were retained as spares, so that they could be refitted when the VFT boiler was in need of overhaul, and indeed were periodically refitted to both cranes Nos. 2 and 3. Photographic evidence shows that one was still in use until the early 1960s, when it was on Newton Abbot's No. 3. The practice of continuing to fit the Turner boiler also explains why the odd arrangement of the rear cab sheets persisted on No. 2 to the end, since the inverted keyhole shape required for the Turner chimney is still present to this day.

The cranes were of extremely sound and substantial construction, specially designed to withstand rough usage and the emergency overloads to which this class of crane was subjected. Mounting the attachment for the derricking tackle on upward extensions of the vertical plates of the jib induced a bending moment opposed to that created by the load of the swan-necked style of jib and in due course all makers would follow suit. The basic design was so successful that most other crane makers were soon obliged to adopt and adapt its previously unique features. Ransomes & Rapier went on to make many further cranes of this type for most of the major railways in Britain, and an even greater number for export, until the firm ceased production of railway steam cranes upon being taken over by Newton, Chambers & Co. in 1958.

Such was the ability of these cranes that when they were considered for a pre-planned lift of 50 tons under exceptional conditions, William Stanier was able to sign on CB Collett's behalf the following letter:

Capacity of 36-ton steam cranes to lift up to 50 tons.

With reference to my conversation with Foreman Robson on Saturday last, I have had this matter in hand with the makers, Messrs. Ransomes & Rapier, as to the capability of our crane No. 2 lifting loads up to 50 tons, and for your information give below extract from their quotations.

"We have not included for strengthening any parts of the crane to suit the 50 ton occasional load which we consider can be applied with comparative safety as the crane in question was tested with 45 tons at 21'4" radius on a 16' base. We have therefore only allowed for the extra counterbalance and attachments for same to render the crane suitable for 50 tons at 20ft. on a 5' 6" base on one side of the crane, as shown in Drawing No. 11364/22348.

"We would point out that the crane would not be stable on its wheels with the extra counterbalance attached, as the extra tail weight which the crane will take, and still be stable on its wheels, is only about 2½ tons. We are therefore including for an instruction plate to be fitted as indicated on Drawing No. 10362.

"With regard to the duty of 50 ton occasional loads, we have assumed that this will be in accordance with your drawing No. 30/32 with the base of 5' 6" on one side of the crane, but if you are only requiring our crane to lift the 50 ton load under normal conditions, i.e. 16'0" base, 8'0" per side, we beg to state that our crane will be quite suitable for this without any alteration or additional counterbalance."

You will note that this crane is allowed to lift 50 ton loads occasionally at 20ft. radius, and no alteration is contemplated to enable a 5' 6" propping base on one side of the crane as the firm suggested, as we should generally be able to use the present 16ft. propping base, i.e. 8ft. on each side.

Yours truly,
for C.B. Collett,
Sgd W.A. Stanier

One wonders whether this crane was being considered as an alternative for the work previously undertaken by the Taff Vale 36 ton crane, see page 146.

Towards the end of its service with BR, the counter-weight seems not to have been used, which meant that the crane's maximum capacity was reduced to 33 tons. The counter-weight has, nonetheless, survived.

Ransomes & Rapier 36-Ton Cranes for GWR							
Date ordered - delivered	Order No	Cost	Running No	Match wagon No		Allocation	Disposal
				GW	BR		
4/2/08 - 1908	B4411	£3,358*	2	2	Dw2, ADW 150434	Swindon Wks *13/8/36-'73*, Bristol on loan '71?, CCE Swindon c12/71-*4/72*	Wdn c'76. Pres
13/10/11 - 7/12	B6113		3	3	Dw3	Wolverhampton *13/8/36*, Worcester '40, Newton Abbot *15/11/56-29/7/57*, Landore *'61*, Neath *mid* '65	Wdn 10/11/66
* Including match wagon.							

Ex-GW 36-ton Ransomes & Rapier steam breakdown crane of 1908 No. 2 with its jib being raised, as it prepares to carry out a lift outside A Shop at Swindon on 23 August 1971. Appropriate lifting tackle on the match wagon is about to be attached. (Author)

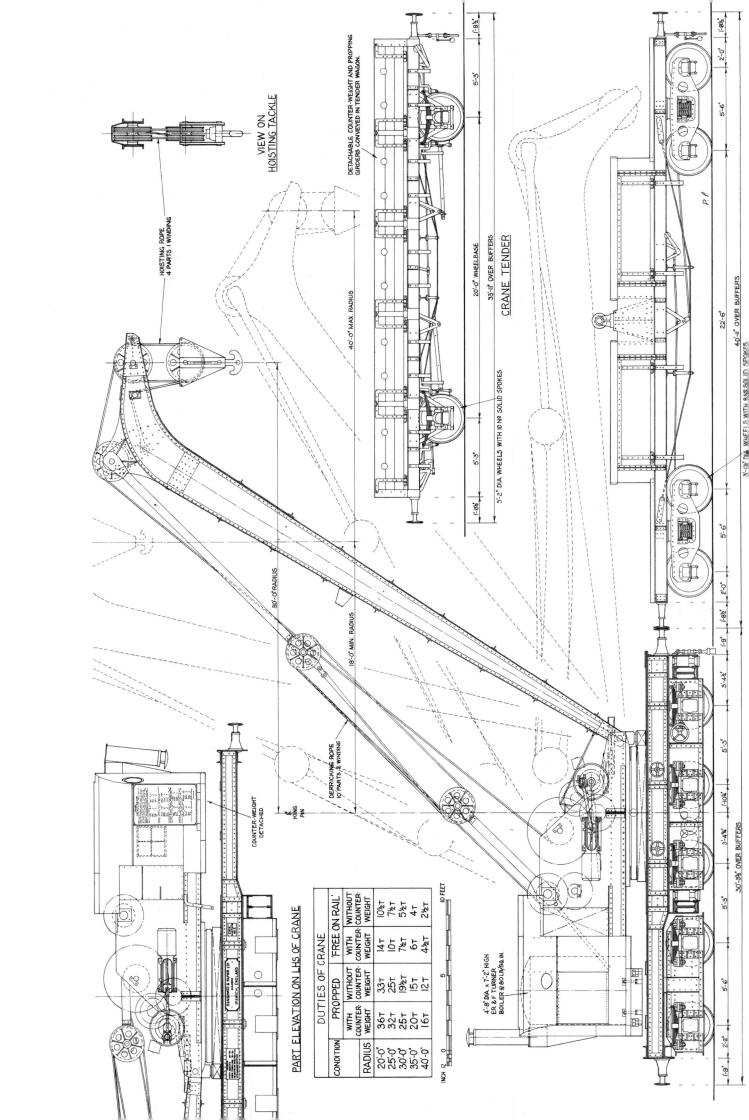

VIEW ON HOISTING TACKLE

HOISTING ROPE 4 PARTS 1 WINDING

DETACHABLE COUNTER-WEIGHT AND PROPPING GIRDERS CONVEYED IN TENDER WAGON.

40'-0" MAX. RADIUS

5'-3"   1'-8½"   2'-0"   5'-6"   5'-3"   1'-8½"

CRANE TENDER

20'-0" WHEELBASE

33'-11" OVER BUFFERS

3'-1½" DIA WHEELS WITH 10 Nº SOLID SPOKES

5'-3"   1'-8½"

22'-6"

40'-11" OVER BUFFERS

3'-1½" DIA WHEELS WITH 8 Nº SOLID SPOKES

P.l.

30'-0 RADIUS

18'-0" MIN. RADIUS

DERRICKING ROPE 10 PARTS 2 WINDING

₵ KING PIN

COUNTER-WEIGHT DETACHED

FRANCIS & RAPIER LTD
IPSWICH, ENGLAND

PART ELEVATION ON LHS OF CRANE

DUTIES OF CRANE

CONDITION	PROPPED		'FREE ON RAIL'	
RADIUS	WITH COUNTER-WEIGHT	WITHOUT COUNTER-WEIGHT	WITH COUNTER-WEIGHT	WITHOUT COUNTER-WEIGHT
20'-0"	36т	33т	14т	10½т
25'-0"	32т	25т	10т	7½т
30'-0"	25т	19½т	7½т	5½т
35'-0"	20т	15т	6т	4т
40'-0"	16т	12т	4½т	2½т

4'-8" DIA. x 7'-2" HIGH
ER & F TURNER
BOILER @ 80 LB/SQ.IN.

3'-4½"   5'-3"   1'-0¼"   3'-4½"   5'-3"   2'-2"   1'-9"

30-3¾" OVER BUFFERS

1'-9"   1'-8½"   1'-9"

INCH 12   0   5   10 FEET

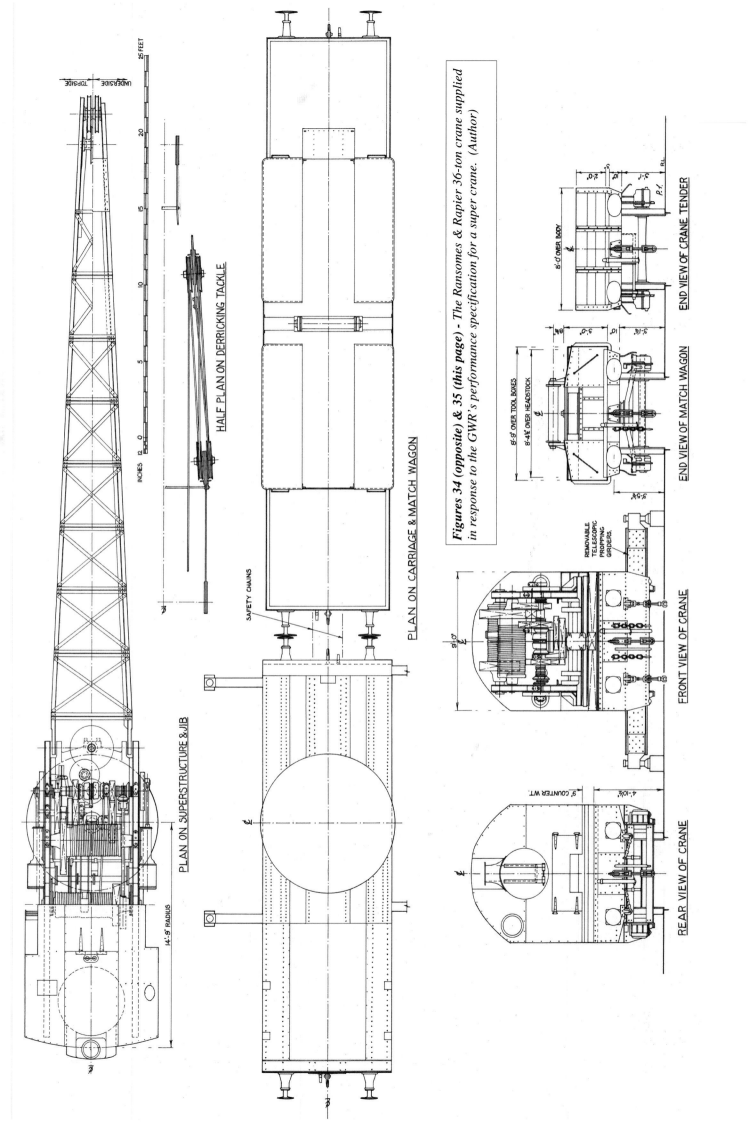

PLAN ON SUPERSTRUCTURE & JIB

14'-9" RADIUS

HALF PLAN ON DERRICKING TACKLE

25 FEET

TOPSIDE

UNDERSIDE

20

15

10

5

0

12

INCHES

SAFETY CHAINS

PLAN ON CARRIAGE & MATCH WAGON

Figures 34 (opposite) & 35 (this page) - *The Ransomes & Rapier 36-ton crane supplied in response to the GWR's performance specification for a super crane. (Author)*

REMOVABLE TELESCOPIC PROPPING GIRDERS.

9'-0"

FRONT VIEW OF CRANE

9' COUNTER WT.

4'-10½"

REAR VIEW OF CRANE

8'-9" OVER TOOL BOXES

8'-4½" OVER HEADSTOCK

3'-0"

10"

3'-1½"

END VIEW OF MATCH WAGON

3'-5¾"

8'-0" OVER BODY

2'-0"

10"

3'-1"

R.L.

P.L.

END VIEW OF CRANE TENDER

Above - No 2 with jib well up as appropriate lifting tackle on the match wagon is attached. (Author)

Opposite page - A rear view of No. 2 in train formation showing the circular cut-outs in the enclosure to accommodate the Turner boiler. (Author)

In 1975, after 67 years of service, No. 2 on the other hand was sold by British Railways to the Dart Valley Light Railway PLC and moved from Swindon to Paignton in Devon, arriving there on 25th November. The crane spent the next fifteen years working on the DVLR's two lines, the Paignton & Dartmouth Railway and the Dart Valley Railway (the line from Buckfastleigh to Totnes, now known as the South Devon Railway), and throughout this period was maintained in 'main line' condition since stock transfers between the two lines entailed running over BR tracks. In addition it was actually used a number of times on BR metals, both at Totnes and at Goodrington.

Nonetheless, in 1989, the board of the DVLR decided to sell the steam crane and replace it with a pair of smaller diesel cranes, and the crane was sold to a private buyer in spring 1989. In autumn 1990 the crane was moved by rail back to Swindon Works, where it was to be exhibited in connection with the 150th Anniversary of the GWR. After a period of storage at the Works, and with the impending final closure and clearance of the Works, the crane was moved to the Rover plant at Swindon, before finally moving to Cranmore on the East Somerset Railway in 1995.

The jib runner with the crane is the original, and dates from the same year as the crane. Originally this was numbered 2, to match the crane, but later it was renumbered (by BR) to ADW150434. Unfortunately the associated weight tender wagon did not survive into preservation.

Stothert & Pitt 36-Ton Crane
for GWR

This crane was built by Stothert & Pitt to the same overall performance specification as Ransomes & Rapier's offering, sharing many outward features. As built in 1909 this crane was fitted with curved lattice jib and inside bearings to the bogie. Whilst it too could achieve a lift of 36 tons at 20 feet radius, despite three sets of propping girders and 15ft 8in tail radius instead of 14ft 9in of the Rapier design, as the radius increased the duties it was able to perform fell off when compared to its rival from the Ipswich stable. Its lifting tackle consisted of six parts one winding, while the derricking tackle was of eight parts with two winding.

The motions of derricking the jib, lifting, slewing and self-propelling were driven by a pair of inclined 10 inch diameter by 12 inch stroke cylinders, for which steam was supplied by a Hopwood 4ft 6in diameter by 7ft 6in tall vertical boiler operating at a pressure of 100lb/sq in. Like the Rapier design, the travelling motion was achieved by a shaft passing through the centre pin of the crane from where it drove a transverse shaft in the carriage, but was coupled to two axles by sprocket wheels and chains. The original lattice jib had been replaced by 1917 by one with solid plate sides, possibly due to an accident.

In 1918, three 35-ton cranes of similar design were ordered (B6083) by the Ministry of Munitions for service in north west France, but differing from the 36-ton crane supplied to the GW in having two rather than three sets of propping girders and a few dimensions, not least in maximum height and width which would have precluded them operating on the British network. The last was scrapped at Leuven in 2001.

Stothert & Pitt 36-Ton Cranes for GWR			
Date delivered	GW Running No	Allocation	Disposal
5/09	1	Old Oak Common *13/8/36-10/5/40*, Bristol 5/40-15/11/56, Ebbw Jct *c'60s*, Worcester '62	Wdn '66

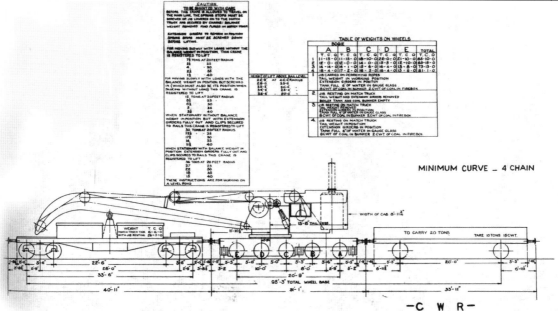

Figure 36 - GW diagram of 36-ton Stothert & Pitt steam crane No. 1. (GW, author's collection)

The Stothert & Pitt version of the 36-ton crane to meet the GW's requirements. It is seen here on 26 April 1910 with its lattice jib and chimney raised and three sets of propping girders in place. (BR, WR, author's collection)

By 23 April 1917 No. 1 had acquired a replacement plate jib with plate sides, presumably due to some accident involving the original lattice one. (BR. WR, author's collection)

No. 1 in the final stages of reassembly and repainting at Swindon Works on 23 July 1961 following probably its last overhaul. (MS Welch)

Ransomes & Rapier 36-Ton Crane
for LNWR

For its second breakdown crane bought in from the trade, the LNWR turned to Ransomes & Rapier for one similar to that recently acquired by the GWR. It will be noticed that the maker reviewed its design for the GWR and made it slightly longer with the 5ft 3in axle spacing increased to 6 feet and deeper frames to the carriage, suggesting that the originals could be improved upon. All subsequent R&R cranes, which were supplied to the GER, LSWR and SR, followed suit, except GWR No. 3. That for the LNWR, nonetheless, was also initially fitted with the Turner type of boiler and was the last to use the tie bar from the crab sides to the tail beam. Its performance at the extreme radius of 40 feet was also a little better than the GW crane at 18 tons, otherwise being the same. The bogie match truck was built specially by the LNWR.

Unlike most cranes which were under the control of the local locomotive running department, this one was retained at Crewe Works until 1939, when it went to Newton Heath. It returned in 1954 to Crewe's CMEE's Department, although it was no doubt made available in the event of a serious accident and sometimes to stand in for cranes away for overhaul.

Ransomes & Rapier 36-Ton Crane for LNWR									
Date ordered - delivered	Order No	Cost	Running No			Match wagon No		Allocation	Disposal
			LNWR	MP	5/41	LMS	BR		
27/9/09 - 1910	B5049	£3,160	25	7	RS1012/36	632	632	Crewe '10-'11, Newton Heath 10/3/39-1/7/47, Crewe Wks 4/54-5/64, Newton Heath 1/10/60	Wdn 11/67

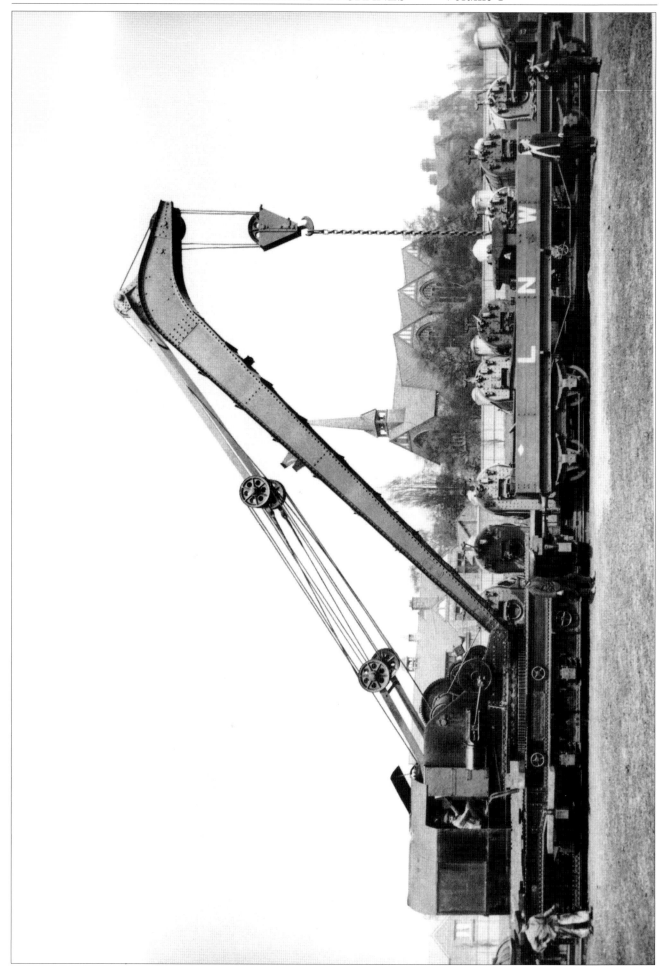

Opposite page - *The LNWR's new 36-ton crane from Ransomes & Rapier with its jib up on 22 April 1912. Whilst it has many of the features in common with that built for the GW, it had an improved and slightly enlarged carriage. (MS Welch collection)*

Right - *Another view, presumably on the same occasion, turned through 180 degrees, from which the smokebox of the Turner boiler can be seen projecting from the rear of the shelter. (HMRS collection)*

Bottom - *With the jib nearly lowered on to the bogie match wagon, the roof of the canopy over the driver is still raised while he was at the controls. The propping girders are still extended with jacks bedded down on timber packing. (HMRS collection)*

Wilson 12-Ton Crane
for GWR

This self-propelled 12-ton crane was acquired by the Great Western Railway from JH Wilson of Birkenhead in 1908 to supplement the impending delivery of their long jib 36-ton cranes. It was presumably intended for lighter work, such as handling wagons and smaller parts of locomotives and coaches. It is known to have assisted in the recovery of an over-turned canal-side crane at Gloucester Docks in March 1909 and continued to be listed as a breakdown crane, first at Old Oak Common, followed by Swindon in 1936 where it remained until at least 1960.

Mounted on four axles, the maximum axle load was 13 tons, which will have given it no trouble in passing down the most load-restricted of lines. Strongly constructed in mild steel sections and plates, the superstructure was mounted on live-ring rollers on a cast

steel roller path. The 9 inch diameter by 10 inch stroke cylinders were mounted vertically on the crab sides. The low carriage permitted the mounting of an 8 foot high by 4ft 6in diameter vertical boiler, which provided steam at 100lb/sq.in.

The crane was capable of lifting 12 tons at 15 foot radius down to 6 tons at 30 foot when propped, or half these values when free on rail. Unusually the brakes were applied by hand-wheels at each end of the front head-stocks, while the travelling gear could be engaged / disengaged by hand wheels low down on the frames between the leading and second axle. To obtain better purchase the steel wire derricking rope passed over a pulley mounted on a strut projecting back over the driver's position and down to a winding drum at floor level. The concurrently built 33ft 5in long 4-wheel match truck was a typical product of Swindon Works to Lot 623.

Wilson 12-Ton Crane for GWR					
Purch'd by	Date deliv'd	Order No	Running No	Match wagon No	Allocation
GW	1908	730	12	12	Old Oak Common, Swindon Wks *13/8/36-10/60*

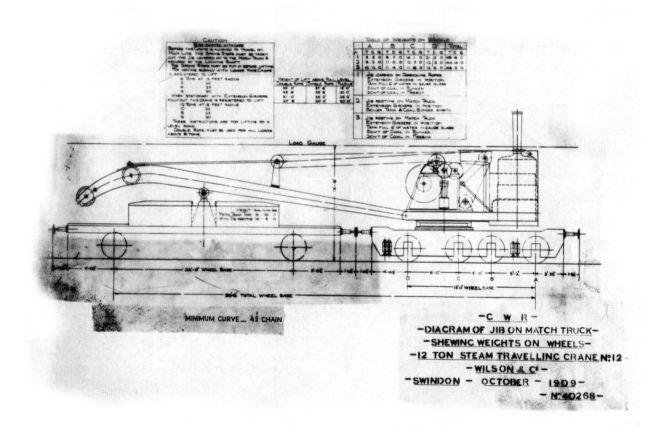

***Figure 37** - Diagram for Wilson 12-ton crane also built in 1908. (GW, author's collection)*

As well as long jib heavy duty cranes, the GW also obtained in 1908 a 12-ton capacity crane from JH Wilson & Co. No. 12 was initially sent to join the Stothert & Pitt crane at Old Oak Common, but subsequently spent much of its time at Swindon. (BR, WR, author's collection)

The 12-ton Wilson crane No. 12 with its jib and chimney raised and with locomotive No. 111 The Great Bear *in the background on 17 June 1909. The relatively lightly constructed 39 foot long jib had plate sides and lattice cross bracing. (BR, WR, author's collection)*

8. Poor Rivals

Cowans Sheldon 35/36-ton cranes of 1911-14
Craven Bros 35/36-ton cranes
Cowans Sheldon 35/36-ton cranes of 1916-17

With the introduction in 1908 of the Ransomes & Rapier 36-ton long jib crane on the GW, soon followed by one for the LNWR, other crane makers found their own designs outdated and they struggled for a few years to prepare designs to match Ransomes and Rapier's product. In the meantime, the GW had added two more 36-ton cranes to its original specification, one from Stothert and Pitt and a second from Rapier.

Cowans Sheldon 35/36-Ton Cranes of 1911-1914

Faced with such competition, between 1911 and 1914 Cowans built three massive 36-ton cranes, one each for the Taff Vale, LNWR and NBR. In these it is possible to identify a scaled-up version of their previous standard 15- to 30-ton cranes. The centrally placed pillar was replaced by live rings on 40 rollers and employing a short post with provision to resist uplift, but the design exhibited a clumsy 4 foot wide parallel-sided lattice jib of 35 feet in length. A long 4-4-4 carriage resulted in a poor outreach in front of the crane. Although reportedly very strong cranes, they must have been difficult to get close to the work. Following on a solitary example of 35 tons capacity in

1914 on a 0-6-4 underframe for Rhymney Railway, in 1916 and 1917 they did considerably better with two more 36/35 tonners of 4-6-0 wheel arrangement with medium length jib for the LNWR and NER, both acquired as replacements for earlier cranes requisitioned by the War Department and sent overseas.

Taff Vale Railway

In an attempt to minimise the impact of the increase in length of the carriage to accommodate six axles, the third and fourth axles were at the unusually close centres of 3ft 4in. To provide stability in the propped mode, four sets of propping girders were installed. The resulting crane weighed in at 94 tons 1 cwt 2 qtrs with the jib up, while with jib resting on match wagon 86 tons 15 cwt 3qtrs was still carried by the crane which produced a maximum axle load of 18 tons 6 cwt 1 qtr. It was variously described as 35 tons capacity on the general arrangement drawing or 36 tons capacity on the diagram.

The superstructure was mounted on a live ring consisting of 40 cast steel rollers. The enlarged, but still old style crab sides carried 9 inch diameter by 14 inch stroke inclined cylinders. The tail extension of the crab

Cowans Sheldon's heavy-handed response to the challenge set by Ransomes & Rapier's 36-ton crane can be seen in the form of their 36-ton Cowans Sheldon steam crane for the Taff Vale Railway in 1911. Stationed at Cathays until 1940, it was photographed with its bogie match wagon No. 10 at Banbury in June 1951. Note the width of the jib head. (JFC Johnston)

sides carried a Spencer-Hopwood boiler and the usual coal and water supplies. The jib was a parallel-sided lattice girder supported by steel wire rope in 16 parts, with just one winding. The single hook and two pulley blocks were carried on four parts with one winding steel wire rope.

The crane was also capable of being used as a fixed crane on the quayside. When appropriately secured and counter-balanced, it was authorised to lift 50 tons at 20 foot radius and even 35 tons, later reduced to 31 tons, out to a radius of 32 feet. To achieve this, the extended propping girders on the landward side had 42 tons of counter weight applied, while on the seaward side the propping girders were only drawn out to a support 5ft 6in from the centre line of the crane. In addition longitudinal beams were drawn out from the rear of the superstructure and upon them a counter-weight was applied.

The crane was delivered to Cathays on 9 December 1911 and the match wagon with diamond frame bogies was built for the TV by SJ Claye the same year. Following grouping in 1923, the GW allocated the number 10, but it remained at Cathays until 1940, when it migrated to Banbury and later Worcester, where, with regional boundary changes, it fell into the hands of the London Midland Region who rechristened it RS1098/36 and then withdrew it in 1969.

Taff Vale 36-Ton Crane by Cowans Sheldon						
Date delivered	Works No	Running No		Match wagon	Allocation	Disposal
		GW/BR-WR	BR-LMR			
19/12/11	3143	10	RS1098/36	10	Cathays 9/12/11-*9/4/40*, Banbury *10/5/40*, to LMR 1/2/58, Worcester 12/59-*10/67*	Wdn '69

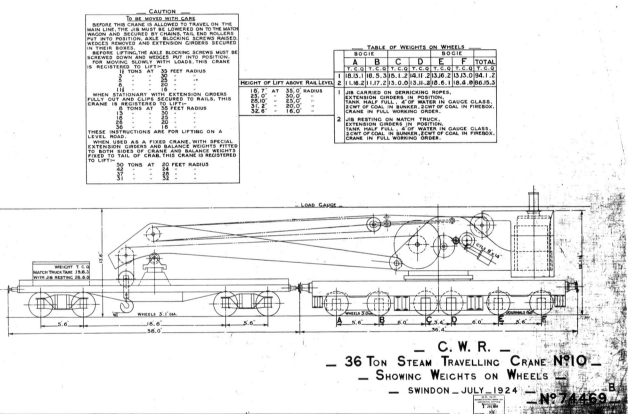

Above - GW diagram of Taff Vale 36-ton Cowans Sheldon crane, GWR No. 10, supplied in 1911. (GW, author's collection)

Left - No. 10 clearing up the debris following an accident at Appleford Crossing on 25 September 1952. The close centres of the middle two axles will be observed. Nonetheless, the carriage is still of considerable length thereby limiting its reach forward. (Kidderminster Railway Museum)

London & North Western Railway and North British Railway

The two closely spaced and heavily loaded axles of the previous crane are not good news to the bridge engineer, so the next version of the Cowans Sheldon 36-ton crane opened the spacing of the third and fourth axles to 6ft 5½in. The NB crane weighed 85 tons 16 cwt and depending on how well the springs were adjusted the axle load could exceed 18 tons for which 7 by 14 inch journals were provided on the centre axles. With the king pin to the superstructure still located at the centre of the carriage the reach forward or backward remained substantial at 18 feet, two feet more than the minimum radius. To accommodate the now slightly more widely spaced bogies, the two sets of propping girders on the outer end of the previous TV crane were replaced by dolly jacks at each corner, leaving two sets of girders, one each either side of the third and fourth axle, making for a very stable crane.

These propping girders were of box section with screw jacks at their ends. The two cranes were equipped with a one-ton auxiliary hoist for handling small items at a faster rate than using the more ponderous main hoist. The NB crane had a wheel diameter of 2ft 10in to enable the crane to pass the somewhat restricted NB loading gauge.

Having taken nearly a decade to realise that it needed to go to the specialist crane builders, the LNWR then embarked on a programme of acquiring top of the range plant, going for its third crane with one from Cowans Sheldon in 1913. The bogie match truck was built specially by the railway company. This massive machine spent most of its life at Preston, only going briefly to Lostock Hall, before being transferred to the Western Region on 31 October 1962. It is reputed to have been allocated to Gloucester, but is believed to have resided out of use at Swindon until withdrawn in 1966, not

				Running Nos		Match		
Purch'd by	Date ordered - delivered	Works No	Cost	Gr'ping	BR-LMR	wagon No	Allocation	Disposal
LNWR	1913	3221	£3,000	MP6	RS1009/36	(DM)636	Preston *'14–1/10/60*, Lostock hall '61, to WR 31/10/62, Gloucester 10/62, Swindon OOU *15/6/63-26/4/64*	Wdn '66
NB	5/3/14 - 1914	3310	£3,290	770517, 971567	RS1062/36 ADRC 95200	770518, 971568	St Margaret's '14, Thornton 3/62, Dundee '66-*4/75*, Carstairs OOU '78	Wdn 17/11/78, SRPS 6/79

Cowans Sheldon 36-Ton Cranes

Cowans Sheldon's design of 36-ton crane supplied to the LNWR and North British in 1913 and 1914 respectively matched the Ransomes & Rapier's capacity, but the 4-4-4 wheel arrangement of the carriage resulted in a serious lack of portée. Ex-LNWR 36-ton Cowans Sheldon steam crane of 1913 was photographed in 10 February 1939. Note the considerable length of the carriage supported by six axles. (Author's collection)

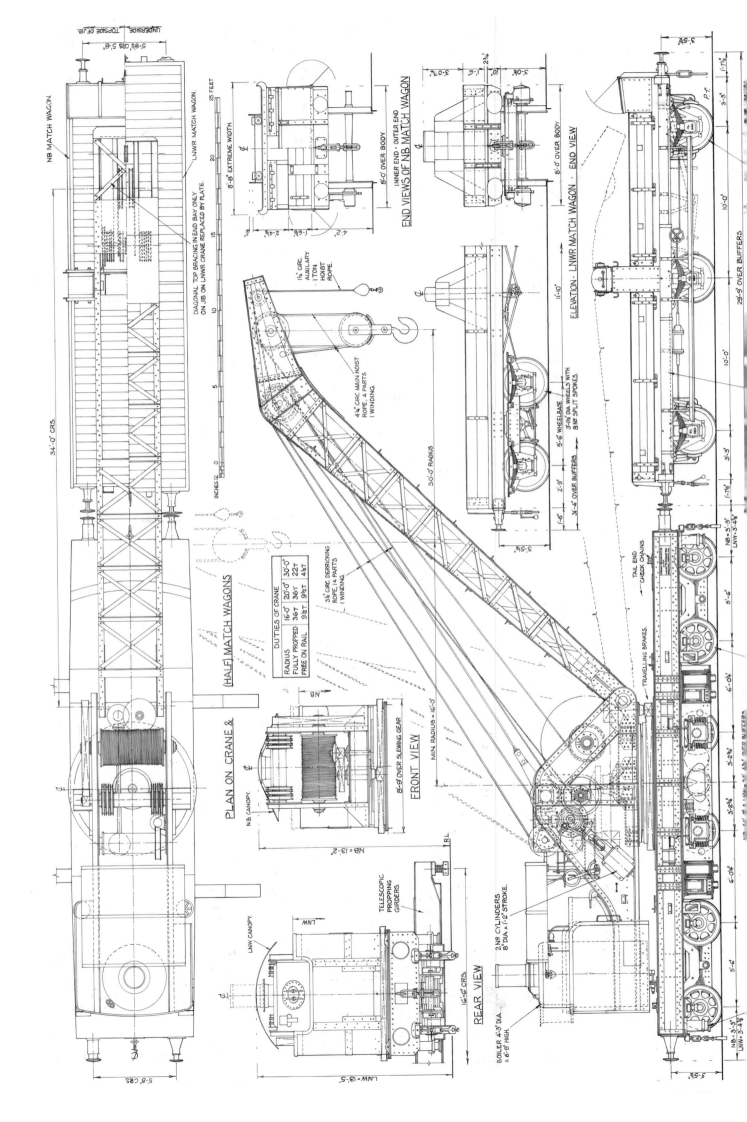

NB MATCH WAGON.

UNDERSIDE. TOPSIDE OF JIB.
5-8½ CRS 5'-8"

LNWR MATCH WAGON.

DIAGONAL TOP BRACING IN END BAY ONLY
ON JIB ON LNWR CRANE REPLACED BY PLATE.

34'-0" CRS.

25 FEET
20
15
10
5
0
INCHES 12

5-8½ CRS.

8'-8" EXTREME WIDTH

INNER END - OUTER END
END VIEWS OF NB MATCH WAGON

8'-0" OVER BODY

3'-0⅞"
2⅝
0
2'-4⅜"
1'-6⅛"
4'-2"

8'-0" OVER BODY

3'-5⅜

3'-0⅝"
10"
3'-0⅜"

END VIEW

ELEVATION - LNWR MATCH WAGON

3-5⅝
1'-1½
3'-3"
10'-0"
10'-0"
3'-3"
1'-7½
NB - 3'-9"
LNW - 3'-4⅝

29'-9" OVER BUFFERS

8 N° SPLIT SPOKES.
3-4½" DIA WHEELS WITH
5'-6" WHEELBASE
34'-4" OVER BUFFERS
1'-6"
2'-9"

1½ CIRC.
AUXILARY
1 TON
HOIST ROPE.

4¼" CIRC. MAIN HOIST
ROPE. 4 PARTS
1 WINDING.

3-0-0" RADIUS

2¾ CIRC. DERRICKING
ROPE. 14 PARTS
1 WINDING.

(HALF) MATCH WAGONS

PLAN ON CRANE &

DUTIES OF CRANE			
RADIUS	16'-0"	20'-0"	30'-0"
FULLY PROPPED	36T	36T	22T
FREE ON RAIL	9½T	9½T	4½T

NB

MIN RADIUS = 16'-0"

8'-9" OVER SLEWING GEAR

FRONT VIEW

NB CANOPY.

NB = 13'-2"

TELESCOPIC
PROPPING GIRDERS

TRAVELLING BRAKES.

TAIL END
CHECK CHAINS

NB - 3'-9"
LNW - 3'-4⅝

5'-6"
1'-6"
6'-0¼
3'-2¼"
6'-0¼

34'-4" OVER BUFFERS

NB - 3'-9"
LNW - 3'-4⅝

3'-5⅜

LNW CANOPY.

LNW

16'-6" CRS.

REAR VIEW

2 N° CYLINDERS
8" DIA × 1'-2" STROKE.

BOILER 4'-3" DIA.
× 6'-9" HIGH

LNW = 13'-5"

Opposite page, Figure 39 - *Drawing of the Cowans Sheldon 36-ton cranes supplied to the LNWR and North British Railway in 1913 and 1914. (Author)*

Above - *No. RS1009/36 standing beside Swindon Workshops on 22 March 1964 awaiting its fate, still showing on the match wagon Preston as its home depot. (MS Welch)*

least because its predecessor remained at Gloucester until at least September 1970.

The North British Railway's example too spent a long time at its first depot, namely St Margaret's, Edinburgh. It was only displaced to Thornton in March 1962 and later Ferryhill, Dundee and Carstairs, before being withdrawn on 17 November 1978 and subsequently

sold to the Scottish Railway Preservation Society in June 1979. After the closure of Falkirk and a sojourn at Perth in storage, it was moved to Bo'ness in 1993. The design of the 6-wheel match wagon appears to lean on those supplied by its southerly neighbour, the North Eastern Railway, for its 35-ton Craven cranes, about to be described below but built a couple of years earlier. During

Right - *Ex-NB 36-ton Cowans Sheldon steam crane as LNER No. 770517 spruced up, including white wheel tyres and burnished buffer heads, and brought up from St Margaret's for public display at Edinburgh Waverley station before World War 2. (LGRP, author's collection)*

149

Centre - *The business end of No. RS1062/36 at Dundee on 12 May 1974, already annotated with its TOPS number TDM1062 and safe working load in kilograms. (JC Dean)*

Left - *Old-fashioned inside bearing Adams bogie with extended axles on to which the blocking out stops were screwed down while the crane was at work. Notice that to achieve the necessary loading gauge on the NB, the wheel diameter had to be reduced to 2ft 10in. (JC Dean)*

Opposite top - *Towards the end of its days No. RS1062/36 stands outside the ex-CR shed at Dundee in April 1971. By this time the 6-wheel match wagon has taken on a considerable sag. (J Templeton, author's collection)*

Right - *The original cast iron notice plate giving the maker's instructions and safe loads. (JC Dean)*

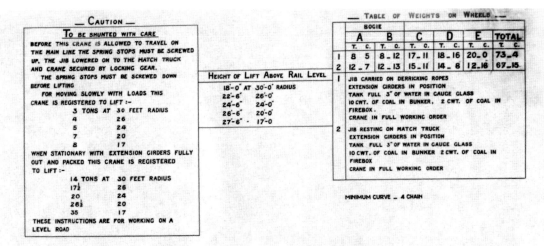

Cowans Sheldon 35-Ton Crane for Rhymney Rly				
Date deliv'd	Works No	GW & match wagon Nos	Allocation	Disposal
20/12/13	3235	9	Caerphilly '22, Newton Abbot 13/8/36-'48, Worcester '50-10/60, Banbury '62-20/6/65	Wdn '65

preservation, however, this match wagon was replaced by a 4-wheel plate wagon in 1987.

Rhymney Railway

Some progress, one feels, was made when Cowans Sheldon did away with the front bogie and substituted a third fixed axle. This considerably reduced the length of the carriage in front of the centre of rotation and that to the rear was no worse than previously. A single example for a British railway, capable of lifting 35 tons, albeit at a radius of only 17 foot, was produced for the Rhymney Railway in late 1913 weighing in at much improved 73 tons 4 cwt and a maximum axle load of 15 tons 11 cwt carried on 6½ by 14inch journals. Just two sets of propping girders, again of box section were fitted between the first and second axles, and between the third and fourth. These were, however, tapered towards the outer end to accommodate screw jacks. The superstructure and jib supporting just a main hook were largely unchanged.

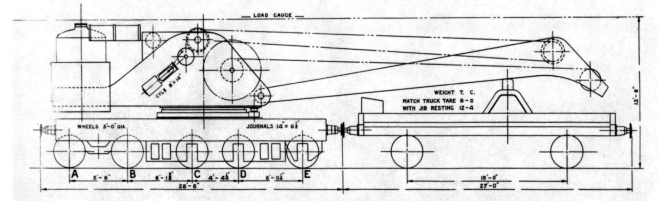

Figure 40 - *Diagram for ex-Rhymney Railway's 35-ton Cowans Sheldon steam crane No. 9 supplied in 1913. (GW, author's collection)*

Top and bottom - *The former Rhymney Railway 35-ton Cowans Sheldon crane at Banbury. Note the much more compact 0-6-4 wheel arrangement to the carriage. The 4-wheel match wagon of unknown origin displays numerous GW standard fittings. There appears to be a Cowans Sheldon 20 ton crane behind No 9.   (Author's collection)*

Initially allocated to the company's locomotive headquarters at Caerphilly, before World War 2 it went to Newton Abbot and under BR was cascaded to Worcester and Banbury before being withdrawn in 1965.

Craven Bros. 35/36-Ton Cranes

Craven Bros. had only recently entered the breakdown crane market in United Kingdom and quickly established a reputation for sound machines. To meet the increase in load capacity now expected, they provided 35-ton cranes, but still with a short jib and on five axles, the outer ones radial, while the third and fourth axles were again closely spaced at 3ft 11in. The second and third axles had a

compensating beam between them. The first of these cranes was built for the L&Y in 1911. Subsequently an improved version, two cranes for the NER in 1912 and one for the GN in 1914 was supplied, followed by orders in 1915 from the War Department for service in Europe. The second version came close to the performance of the Rapier crane except at the larger radii.

As well as the extra axle to carry the increase in weight, the machinery was totally redesigned to achieve improved accessibility for maintenance. The crab sides were stepped down to allow the critical items to be lifted straight out of their journals without having to dismantle the sides. Likewise, the Walschaerts valve gear was

Craven 35/36-Ton Cranes									
Purch'd by	Date ord'd - deliv'd	Order No	Cost	Running No		Match wagon No		Allocation	Disposal
				1st	2nd LMS / BR	Pre-group	Grp'ing		
L&Y	3/11 - 1911	9158	£2,585	2048, MP11	RS1017/ 35	34450	164450	Sandhills '11/Bank Hall -5/64, Edge Hill 11/66	Scrapped 4/67
NER	7/11 - 1912	9372	£3,020	CME 15, 770569	971569, RS1063/ 35	03435?, 3775	770570 971570	York '13-*1/22*, Eastfield 29/11/27-*10/5/40*, Thornton '40-*1/10/60*, Ferry-hill '62, Perth *26/6/67*	Scrapped '67/8?
NER	7/11 - 1912	9372, 10063	£3,020	WD No. 1	SNCB 310.04	03435?, 40 958 4 800-5		Gateshead '12, to WD '14, rebuilt '15, SNCFB, Kinkenpois	Preserved
GN	6/13 - 1914	9780	£3,975	A343, SB2, 941592	123, RS1096/ 35		343AA	Peterboro '27-'*38*, Gorton, Neasden *10/5/40*, Gorton *16/9/42*, Woodford Halse *7/44-6/11/61*, to LMR 1/2/58, Banbury 14/6/65-*16/3/66*	Wdn 7/4/66 Scrapped 8/10/66
WD	1915	10064		WD No. 2				Outriggers	
WD	11/16	CS3750	£5,100	90?				Craven design, Shoeburyness 11/16, Cohens 19/10/49, RW Greenwell & Co, River Wear Commissioners *6/6/50*	Scrapped '65

The first 35-ton crane supplied by Craven Bros to a British railway company, in this case the Lancashire & Yorkshire in 1911. Note the outside Walschaerts valve gear. (H Morris, author's collection)

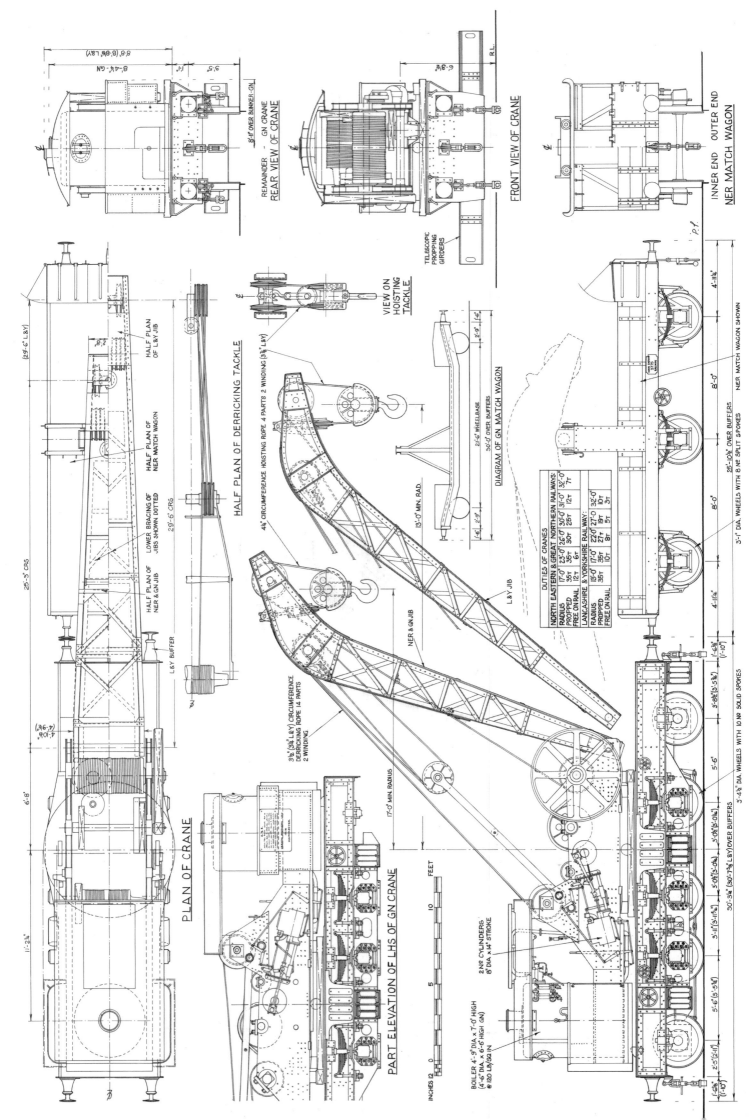

REAR VIEW OF CRANE

REMAINDER – GN CRANE
8'-1" OVER BUNKER – GN

FRONT VIEW OF CRANE

TELESCOPIC
PROPPING
GIRDERS

INNER END   OUTER END
NER MATCH WAGON

NER MATCH WAGON SHOWN

HALF PLAN
OF L&Y JIB

HALF PLAN OF
NER MATCH WAGON

LOWER BRACING OF
JIBS SHOWN DOTTED

HALF PLAN OF
NER & GN JIB

L&Y BUFFER

PLAN OF CRANE

HALF PLAN OF DERRICKING TACKLE

VIEW ON
HOISTING
TACKLE

4½" CIRCUMFERENCE HOISTING ROPE 4 PARTS 2 WINDING (3⅜ L&Y)

L&Y JIB

NER & GN JIB

DIAGRAM OF GN MATCH WAGON

13'-0" MIN. RAD.

21'-6" WHEELBASE
30'-0" OVER BUFFERS

3½" (3¾ L&Y) CIRCUMFERENCE
DERRICKING ROPE 14 PARTS
2 WINDING

17'-0" MIN. RADIUS

PART ELEVATION OF LHS OF GN CRANE

2 N° CYLINDERS
8" DIA x 14" STROKE

BOILER 4'-9" DIA x 7'-0" HIGH
(4'-6" DIA x 6'-6" HIGH GN)
@ 120 LB/SQ IN

DUTIES OF CRANES			
NORTH EASTERN & GREAT NORTHERN RAILWAYS:			
RADIUS	17'-0	23'-0	26'-0	30'-0	31'-0	32'-0
PROPPED	35T	35T	30T	28T	12T	7T
FREE ON RAIL	12T	6T				
LANCASHIRE & YORKSHIRE RAILWAY:			
RADIUS	13'-0	17'-0	22'-0	27'-0	32'-0
PROPPED	35T	27T	21T	19T	3T
FREE ON RAIL	10T	8T	5T		

NER MATCH WAGON SHOWN

25'-10⅞ OVER BUFFERS

3'-1" DIA WHEELS WITH 8 N° SPLIT SPOKES

3'-4½ DIA. WHEELS WITH 10 N° SOLID SPOKES

30'-3¼ (30'-7⅞ L&Y) OVER BUFFERS

INCHES 12   0   5   10   FEET

positioned outside the sides controlling the admission of steam to 8 inch diameter by 14 inch stroke cylinders. The gears to the final drive of the hoisting drum were of the double helical type rather than the more usual straight cut. Like the 20/25-ton cranes built in 1907/8 the lifting tackle to the main block was of four parts, or falls rigged to a snatch block on the underside of the jib. With the latter unhooked and the main block removed, 17½/18 tons could be lifted at twice the speed. They were self-propelled at a speed of up to 12 mph, with steam and hand brakes acting on the wheels of the outer fixed axles.

Lancashire & Yorkshire Railway

In 1911, instead of returning to Cowans Sheldon for a further crane, the L&Y turned to the local firm Craven Bros. in Manchester and ordered a 35-ton crane, allocating it to Sandhills shed, from 1920 known as Bank Hall, Liverpool. It remained here until almost the end, when it went briefly to Edgehill, Liverpool before being withdrawn in April 1967.

With its jib resting on the match wagon, this crane weighed 65 tons 12 cwt and had a maximum axle load of 17 tons 4 cwt. It had a 29ft 6in long jib necessitating five cross braced panels and enabling the

Top - *The L&Y's breakdown train at Sandhills made up of the 35-ton Craven crane and match truck in train formation with tool and riding vans. (AG Ellis, author's collection)*

Bottom - *Four of the crane crew stand proudly by their crane in L&Y livery at Sandhills. (E Mason, courtesy BC Lane)*

Opposite page, Figure 41 - *Drawing of Craven 35-ton cranes for L&Y, NER and GN. (Author)*

crane to lift its maximum load of 35 tons at a radius of 20 feet, but later reduced to 17 feet down and to 10 tons at its maximum radius of 32 feet when fully propped. Free on rail these values dropped to 10 and 3 tons respectively. It and the match wagon were fitted with vacuum brake gear, together with passenger-rated buffers and draw-gear, to enable it to run at greater speed.

The match wagon No. 34450 was designed on a standard 21ft 6in by 8 foot wagon underframe and built in 1911 by the L&Y at a cost of £106-4-2, a drawing for which will be found in *Lancashire & Yorkshire Wagons, Volume 2*, Wild Swan Publications, 2006, p 434.

North Eastern Railway

Well satisfied with the three 25-ton cranes the NER had purchased from Craven Bros in 1907, they ordered two more from the company of 35 tons capacity. These and subsequent 35-ton cranes had shorter jibs than the L&Y's at 25ft 3in and a reduction in the number of cross-braced panels to four, similar to the 25-ton cranes. The two NER cranes were allocated to York and Gateshead, allowing a couple of the 25-ton cranes there to be cascaded to others depots. The new Gateshead crane was, however, requisitioned by the War Office and rebuilt to provide a gantry and pile driving equipment. Craven Order No. 10064 from the War Department was for a similar new crane, but this time with outriggers rather than propping girders. The Gateshead machine was not returned to the NER and after war service with the Railway Operating Department who based it at their Audruicq Depot and St. Etienne du Rouvray Workshops, it went via the Nord Belge to Belgian Railways, and still exists, stored in the old depot at Leuven.

The remaining NER crane continued at York, being numbered CME 15, until 1927 when it was transferred to the Scottish Area of the LNER. Here it was allocated to Eastfield shed and renumbered 770569 and the match wagon to 770570, only for these to be further altered to 971569 and 971570 in 1938. With the arrival of a 45-ton crane at Eastfield in 1940 the Craven crane was moved to Thornton, where following nationalisation it was renumbered yet again as RS1057/63, while the match wagon became DE971570. Even when at Thornton, it frequently travelled to Cowlairs Works at weekends where its short jib was useful in repositioning locomotive boilers. Short sojourns at Ferryhill and Perth culminated in withdrawal by 1967/8.

Opposite page - *One of the two North Eastern Railway's 35-ton Craven cranes of 1912 now transferred to Scotland and based at Eastfield. LNER No. 770569 and associated 6-wheel match truck stand ready for duty sometime prior to World War 2. The radius and safe load indicator can be discerned under the canopy towards the right-hand end. (GN Heathcote)*

Above - *The crane after the war and nationalisation in similar pose at Eastfield on 23 March 1952, despite in the meantime having been transferred to Thornton, and renumbered 971569. (J Templeton, author's collection)*

Bottom - *Towards the end of its life, the same crane now No. RS1063/35, shelters under the roof of the nearly empty Perth shed on 26 June 1967, probably totally unaware that its sister was still in service on the Belgian Railways. (Author)*

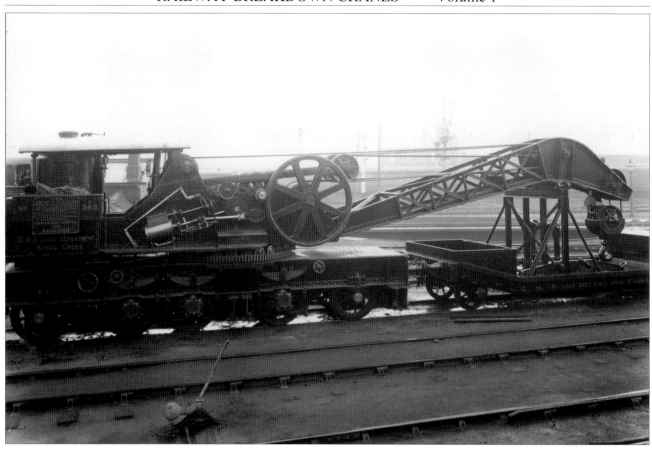

Above - Almost new Craven 35-ton steam crane No. A343 and match wagon No. 343AA both duly lettered GNR Loco Department Kings Cross. Notice the four panels to the jib of this and the NER Crane compared with five on the L&Y's. *(RJ Essery collection)*

Bottom - A party of visitors examine the GN 35-ton Craven crane No. A343 at Peterborough circa 1920. *(HMRS collection)*

Great Northern Railway

Finally the Great Northern Railway also acquired such a 35-ton crane from Craven Bros. in 1914. The match wagon was a former GN 15-ton low machine wagon, its brothers being coded Mac M by the LNER, upon which a trestle jib support was erected along with tool boxes at each end. At some point in the crane's life the buffers were altered so that they were mounted on hinges, thus allowing them to be folded back to enable the crane to approach closer to the load. Replacement water tank and coal bunker were fitted at some stage, no doubt because the previous ones were life expired.

Although, when new, it was clearly painted with the home depot as Kings Cross, it is believed this had merely been done to convince the directors of the company that their latest investment was stationed at the prestigious London terminal. Strategy dictated, however, that Peterborough was geographically much to be preferred and it is understood this crane spent its early years there from where it could be more readily despatched up and down the East Coast main line, or round by some of the secondary routes, as needs be. When Peterborough received its 45-ton crane in 1940, the Craven crane, by then No. 941592, moved on to Gorton and then Woodford Halse on the Great Central Section. After this line was transferred to the London Midland Region at the beginning of 1958, it was renumbered RS1096/35 and subsequently moved on to Banbury from where it was withdrawn on 7 April 1966 and scrapped by 8 October the same year.

A further crane of this type was supplied by Craven to the War Department with hinged outriggers, while others of their design, with a jib as used for the L&Y order, appear to have been built by Cowans Sheldon. At the time, mechanically the Craven product was first class: is it possible, therefore, that Cowans were able to benefit from this design in their own future work?

One of the WD cranes seems to have led a somewhat chequered career. It was delivered to Shoeburyness in November 1916, where it was named *Hood,* before passing through the hands of George Cohen Ltd at Wood Lane in October 1949 and being sold to RW Greenwood, who appear not to have used it, or were acting as agents. It then found its way to the River Wear Commissioners as No. 90, who christened it *Black Prince* and used it in the maintenance of harbour works. It was last noted being employed on repair work to the Sea Lock, following storms of Jan/Feb.1953, lifting blocks of up to 20 tons in weight. Before being scrapped in 1965, the crane was offered to Mr F Atkinson, Museums Director of the Durham County Council, but at a cost of £500, the Director preferred to invest in a more representative machine, thereby passing up an opportunity to acquire it for the Beamish Museum.

Shortly before the end, No. RS1096/35, still lettered Woodford Halse MPD but at Banbury shed on 16 March 1966. By now much superficially altered; note the hinged buffers, the provision of a ladder for the driver and taller replacement water tank and coal bunker, while a turbo-generator has been mounted on the counter-weight. (Colin Stacey, Initial Photographics)

A Cowans Sheldon built 35-ton crane of Craven design with five cross-braced panels to the lattice jib, acquired after the war by the River Wear Commissioners. Here it lies derelict on 21 May 1957. The Cowans builder's plate is over the right-hand axle. Screw jacks are fitted to the propping girder ends. (JM Fleming)

Cowans Sheldon 35/36-Ton Cranes of 1916/7

Having found a more satisfactory wheel arrangement for large cranes and replaced the central pillar by the live ring, Cowans Sheldon at last grasped the nettle, anticipated by other makers, and modernised the superstructure to be more amenable to the needs of maintenance by enabling most of the major components to be readily removed for overhaul. The arrangement of machinery developed was to carry the company forward for the next 40 years. A pair of heavy plate crab sides tapered upwards from the jib foot and a relatively low front to support the journals of the various transverse lay-shafts, culminated in a step up at the rear to accommodate the derricking drum as high as practical.

The wheel arrangement of the Rhymney crane was reversed to become a 4-6-0, which seems a retrograde step when the crane would be more stable while travelling with the fixed axles better placed centrally under the centre of rotation of the superstructure. Again within this, three sets of propping girders were accommodated, at the front and rear of the bogie and between the fourth and fifth axles, when with the alternative wheel arrangement two sets would have been more than adequate. The Adams bogie was, however, replaced by a plate frame one with independent springs to each axle journal. Instead of the post and cross-bracing to the lattice jib, opposing diagonal bracing, of the Warren form, was adopted to support at the outer end a main hoist and 2 ton auxiliary hoist.

The NER crane carried a 4ft 3in diameter by 6ft 9in tall boiler (the LNWR one was 4ft 6in by 8ft 6in) pressed to 100 lb/sq. in. The steam therein produced fed a pair of 8 inch diameter by 14 inch stroke cylinders. This enabled the crane to raise its jib from resting on the match wagon to minimum radius in about 10 minutes. It could lift 35/36 tons at a speed of 20 feet a minute; 17½ tons could be raised at 40 feet per minute, while 2 ton could be hoisted at 200 feet per minute. Slewing under full load could be achieved at a rate of 2 revolutions per minute and travelling under its own steam with no load at 350 feet per minute (4 mph).

The Crane's Motions

In the description and drawing below of this machinery, the terminology adopted is similar to, where possible, that used earlier to describe the Cowans Sheldon 15-ton cranes of the 1880-1910s:

Derricking the Jib

Upon arrival at the site of operations after rendering the springs inoperative, the first job was to raise the jib. The spur pinion E on the crank-shaft permanently rotated the rear lay-shaft by means of pinion wheel F. To raise or lower the jib, mitre wheel Q was locked to the shaft by means of a dog-clutch and drove, through another mitre gear R, a shaft at the end of which was worm gear S meshed with worm wheel T on the derricking drum. As a worm is non-reversible (i.e. the worm wheel cannot drive the worm), the jib cannot run down of its own accord. Nonetheless, to prevent vibration causing the jib to creep, a screw-operated hand brake was provided on the worm shaft. On the subsequent 45-ton cranes the brake was applied by a weight which was automatically released when the derricking gear was engaged.

Hoisting a Load

To achieve a lift at maximum load, the degree of step down required by the gear chain caused the load to rise at only a very slow speed. The provision, however, of two sets of gears between the crank-shaft and the front lay-shaft gave the option to raise a reduced load of up to half the maximum at twice the speed. These options were obtained by either engaging sliding pinion A1 with spur wheel B1 for maximum lift, or alternatively a dog-clutch brought spur pinion A2 into mesh with spur wheel B2 for reduced loads. In both cases this then drove spur pinion C and spur wheel D, which was permanently engaged with the hoisting drum. A foot-operated pedal applied the hoist brake attached to the front lay-shaft.

Slewing the Superstructure

To enable adjustments either way in the alignment of the jib without reversing the engine, a pair of mitre wheels H1 or H2 mounted on the rear lay-shaft could be engaged by means of one or other of the double cone friction clutches. The mitre wheel G meshed with H1 and H2 then rotated a short vertical shaft at the foot of which a further set of mitre gears K and L transformed the motion into a long horizontal shaft. At the forward end of this shaft a small bevelled pinion M acted on a bevelled wheel N, which in turn drove another short vertical shaft at the bottom of which spur pinion O acted on the outside of spur rack P attached to the carriage, so rotating the superstructure.

Self-Propelled Travel

The elimination of the large vertical pillar of earlier cranes and the adoption of the live ring with stub king pin secured at the top to resist uplift, enabled a vertical drive spindle to pass down the centre from the superstructure to the carriage. A further set of mitre wheels I1 and I2 on the rear lay-shaft, this time engaged in one direction or the other by a double-sided dog clutch, rotated mitre wheel J on a third short vertical shaft. At the foot of this, spur pinion U was meshed with spur wheel V at the head of the drive spindle down the centre of rotation. In the carriage two further sets of mitre wheels X and Y, together with Z and C1 at each end of a longitudinal shaft provided motion to matching sets of spur wheels and pinions D1, E1 and E2, and F1 and F2, which in turn drove the leading and middle fixed axles of the crane. The train of gears could not, however, remain in gear while the train was being hauled by a locomotive. So it was arranged that idler spur wheel D1 could be withdrawn prior to movement in train formation for which purpose a hand-wheel was mounted on the carriage side.

The controls for the above improved design of

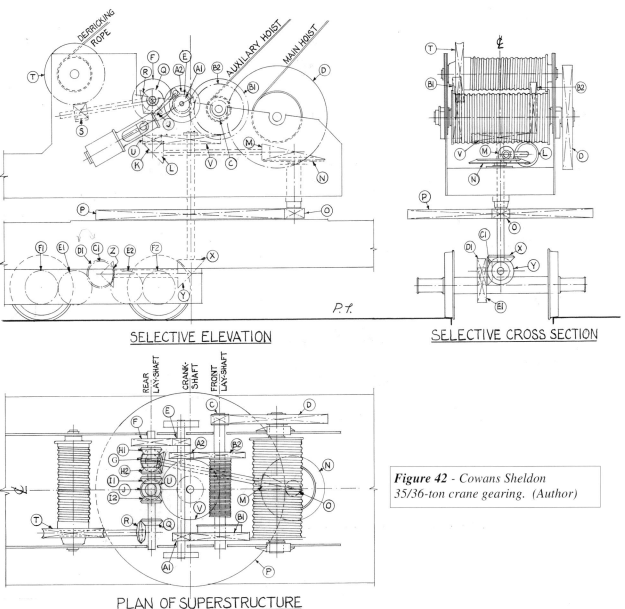

SELECTIVE ELEVATION

SELECTIVE CROSS SECTION

PLAN OF SUPERSTRUCTURE

Figure 42 - *Cowans Sheldon 35/36-ton crane gearing. (Author)*

superstructure were now grouped conveniently within easy reach of the crane driver. In due course, a series of levers in the form of a miniature signal frame, together with close by hand wheels and firebox damper levers were provided.

As part of their contribution to the war effort, the North Eastern Railway released two cranes, and the LNWR one crane, for military service, all of which, as it turned out, failed to be returned to their respective companies. Despite the demands on industry during the conflict, it appears authority was obtained for their replacement, the orders being placed with Cowans Sheldon who delivered respectively in 1916 and 1917.

There were several differences in the jib and hook/block between the 35-ton NER (3335) and LNWR 36-ton (3765), namely in the length and arrangement of the main and auxiliary hoists. The NER crane had a jib 29ft 1in between centres of the jib foot and the pulley of

the main block and full construction extended to carry the pulley wheel for the auxiliary hoist. The jib of the LNWR crane, on the other hand, was at 30ft 9in centres beyond which the main construction shortly ceased at the upper end, after which subsidiary brackets carried the pulley to the auxiliary hoist. At the end of the hoisting tackle, the support to the single main hook to the NER crane was between the two pulleys, which were spaced out to accommodate it, whereas the LNWR's block was of the more conventional form with the hook hung on a pair of straps below the more closely spaced pulleys. At the jib head the auxiliary rope on both was carried on a third pulley wheel between and of the same diameter as the main rope pulley.

The counterbalance to the NER crane was positioned behind the boiler, whereas the on the LNWR crane it was underneath. The tail swings were therefore 15ft 6in, compared with 14ft 7in.

Cowans Sheldon 35/36-Ton Cranes

Purch'd by	Date ord'd - del'd	Works No	Cost	Running No			Match wagon No		Allocation	Disposal
				1st	2nd	BR	Pre-group	Grouping		
NER	12/12/14 -1916	3335	£5,550	CME 1	901626	(331) 151	9024	901697 & 901733	Gateshead 1/9/21, York '32-1/10/60, Dairycoates 3/63- 11/67	Wdn '68
LNWR	u/k-1917	3765	£4,525	MP5	RS1008/36	RS1008/36	(1) u/k	(2) 770000	Willesden '17-14/4/34, Kentish Town 12/38-'57, Llandudno Jct 3/64	Wdn 2/10/64 Scrapped 10/12/64

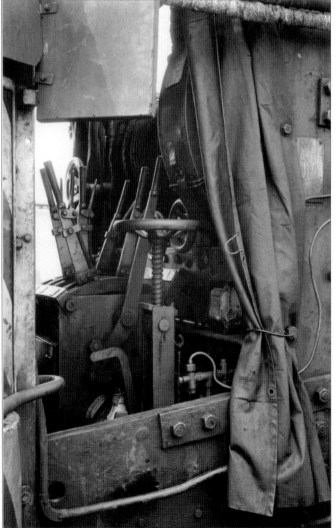

North Eastern Railway 35-ton crane

In accordance with its custom, the NER specified a maximum capacity of 35 tons. The quoted duties were limited to 35 tons, if propped, and 7½ tons free on rail at any radius between the minimum of 15 feet to a maximum of 23 feet. The possibility of lifting beyond this radius does not appear to have been considered, although obviously this will have occurred, but no guidance was apparently offered to the users.

The jib was supported while in train formation on a 4-wheel match truck, wagon No. 9024 of the well type which was built in 1899. The purpose of adopting the well was to make it easier for the breakdown crew to access the various items of heavy equipment carried on the wagon, such as spreader beams, lifting chains; shackles; timber packing; bridging rails etc. The match wagon, as was the practice at the time of its construction, was fitted with safety chains and despite these being absent from the crane, they remained on the wagon for much of the rest of its existence. The crane and match wagon were originally fitted with through pipes for both vacuum and air brakes, but the latter were removed before 1940.

Replacing the requisitioned crane from Gateshead, this crane moved to York in the twenties and finished up at Hull, Dairycoates in March 1963. Prior to its retirement in 1968, the crane received the full all over red livery, following probably its last overhaul. As well as a white jib head and lettering, the hand-wheels were picked out in white while the cab roof, match wagon axle -guards, jib rest and well were black.

The controls to LNER 45-ton Cowans Sheldon crane of 1926, grouped for the convenient use of the driver. (Author)

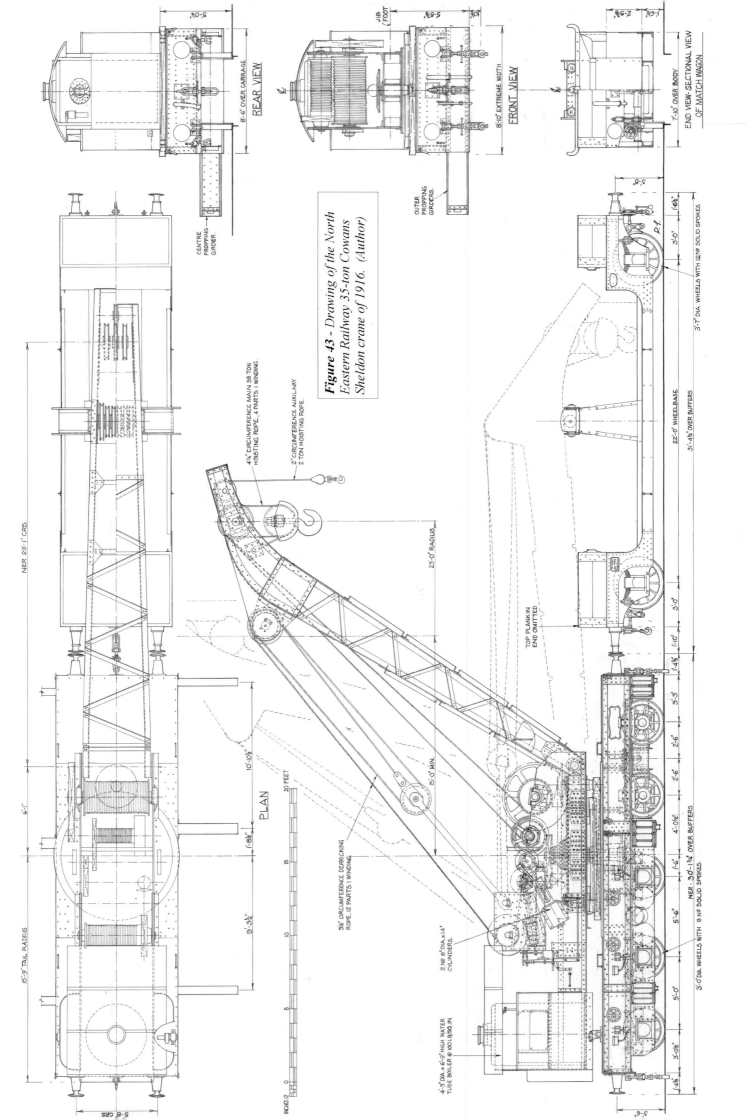

REAR VIEW

FRONT VIEW

END VIEW-SECTIONAL VIEW
OF MATCH WAGON

CENTRE PROPPING GIRDER.

JIB FOOT

OUTER PROPPING GIRDERS.

8'-6" OVER CARRAGE

8'-10" EXTREME WIDTH

7'-10" OVER BODY

Figure 43 - *Drawing of the North Eastern Railway 35-ton Cowans Sheldon crane of 1916. (Author)*

4¼" CIRCUMFERENCE MAIN 35 TON HOISTING ROPE, 4 PARTS 1 WINDING.

2" CIRCUMFERENCE AUXILIARY 2 TON HOISTING ROPE.

23'-0" RADIUS

3½" CIRCUMFERENCE DERRICKING ROPE, 12 PARTS 1 WINDING.

15'-0" MIN.

2 N⁰ 8"DIA x 14" CYLINDERS.

4'-3"DIA x 6'-9" HIGH WATER TUBE BOILER @ 100 LB/SQ IN

PLAN

NER 29'-1" CRS.

15'-9" TAIL RADIUS

6'-1"

1'-8½"

9'-3½"

10'-10½"

5'-6' CRS.

INCHES 12   0   5   10   15   20 FEET

NER · 30'-1¾' OVER BUFFERS

22'-0" WHEELBASE

31'-4¾" OVER BUFFERS

3'-0' DIA WHEELS WITH 9 N⁰ SOLID SPOKES.

3'-7" DIA WHEELS WITH 12 N⁰ SOLID SPOKES.

3'-6"

3'-0½"

5'-0"

5'-6"

1'-6"

4'-0½"

2'-6"

2'-6"

3'-3

1'-10'

3'-0"

1'-4½

TOP PLANK IN END OMITTED

3'-0"

1'-6½

P.I.

Ex-NER 35-ton Cowans Sheldon crane handling a locomotive tender wheel set at York, circa 1940. Note the match truck and rest of the breakdown train on the siding behind. Both vacuum and air brake pipes are still in place, whilst the auxiliary hoist appears to be absent. To gain extra height of lift the hook is suspended between the two pulleys of the block. (Author's collection)

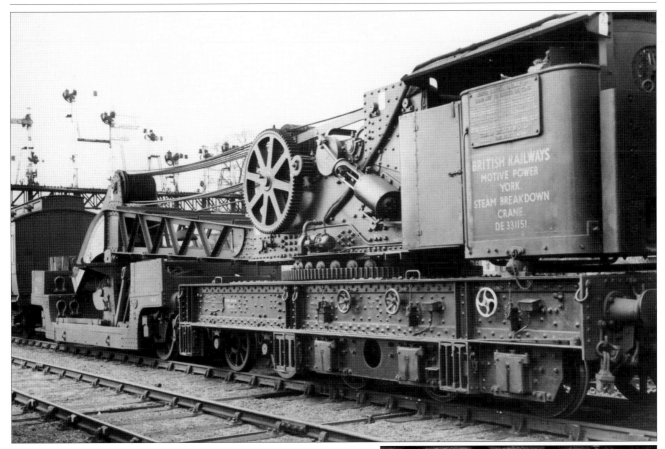

Above - *By 1 May 1962 this crane had been repainted in BR's black livery with straw lettering and renumbered as DE 331151, when seen at Scarborough. Note the large vertical counter-weight attached to the rear of the superstructure. (NEW Skinner)*

Bottom *- A view from the front on the same occasion. Numerous items of lifting gear are stowed on the match wagon, including several shackles and chains. (NEW Skinner)*

Insert - *The Cowans Sheldon works plate No. 3335 of 1916 mounted on the carriage, pictured on 29 July 1962. (NEW Skinner)*

London & North Western Railway 36-ton crane

Like the NER, having in 1916 sold their somewhat unsatisfactory home-produced 20-ton crane to the War Department, the LNWR in October 1916 ordered a crane of 36 tons capacity from Cowans Sheldon. The differences in the LNWR crane from the one supplied to the NER are noted above. The crane was initially coupled to a bogie match wagon 39ft 1in long over buffers, number unknown. This overall length and the displacing of the jib rest off centre suggest a longer jib crane had

originally been envisaged. In 1937 this was replaced by a brand new 26ft 9in over headstocks 4-wheeled match wagon to diagram 1998, LMS No. 770000 to Lot 1069.

The LNWR crane was initially allocated to Willesden where it continued to serve until a reassessment of capacity necessary to handle Stanier's Pacific locomotives led to its being transferred to Kentish Town in 1938. Finally it was briefly moved on to Llandudno Jct before being withdrawn on 2 October 1963 and scrapped by 10 December the same year.

Above - As LMS No. MP5, the ex-LNWR 36-ton Cowans Sheldon steam crane stands at Crewe Works on 14 April 1934 still paired with its original LNWR-built bogie match wagon. On this crane the counter-weight is positioned under the boiler and water tanks. A tarpaulin curtain protects the driver's position and another is placed over the tool box at the far end of the match wagon. (ER Morton)

Above - August 1937 saw a brand new purpose built 4-wheel match wagon supplied for the crane, photographed soon after it was built. Based on a design for the six new 36-ton cranes supplied to the LMS in 1931 with small diameter wheels and low solebars, the tool box doubles up as a jib rest. (RJ Essery collection)

Opposite page, Figure 44 - *Drawing of the London, North Western Railway 36-ton Cowans Sheldon crane of 1917. (Author)*

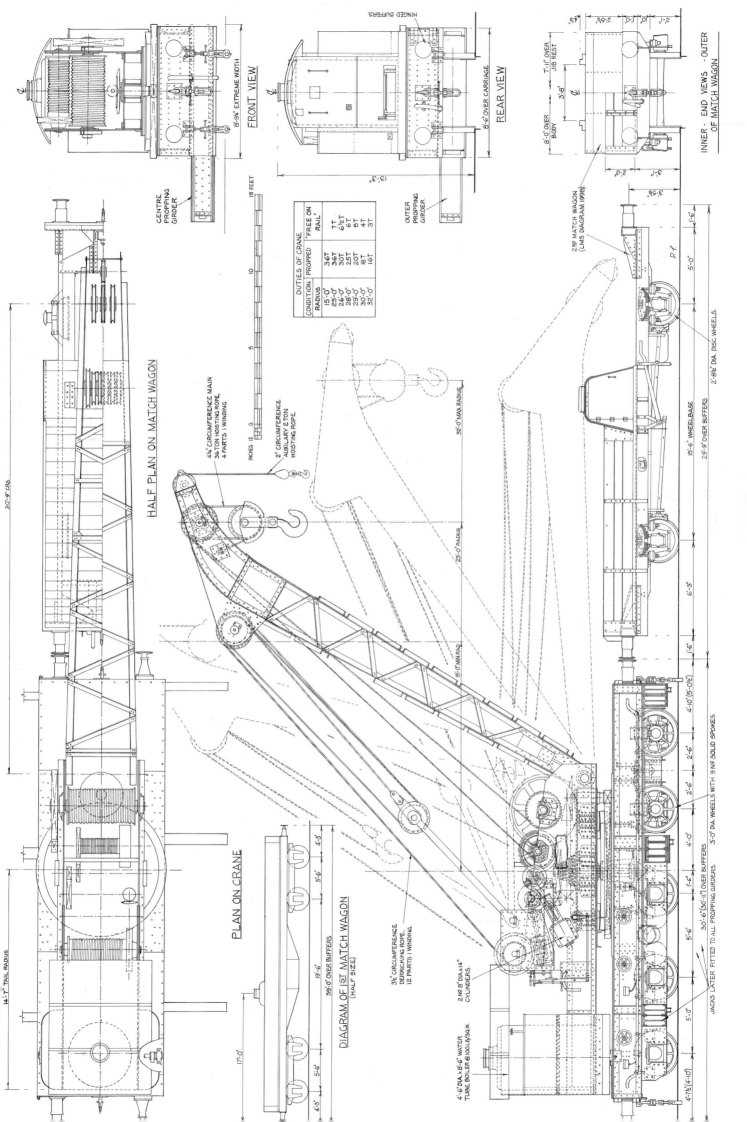

FRONT VIEW

8'-9¾" EXTREME WIDTH

CENTRE PROPPING GIRDER.

REAR VIEW

HINGED BUFFERS.

8'-6" OVER CARRIAGE

13'-3"

OUTER PROPPING GIRDER.

INNER - END VIEWS - OUTER OF MATCH WAGON

7'-11" OVER JIB REST
3'-8"
8'-0" OVER BODY

2'-6½"

HALF PLAN ON MATCH WAGON

30'-9" CRS.

14'-7" TAIL RADIUS

PLAN ON CRANE

17'-0"
19'-6"
39'-0" OVER BUFFERS
5'-6"
4'-3"

DIAGRAM OF 1ST MATCH WAGON
(HALF SIZE)

4'-3"
5'-6"

15 FEET
10
5
INCHES 12
5

DUTIES OF CRANE		
CONDITION	PROPPED	"FREE ON RAIL"
RADIUS		
15'-0"	36T	7T
25'-0"	36T	6½T
26'-0"	30T	6T
28'-0"	25T	5T
29'-0"	20T	5T
30'-0"	18T	4T
32'-0"	16T	3T

4½" CIRCUMFERENCE MAIN 36 TON HOISTING ROPE, 4 PARTS 1 WINDING.

2" CIRCUMFERENCE AUXILIARY 2 TON HOISTING ROPE.

32'-0" MAX RADIUS

23'-0" RADIUS

15'-0" MIN RAD.

3½" CIRCUMFERENCE DERRICKING ROPE, 12 PARTS 1 WINDING.

2 N° 8" DIA x 14" CYLINDERS

4'-6" DIA x 8'-6" WATER TUBE BOILER @ 100 LB/SQ.IN.

2 N° MATCH WAGON (LMS DIAGRAM 1998)

P.L.

5'-0"

15'-6" WHEELBASE
29'-9" OVER BUFFERS

2'-8½" DIA DISC WHEELS.

1'-6"

6'-3"

1'-6"

4'-10" (5-0½)

2'-6"
2'-6"
4'-0"
1'-6"
5'-6"

30'-6" (30'-11") OVER BUFFERS
3'-0" DIA WHEELS WITH 9 N° SOLID SPOKES.

4'-7½" (4'-10")

JACKS LATER FITTED TO ALL PROPPING GIRDERS.

3'-5½"
2'-0"
3'-1"

A little incident at Cardington on 9 April 1940, when LMS Stanier 2-6-T No. 165 left the rails, resulted in a summons for Kentish Town's breakdown train, see British Railways Illustrated, *March 1995, pp 293-294. Here No. RS1008/36 is blocked up, swung round and has slings attached to the front frames of the locomotive. The lower view shows the driver and another at the controls. (AE West)*

With its jib raised, the crane posed for the official photographer on 10 February 1939 with its replacement match wagon. Note the auxiliary hoist and the supplementary trapezoidal shaped tool box added against the jib rest/tool box. (BR, LMR, author's collection)

In early BR days No MP5 awaits the call of duty. The form of the coaling tower suggests this may be at Cricklewood, which seems to have hosted this and earlier cranes from time to time. (Author's collection)

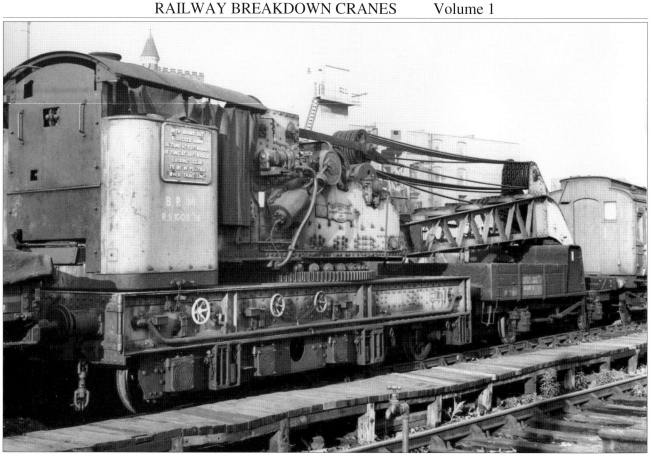

By now fitted with hinged buffers to enable the crane to approach just that little bit closer to the load or other obstruction, No. RS1008/36 awaits the call to duty at Kentish Town around 1959. (MS Welch)

At its final depot, No. RS1008/36 at Llandudno Jct on 12 July 1964. Compare the jib head and provision for the auxiliary hoist of this ex-LNWR crane with that of the NER. (E Sawford)

9. Ransomes & Rapier Consolidates Its Position

Ransomes & Rapier 35-ton cranes for GER
Ransomes & Rapier 36-ton cranes of 1918 & 1927
Cowans Sheldon 36-ton crane for LSWR

Apart from one example of a crane equipped with relieving bogies ordered by the Midland Railway in 1914 and the initial subject of Volume 2, before more cranes of this type were ordered, further 35/36-ton cranes of the 0-6-4 wheel arrangement and three of 0-4-4 configuration of 25/30 ton capacity, together with two 45-ton cranes on a pair of 4-wheel bogies were supplied to other railways by several builders.

The Great Eastern received a pair of 35-ton cranes from Ransomes and Rapier with medium length jibs, whilst the London and South Western had one 36-ton each from Rapier and Cowans and, following grouping, two more similar for the Southern Railway from Rapier. The examples for the southern companies and GER, whilst similar to the long jib design of 1908 for the GWR, had redesigned heavier carriages, like that for the LNWR, and hence slightly different characteristics, including improved distribution of axle loads.

Ransomes & Rapier 35-Ton Cranes
for GER

Despite having successfully built in-house a couple of 20-ton cranes in 1908, the Great Eastern Railway nonetheless elected to employ the highly successful Ransomes & Rapier company, located at Ipswich on their system.

Instead of a jib over 40 feet in length, however, it chose one of medium size, viz: 29ft 10¼in, which in turn led to the jib end pulleys to the derricking tackle being repositioned at the jib head, while the minimum radius was 15 feet. Like the previous Ransomes & Rapier designs, these 35-ton cranes relied for their maximum capacity on the presence of a 6-ton counter-weight, which was carried while in train formation on the match wagon. On the other hand the propping girders remained in position in the crane carriage, although the screw jacks had to be carried in the match wagon. The crane could, nonetheless, be safely worked without the counter weight in place at reduced loads of typically 30 tons when propped and 14 tons free on rail.

The first, built in 1915, was promptly requisitioned for war service in Northern France. Reallocation under LNER management led to this crane being transferred to Kings Cross, where it stayed until displaced in 1940 to Neasden. Following a change in regional boundaries to the Western Region it was renumbered 54, and later, on take-over by the London Midland Region, it became RS1095/35. The second crane remained in Great Eastern territory, moving from Stratford to Norwich in 1940, and to March in the early 1960s.

Ransomes & Rapier 35-Ton Crane for GER								
Date ordered - delivered	Order No	Cost	Running No			Match wagon No	Allocation	Disposal
			GER	LNER	BR			
30/1/14 - 1915	B7478	£2,990	6A	941593	W Reg 54, RS1095/35	u/k	Stratford '15, requisitioned by Govt, Kings Cross '26-*10/5/40*. Neasden *7/44*–18/6/62, to WR '49, to LMR 1/2/58, Bristol '61?	Scrapped 8/65
8/1/19 - 1919	C413	£7,930	7A	SB4, 961600	(330)135	LNER 961650	Stratford '19/'20?- *c'37* Thorpe *'40-6/11/61*, March *3/64-8/67*	Wdn c'68

Transferred to Neasden in LNER days, this GER crane, formerly No. 6A and LNER No.941593, with nationalisation found itself in 1949 on the Western Region as No. W54 and subsequently on the London Midland Region as No. RS1095/35. (Author's

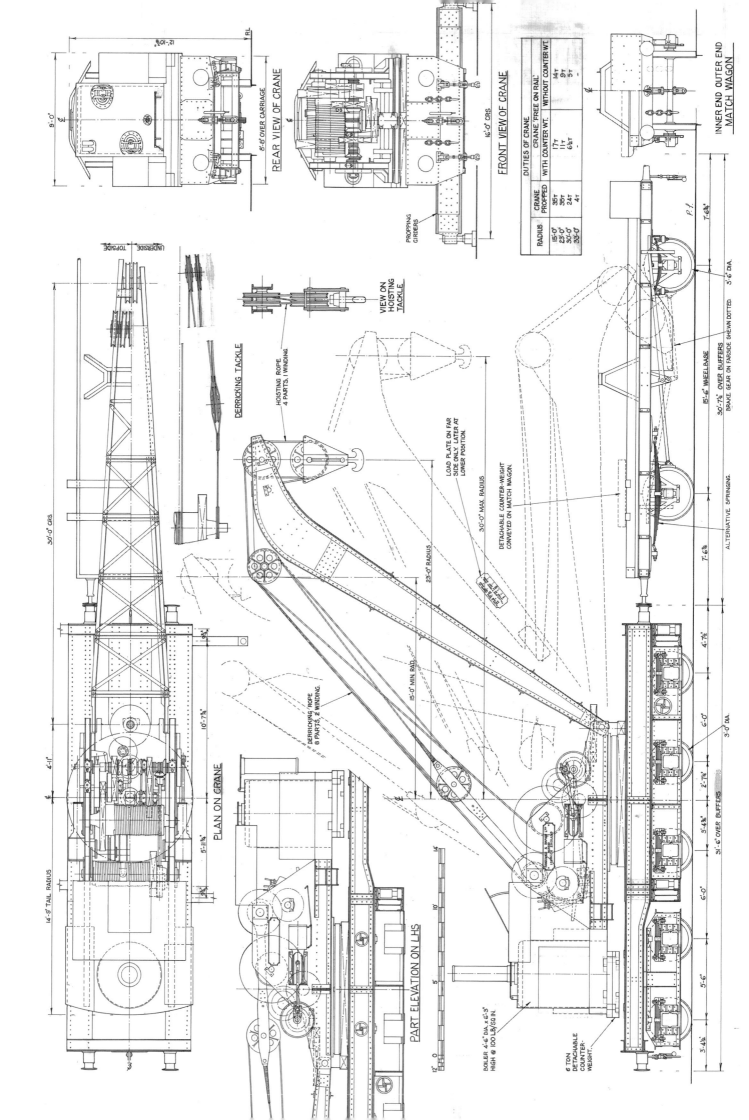

REAR VIEW OF CRANE

8'-6" OVER CARRIAGE

12'-10⅝"

9'-0"

FRONT VIEW OF CRANE

16'-0" CRS

PROPPING GIRDERS

DUTIES OF CRANE

RADIUS	CRANE PROPPED	CRANE FREE ON RAIL	
		WITH COUNTER WT.	WITHOUT COUNTER WT.
15'-0"	35т	17т	14т
23'-0"	35т	11т	9т
30'-0"	24т	6½т	5т
33'-0"	4т	—	—

INNER END   OUTER END
MATCH WAGON

3'-6" DIA.

7'-6¾"

15'-6" WHEELBASE

30'-7⅞" OVER BUFFERS

BRAKE GEAR ON FARSIDE SHEWN DOTTED.

ALTERNATIVE SPRINGING.

7'-6"

4'-7½"

6'-0"

3'-0" DIA.

2'-7¼"

3'-4¾"

6'-0"

5'-6"

3'-4¾"

31'-6" OVER BUFFERS

VIEW ON HOISTING TACKLE

DERRICKING TACKLE

HOISTING ROPE 4 PARTS, 1 WINDING.

UNDERSIDE   TOPSIDE

30'-0" CRS.

10'-7¾"

4'-11"

5'-11¼"

14'-9" TAIL RADIUS

PLAN ON CRANE

LOAD PLATE ON FAR SIDE ONLY, LATER AT LOWER POSITION.

33'-0" MAX. RADIUS

23'-0" RADIUS

DETACHABLE COUNTER-WEIGHT CONVEYED ON MATCH WAGON.

15'-0" MIN RAD.

DERRICKING ROPE 8 PARTS, 2 WINDING.

PART ELEVATION ON LHS

BOILER 4'-6" DIA. x 6'-3" HIGH @ 100 LB/SQ IN.

6 TON DETACHABLE COUNTER-WEIGHT.

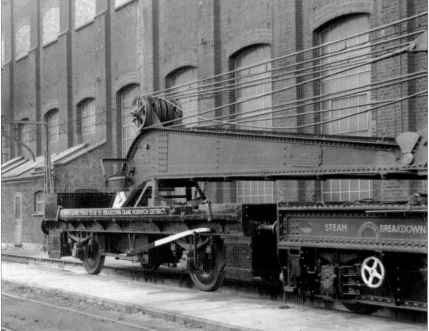

Above - *Ex-GER 35-ton Ransomes & Rapier steam crane as BR(ER) No. 135, allocated to Norwich, outside Stratford North Works in July 1956. (Denis Seagrave, courtesy HMRS collection)*

Centre and bottom *- A couple of views of ex-GER 35-ton Ransomes & Rapier steam crane on the same occasion showing the jib on match wagon DE 961650 and the crane itself. (both Denis Seagrave, courtesy HMRS collection)*

Opposite page, Figure 45 - *Drawing of the 35-ton steam cranes supplied by Ransomes & Rapier to the Great Eastern Railway in 1915 and 1919. (Author)*

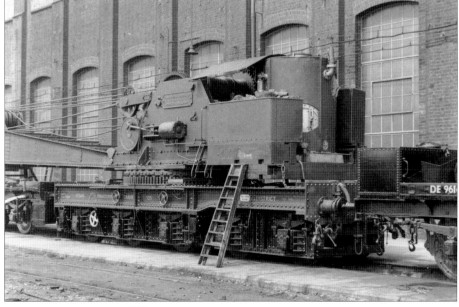

The guard truck No. DE 961651 for steam crane No. 135 outside Stratford North Works in July 1956. At the left-hand end there is a water tank and a tool box at the other end, between which are a pair of bogies to place under heavy loads for moving short distances. (Denis Seagrave, courtesy HMRS collection)

Ransomes & Rapier 36-Ton Cranes of 1918 & 1927

London & South Western Railway

Impressed by the long jib cranes introduced by the Great Western Railway in 1908, seven years later, when the need for enhanced crane capacity on the LSWR became imperative with the increasing number of large locomotives being placed in service, the Chief Mechanical Engineer, RW Urie, turned in early 1915 to Ransomes and Rapier. The 36-ton crane supplied in 1918 was of similar form to the LNWR example, rather than the GWR's pair of cranes. Although a delivery period of six months was envisaged at the time of placing the order, the delay was presumably due to the difficulties in allocating priority in obtaining materials and labour to fulfil the order.

The match truck was cobbled up from a pair of redundant locomotive tenders by the expedient of placing a pivoted beam between them upon which was placed the jib rest. This, however, made the combination difficult to lift; as a consequence it was preferable to shunt it into a convenient siding or on to the adjacent line and propel the crane to the mishap without it.

Allocated to the LSWR's principal London depot, Nine Elms, No. 6 remained there until 1938 when it went to Fratton, being renumbered 35S soon after the SR took over. By June 1940 it was at Eastleigh from where it was withdrawn on 9 January 1965. The occasional requirement to undertake the replacement of tall chimneys to the boilers for the steam hammer in Eastleigh Works led to the fabrication of an almost exact half-scale replica of the crane's jib which was attached to the top of the jib to afford sufficient reach.

				Running No			Match wagon No			Allocation	Disposal
Ransomes & Rapier 36-Ton Cranes											
Purchased by	*Date ordered - delivered*	*Order No*	*Cost*	*Pre- / Group 'ing*	*1st BR*	*BR-CEPS*	*Pre-group*	*Group ing*	*BR*	*Allocation*	*Disposal*
LSWR	3/3/15 - 1918	B7999	£4,494	6/ 35S	Ds35	-	67S +68S	35SM+ 34SM	Ds3083+ Ds3084	Nine Elms '18-*7/37*, Fratton *5/38*, Eastleigh *6/40*	Wdn 9/1/65
SR	2/2/26 - 1927	C6553	£6,271	-/80S	Ds80	ADRR 95225	-	80SM	Ds3087	Bricklayers Arms 10/27, Ashford (K) *5/38*, Guildford 6/62, Stewart's Lane (spare) 7/67-*1/79*	Scrapped at Stewart's Lane 3/86 2/89?
SR	2/2/26 - 1927	C6553	£6,271	-/81S	Ds81	ADRR 95201	-	81SM	Ds3088	Brighton 11/27-*5/38*, Fratton 6/46-*'58*, Guildford 8/4/59-23/4/60, Feltham *10/60* Stewart's Lane 2/63-*11/86*	Wdn 9/9/86. Sold to K&ESR 1/87

Nine Elms' 36-ton Ransomes & Rapier crane No. 35S attends to the derailed tender of 4-6-0 Lord Nelson class No. 857 Lord Howe, somewhere in south London. This engine was fitted with a short-lived experimental boiler and round-topped fire box sometime after 1936. The shape of the top edge of crab sides and mounting of the hoisting barrel of this and the LNWR 36-ton Rapier crane should be compared with that of the cranes subsequently supplied in 1927 to the SR. (Author's collection)

No. 35S in SR black livery soon after its transfer to Eastleigh. Note the hose pipe strung out across the back of the shelter. (W Bishop collection)

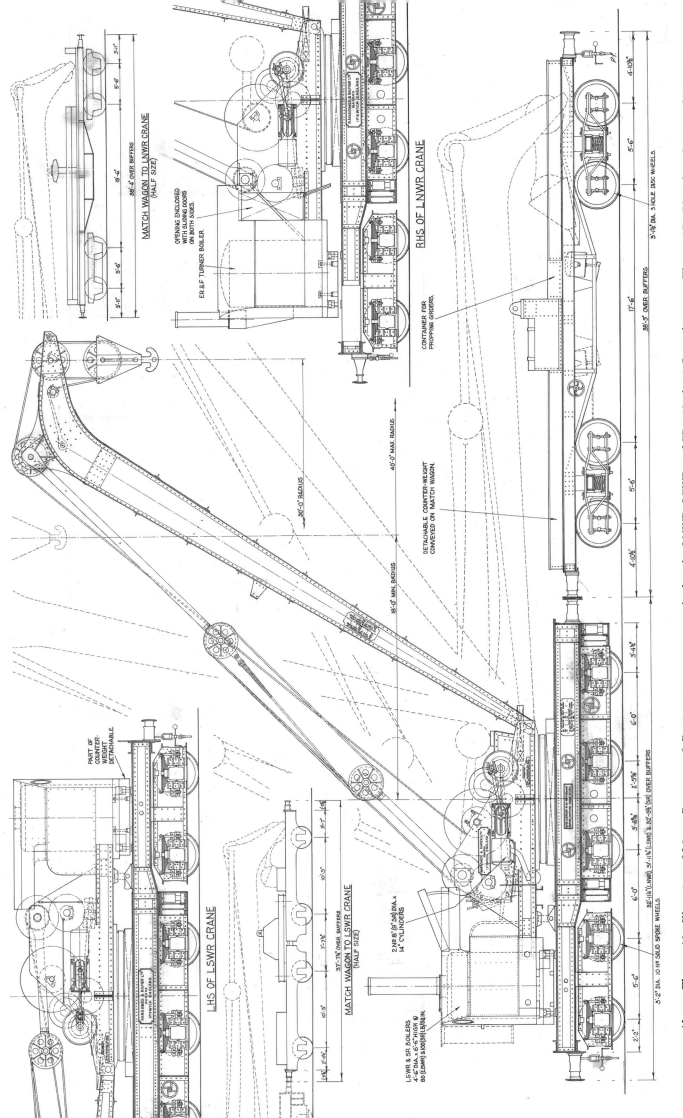

MATCH WAGON TO LNWR CRANE
(HALF SIZE)

OPENING ENCLOSED
WITH SLIDING DOORS
ON BOTH SIDES.

ER & F. TURNER BOILER

RHS OF LNWR CRANE

RANSOMES & RAPIER LTD
ENGINEERS
IPSWICH ENGLAND

CONTAINER FOR
PROPPING GIRDERS.

3'-1½" DIA. 3 HOLE DISC WHEELS.

DETACHABLE COUNTER-WEIGHT
CONVEYED ON MATCH WAGON.

40'-0" MAX. RADIUS

30'-0" RADIUS

18'-0" MIN. RADIUS

PART OF
COUNTER-
WEIGHT
DETACHABLE

LHS OF LSWR CRANE

RANSOMES & RAPIER LTD
ENGINEERS
IPSWICH ENGLAND

MATCH WAGON TO LSWR CRANE
(HALF SIZE)

2 N⁰ 8" (9" 5R) DIA.×
14" CYLINDERS

RANSOMES & RAPIER LTD
IPSWICH ENGLAND

LSWR & SR BOILERS
4'-6" DIA.× 6'-6" HIGH @
80 (LSWR) & 100 (SR) LB/SQ IN.

3'-2" DIA. 10 N⁰ SOLID SPOKE WHEELS.

32'-11¼"(LNWR), 31'-11¾"(LSWR) & 32'-9¾"(SR) OVER BUFFERS

Above, Figure 46 - Elevation of 36-ton Ransomes & Rapier steam crane supplied to the LNWR, LSWR and SR. (Author) Opposite page, Figure 47 - Plan & end views of 36-ton Ransomes

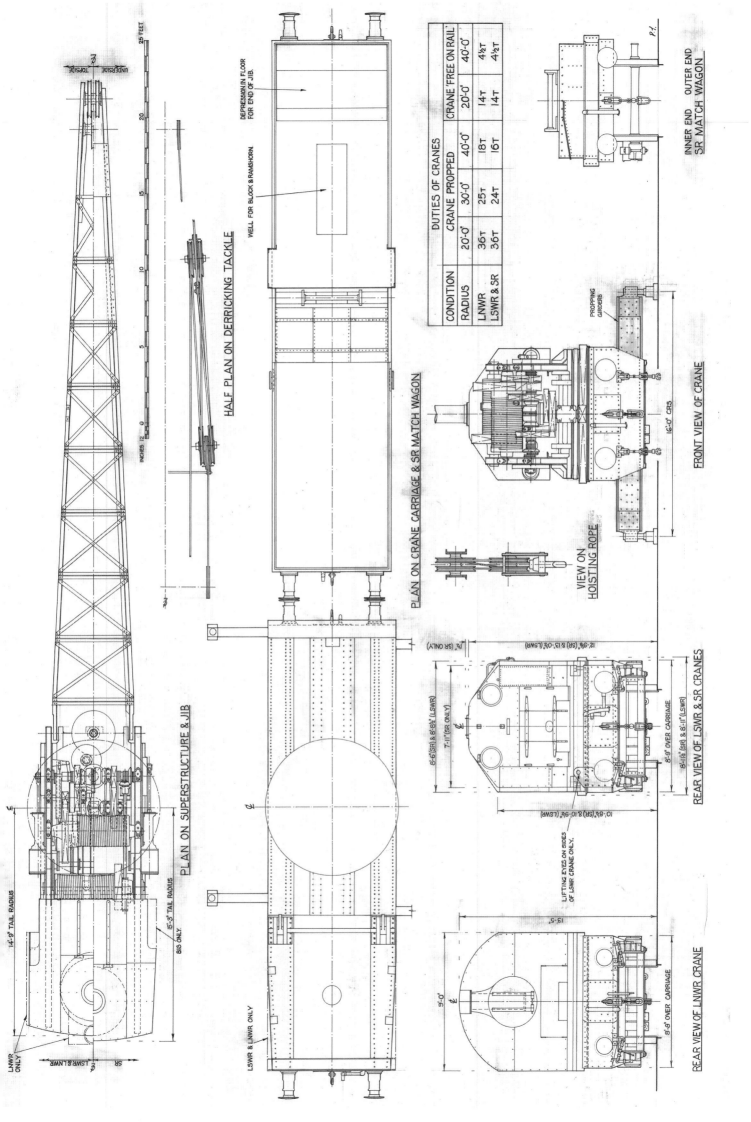

PLAN ON SUPERSTRUCTURE & JIB

HALF PLAN ON DERRICKING TACKLE

DEPRESSION IN FLOOR FOR END OF JIB.

WELL FOR BLOCK & RAMSHORN.

PLAN ON CRANE CARRIAGE & SR MATCH WAGON

LSWR & LNWR ONLY

INNER END   OUTER END
SR MATCH WAGON

CONDITION	DUTIES OF CRANES			CRANE 'FREE ON RAIL'	
	CRANE PROPPED				
RADIUS	20'-0"	30'-0"	40'-0"	20'-0"	40'-0"
LNWR	36T	25T	18T	14T	4½T
LSWR & SR	36T	24T	16T	14T	4½T

PROPPING GIRDERS

16'-0" CRS

FRONT VIEW OF CRANE

VIEW ON HOISTING ROPE

12'-9¾" (SR) & 13'-0¾" (LSWR)

1'-2" (SR ONLY)

8'-6" (SR) & 8'-8¾" (LSWR)

7'-11" (SR ONLY)

8'-9" OVER CARRIAGE

8'-11½" (SR) & 8'-11" (LSWR)

10'-6½" (SR) & 10'-9¾" (LSWR)

LIFTING EYES ON SIDES OF LSWR CRANE ONLY.

REAR VIEW OF LSWR & SR CRANES

13'-5"

9'-0"

8'-8" OVER CARRIAGE

REAR VIEW OF LNWR CRANE

14'-9" TAIL RADIUS

15'-3" TAIL RADIUS
BIS ONLY.

LNWR ONLY

SR
LSWR & LNWR

25 FEET
20
15
10
5
0
INCHES 12 0

TOPSIDE
UNDERSIDE

By 26 May 1957, now renumbered Ds35 and repainted in BR livery, photographed at Eastleigh again. The counter-balance and propping girders are in place on the crane. The pair of lifting eyes riveted to the rear headstock appears to be unique to this crane. (L Elsey)

Top - *The two match trucks given the Nos. Ds3084 and Ds3083 by BR carry the jib of No. Ds35 while in train formation, as seen here at Eastleigh on 1 June 1962. (AE West).*

Bottom - *No. Ds35 with its jib up stands outside Eastleigh Works for an open day during the 1950s. (Paul Hersey collection)*

Southern Railway

As well as highlighting deficiencies in track maintenance and questioning the wisdom of large express tank engines, the disastrous accident at Sevenoaks on 24 August 1927 drew attention to the inadequacies of the breakdown arrangements on the Eastern Division of the Southern Railway. In fact two steam breakdown cranes were already on order with Ransomes & Rapier Ltd in accordance with the specification of REL Maunsell, Chief Mechanical Engineer, the builders employing their standard practice in regard to the structural features and details, largely following the crane supplied to the LSWR seven years earlier, modified to suit the SR composite loading gauge. The crab sides were, nonetheless, modified to improve the accessibility of the journals to the derricking and hoisting winding barrels. The boiler of the Spencer-Hopwood patent type had a working pressure of 100lb per sq. in, and was lagged with an asbestos mattress covered with planished steel sheets in removable sections. The usual boiler mountings were fitted, including two injectors of the Simplex type.

The cranes were each capable of lifting and slewing the following loads when propped up: 36 tons at 20 feet radius and 16 tons at 40 feet. Free on rail they could lift, slew and travel with 14 tons at 20 feet radius and 4½ tons at 40 feet. They could also derrick with the full loads, consistent with the radius of the jib head.

In working order each crane weighed about 88 tons. To achieve an axle-load not exceeding 15 tons in a train order with the jib, snatch block, etc on the match wagon, it was necessary, like the cranes for the GWR, to remove the counter-weight and propping girders and place them also on the match wagon. This resulted in a crane weight of 72 tons 7cwt and afforded the necessary route availability, but this was a time-consuming process. Once bridge strengthening and upgrading of the track had taken place, from about 1947/8 the practice was discontinued and the girders and tail weight were left in position on the crane with only the jib resting on the match wagon. This had the effect of increasing the crane weight to 83 tons 11 cwt and the maximum axle-load to 17 tons 6 cwt. A diagram of altered axle weights for the SR crane was submitted to the CCE for approval, but the diagram for the ex-LSWR crane was not amended until 3 February 1954.

The automatic vacuum brake-fitted bogie-type match trucks were built by the Gloucester Railway Carriage & Wagon Co in 1927. These were also awkward to lift and it was, therefore not uncommon for these to be shunted into a siding or adjacent line and for the crane to be propelled to the mishap without it.

As mentioned, these two cranes had been on order at the time of the Sevenoaks accident. The need to bring over No. 35S from Nine Elms had emphasised the urgent requirement for enhanced crane power on both the Eastern and Central Divisions of the SR, so once the new cranes were delivered they were allocated to Bricklayers Arms and Brighton. In turn they were cascaded, one to Ashford (Kent), following the arrival of further cranes in 1937, and in due course the other to Fratton. Ds80 found its way to Guildford in June 1962 and, following the withdrawal of steam on 10 July 1967, instead of joining the locomotives on the scrap heap it went for an overhaul at Doncaster Works. It duly returned painted in bright red and still lettered "Guildford", but it remained at Stewart's Lane as regional spare, in the company of its sister. By then ADRR95225, it was scrapped in March 1986, while Ds81 (ADRR95201) was sold to the Kent & East Sussex Railway in January 1987.

On formation of the Southern Railway the LSWR had two modern 36-ton long jib cranes. To remedy the deficiency on the systems of the other two constituents, two further 36-ton cranes were ordered from Ransomes & Rapier and allocated initially to Bricklayers Arms and Brighton in October and November 1927. Southern Railway 36-ton Ransomes & Rapier steam crane No. 80S is seen at Swanley Jct. Note the member of the engineering staff standing by his theodolite, perhaps in connection with the reconstruction of the station carried out as part of the extension electrification of the line to Gillingham (Kent) opened in July 1939. (Author's collection)

Top - No. 80S stands ready at Ashford (Kent) on 29 August 1948 still in SR livery, believed to have been grey with white lettering. Note the business-like bogie match wagon, not the easiest thing to place out of the way. The propping girders are in position on the crane, but the counter-weight is not and presumably is on the match wagon. The necessary light chains for manipulating the counter-weight are apparent on the underside of the jib. (JH Aston)

Bottom - A view of now renumbered No. Ds81 at Stewart's Lane in BR black with 'ferret and dart board' style totem on the side of the water tank and notice plates nicely picked out in red and white, together with red flywheel. Both the counter-weight and all the propping girders are carried on the crane thereby permitting the removal of the light chains from the jib. (Lens of Sutton, author's collection).

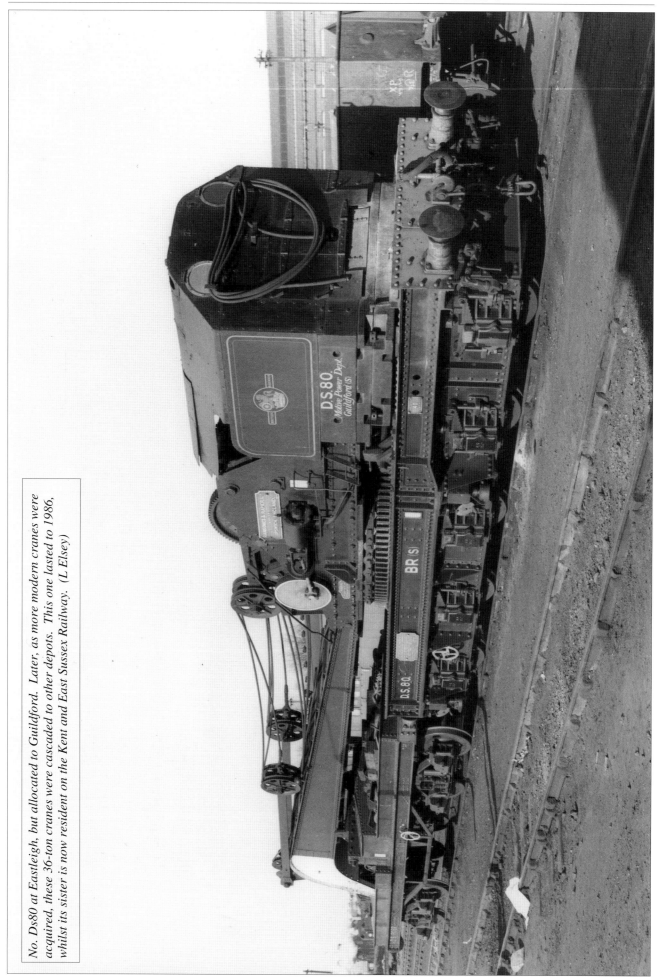

No. Ds80 at Eastleigh, but allocated to Guildford. Later, as more modern cranes were acquired, these 36-ton cranes were cascaded to other depots. This one lasted to 1986, whilst its sister is now resident on the Kent and East Sussex Railway. (L Elsey)

By 26 January 1966 looking a little more care worn, Ds. 80 unloads pre-tensioned concrete beams in Havant goods yard for subsequent use in the reconstruction of the road approach viaduct to Portsmouth Harbour station. (Author)

The driver's view looking up the jib of Ds80 at Vauxhall on 27 March 1971 showing ten-part two-winding derricking tackle and single hoisting rope between. (Author)

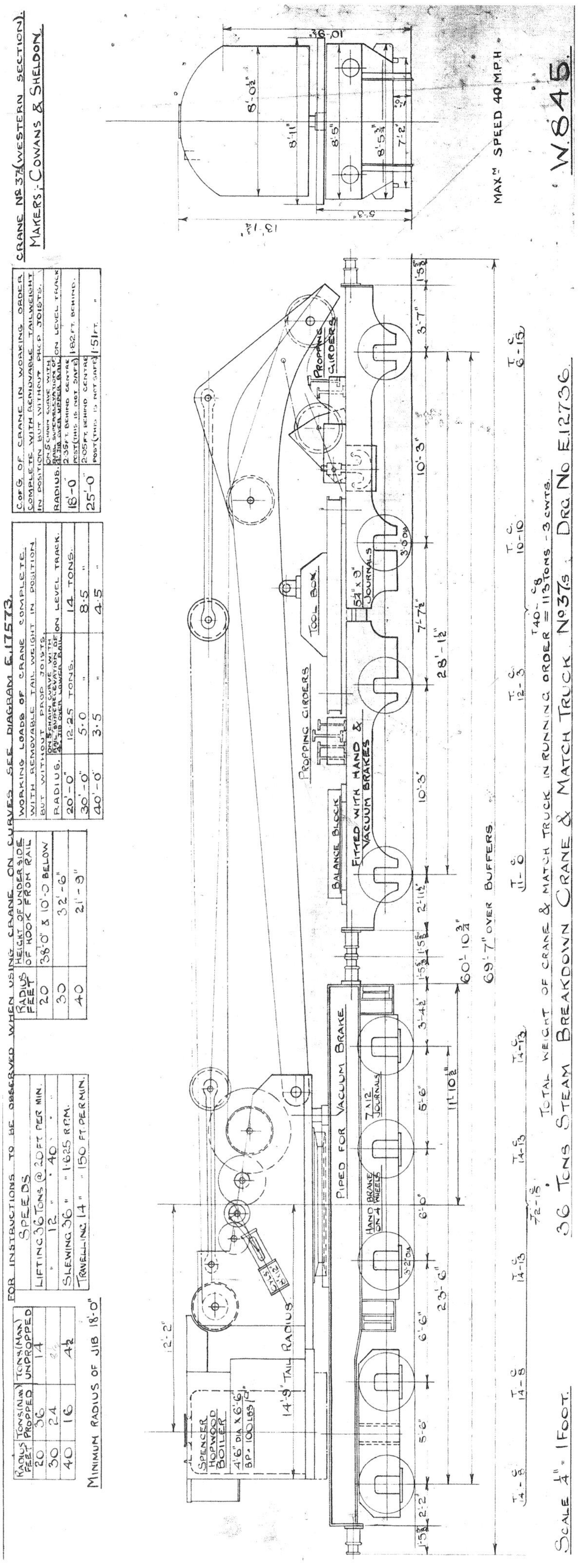

Cowans Sheldon 36-Ton Crane
for LSWR

Having waited so long for their first long-jibbed 36-ton crane, one presumes that when the LSWR came to considering the purchase a further 36-ton crane, they found Ransomes & Rapier already fully committed and/or their bid over-priced. It was a time of high demand, as firms and undertakings of all sorts sought to restore their businesses to full capacity after World War 1, as a consequence of which prices soared. For whatever reason, the LSWR turned instead to Cowans Sheldon, who built them a 'look alike', presumably to fulfil the requirements of the client's specification. In doing so, it set the trend for much of Cowans future work. Whilst the machinery follows the design of the recent 35/36-ton cranes of 1916/7, the carriage, 0-6-4 in lieu of a 4-6-0, and a plate jib clearly owe much to Ransomes & Rapier. The cylinder stroke was reduced from 14 to 12 inches, compensated by an increase in boiler pressure from 80 to 100 lb/sq in. This enabled the crane to lift 36 tons at a speed of 20 feet a minute, while 12 tons could be raised at 40 feet per minute. Slewing under full load could be achieved at a rate of 1.625 revolutions per minute and travelling under its own steam at 150 feet per minute (1¾ mph).

The wheel sets complete with axle-boxes, spring detail, draw-gear, buffers, screw couplings and vacuum piping were all supplied by the railway company. The match wagons were again provided by them and exactly followed previous practice of a pair of redundant locomotive tender underframes.

While under the control of the southern companies, this crane remained at Salisbury, but, with the introduction of electric traction to Bournemouth and the withdrawal of steam power from the Southern Region on 10 July 1967, Salisbury depot closed and its crane was transferred to the Western Region. Having been successively LSWR No. 7, Southern No. 37S and BR (SR) No. Ds 37, the WR renumbered it 376 and down-rated its load capacity to 32 tons before sending it initially to Worcester and later Landore. The state of its boiler led to the crane being scrapped in 1971, still painted grey.

*Left, **Figure 48** - Diagram of ex-LSWR 36-ton Cowans Sheldon steam crane. (SR, author's collection)*

CRANE No 37S (WESTERN SECTION)
MAKERS - COWANS & SHELDON

RADIUS FEET	TONS(MAX) PROPPED	TONS(MAX) UNPROPPED
20	36	14
30	24	16
40	16	4½

FOR INSTRUCTIONS TO BE OBSERVED WHEN USING CRANE ON CURVES SEE DIAGRAM E.17573.

SPEEDS
LIFTING 36 TONS @ 20 FT PER MIN.
12 " " 40 '
SLEWING 36 " 1.625 R.P.M.
TRAVELLING 14 " 150 FT PER MIN.

MINIMUM RADIUS OF JIB 18'-0"

MAX.ᴹ SPEED 40 M.P.H.

36 TONS STEAM BREAKDOWN CRANE & MATCH TRUCK No 37S. DRG No E.12736

SCALE ¼" = 1 FOOT.

Date ordered - delivered	Works No	Cost	Running No			Match wagon No			Allocation	Disposal
			Pre-group	Group 'ing	BR	Pre-group	Group ing	BR		
18/12/20 - 1922	4193	£9,939	7	37S	Ds37, WR 376	115S+ 116S	37SM+ 38SM	Ds3085+ Ds3086	Salisbury '22-10/5/40, Exmouth Jct (tempy) 7/44, Salisbury '46-10/67, WR 7/67, Worcester 10/67-'70, Landore 12/9/70	Scrapped 8/71

Cowans Sheldon 36-Ton Crane for LSWR

Ex-LSWR 36-ton Cowans Sheldon steam crane No. 37S, reportedly at Exmouth Jct. circa 1935, displaying its SR livery. At this time too it has its propping girders in position, but not the counter-weight. Note the vacuum pipe hose, but three-link couplings. (BP Hoper Railway Photographs)

Serving out its time on the Western Region at Landore, Swansea on 12 September 1970, still in grubby SR grey. Note the water hose neatly coiled and hung on a hook at the rear of the enclosure. (Author)

10. Further Smaller Cranes

Cowans Sheldon 25-ton cranes of 1917-19
Cowans Sheldon 20/30-ton crane for Met Rly
Ransomes & Rapier 30-ton crane for LER

The design of this type of smaller crane appears to originate in 1916 with an order by the War Department for a 20-ton crane of 0-4-4 wheel arrangement for use on the Continent, this being Works Order No. 3823 for the Inland Water Transport Department. To provide stability for heavier lifts, three sets of propping girders without jacks were fitted to the underside of the carriage at each end and in the centre. Following the war this crane was taken over by the SNCB as No. A320/06, later 214.3.17.00 allocated to Merelbeke. After being held in store for preservation at Leuven, Belgium, it is now on the ZLSM heritage line in Simpelvald, South Limburg, Netherlands, where it is under active restoration.

A further order was placed by the WD on 10 March 1917 for two 25-ton cranes, Works Order Nos. 3855-6, which went to Palestine, followed by another order on 10 May 1918, Works No. 4047, later acquired by the NER. On 20 May 1919 the Barry Railway ordered another, Works Order No. 4099. Both 20- and 25-ton versions had lattice jibs, the first group having external bracing, while the 25-ton had bracing inside the longitudinal angles.

Cowans Sheldon 25-Ton Cranes of 1917-1919

The NER purchased Works Order No. 4047 as war surplus, no doubt at a knock-down price. Instead of putting it on breakdown duties, however, it was stationed at Stooperdale Works, Darlington, where it will have handled heavy loads in the yard, such as locomotive boilers. At some time during LNER days, the crane appears to have had 2½ inch longer buffers fitted.

Match Trucks

The match trucks to the 25-ton version appear to have been supplied with the cranes, rather than being provided by the purchasing company. The General Arrangement drawing shows 1ft 8in long self-contained buffers, but standard 1ft 6in may have been fitted. If so, the length of the underframe must have been increased in order to maintain the total length over buffers quoted of 27 foot. The GA drawing also shows a single brake shoe on a hanger, operated by long hand lever and drop arm acting through a fulcrum on a short push arm.

The Barry crane, probably in GW days, had various modifications implemented. Plate axle-guards on the match wagon were changed to W irons with split axle-boxes; and buffer-housings changed from parallel to GW tapered design. If the original brake was on one side only, additional brake gear was added on the second side with double vee hangers. The jib rest was either strengthened or replaced including the addition of side plates. On the NER crane the brake gear was of the Morton type.

Cowans Sheldon 25-Ton Cranes

Purchased by	Date ordered - delivered	Works No	Cost	Running No			Match wagon No	Allocation	Disposal
				Pre-group	Group 'ing	BR			
WO	10/9/17 - 1918	3855						Palestine Rlys	Preserved at Haifa Museum, Israel
WO	10/9/17 - 1918	3856						Palestine Rlys	Scrapped Lod 2/90
WO/NER	10/5/18 - 1918	4047		CME30	902705	337	902705	Stooperdale '22-14/8/71	
Barry	20/5/19 - 6/20	4099	£5,928 *	-	14	14	14	Barry 13/8/36, Radyr '48, Barry 15/11/56, Margam '65-, to CCE late '70, Radyr 12/9/70	Wdn '70
* including match wagon									

Opposite top - By now down-rated to 32 ton maximum capacity, the front quarter view of what was now formally Western Region No. 376. Although in many respects following the Ransomes & Rapier equivalent, the derricking tackle was ten parts, but only one winding. (Author)

Opposite bottom - A closer up view of the crane, still displaying No. Ds37 on the carriage and elsewhere BR SR. The diagonal rod passing behind the cylinder and bar at the jib foot provided an indication to the driver of the radius of the jib. The 6-wheel former milk-tank wagon will probably have been included in the make-up of the breakdown train to provide a source of water for the crane in the absence of such facilities following the replacement of steam by diesel power. (Author)

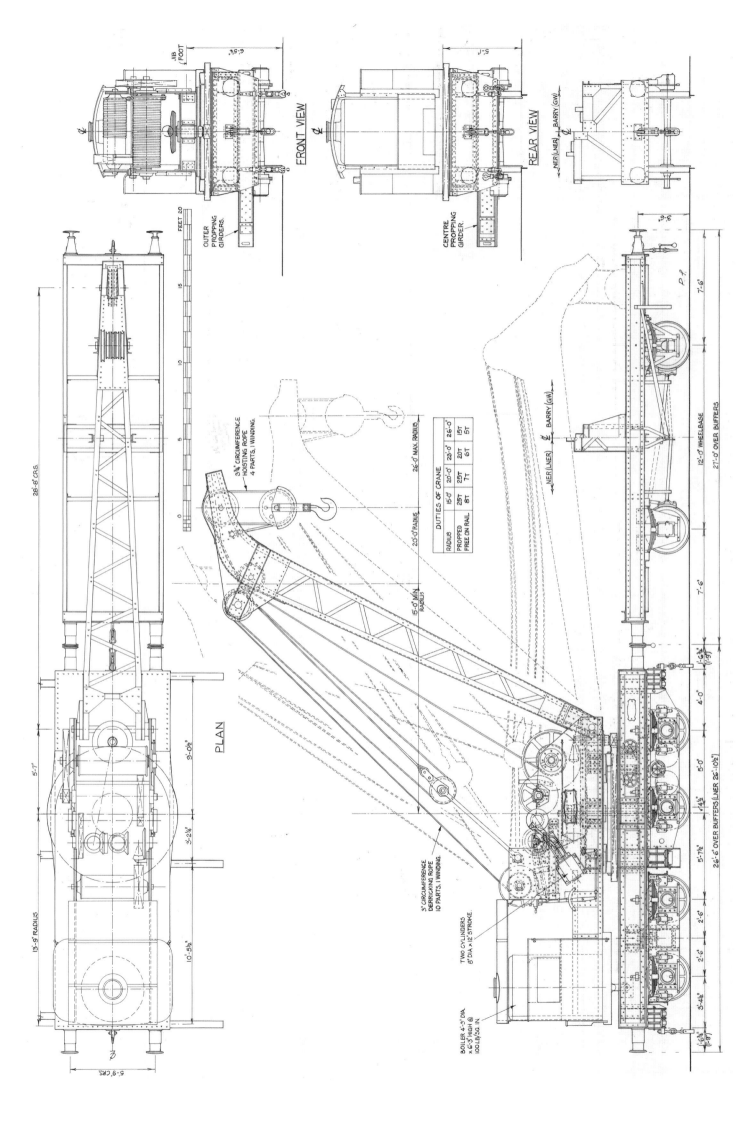

FRONT VIEW

REAR VIEW

PLAN

JIB FOOT

9'-6"

9'-1"

NER (LNER)
BARRY (GW)

OUTER PROPPING GIRDERS.

CENTRE PROPPING GIRDER.

FEET 20 15 10 5 0

28'-8" CRS.

5'-7"

9'-0½"

3'-2¼"

10'-5½"

13'-9" RADIUS

5'-9" CRS.

3¾" CIRCUMFERENCE HOISTING ROPE 4 PARTS, 1 WINDING.

26'-0" MAX. RADIUS

20'-0" RADIUS

15'-0" MIN RADIUS

DUTIES OF CRANE					
RADIUS	15'-0"	20'-0"	23'-0"	26'-0"	
PROPPED	25T	25T	20T	15T	
FREE ON RAIL	8T	7T	6T	5T	

3" CIRCUMFERENCE DERRICKING ROPE 10 PARTS, 1 WINDING.

TWO CYLINDERS 8" DIA × 12" STROKE.

BOILER 4'-3" DIA. × 6'-3" HIGH @ 100 LB/SQ. IN

3'-6"

7'-6"

7'-6"

NER (LNER)
BARRY (GW)

12'-0" WHEELBASE

27'-0" OVER BUFFERS

26'-6" OVER BUFFERS (LNER 26'-10½")

1'-6½"
(1'-9")

4'-0"

5'-0"

1'-4½"

5'-7½"

2'-6"

2'-6"

5'-4½"

1'-6½"
(1'-9")

P.7.

Opposite page, Figure 49 - *Drawing of Cowans Sheldon 25-ton steam crane of 1918/9. (Author)*

Above - *Ex-WD 25-ton Cowans Sheldon steam crane of 1918, later acquired by the NER, as BR ER No. DE902705 standing at Darlington North Road on 3 August 1967. (Author)*

Bottom - *No. DE902705 and match wagon under cover at Darlington North Road on 14 August 1971. (JC Dean)*

Barry Railway's 25-ton Cowans Sheldon crane in the last year of GW ownership lifting the front end of a locomotive at Barry shed on 31 August 1947. (Author's collection)

No. DW14 at Radyr on 12 September 1970 with its boiler out and journal brasses removed, an operation from which it did not recover. (Author)

Cowans Sheldon 20/30-Ton Crane for Metropolitan Railway

A development of the original 20-ton crane of 1918 was ordered by the Metropolitan Railway in 1924, Works No. 4475. Based on the 1917 design for the War Department, Cowans Sheldon supplied a crane in 1925 capable of lifting 20 tons at a radius of 20 feet. This had a different superstructure, possibly because the overall height was limited to 12ft 4in. In August 1930 the crane's duties were up-rated to 30 ton capacity at the minimum radius of 16 feet, necessitating a larger snatch-block. Hinged buffers were fitted in June 1931, resulting in an increase in overall length of ¾ inch. In 1944 the straight axle horn block tie bars were replaced by downward cranked ones to increase the clearance to the underside of the axle-boxes.

When the London Passenger Transport Board took over the assets on 1 July 1933, these included those of the Metropolitan Railway, in turn becoming the London Transport Executive after 1947. One assumes that at the outset this crane was based at Neasden, but it had moved to Lillie Bridge by July 1947. Upon withdrawal it was sold to Cashmore circa 1966.

Cowans Sheldon 20/30-Ton Crane for Met Rly					
Date delivered	Works No	Running No LPTB	Match wagon No	Allocation	Disposal
1925	4475	C604	14	To LPTB 30/6/33, Neasden *10/5/40*, Lillie Bdg *7/47*	Wdn sold to J Cashmore c'66

In the pristine conditions of London Transport's depot at Neasden, ex-Metropolitan Railway 30-ton Cowans Sheldon crane No. C604 languishes under cover. (JFC Johnson)

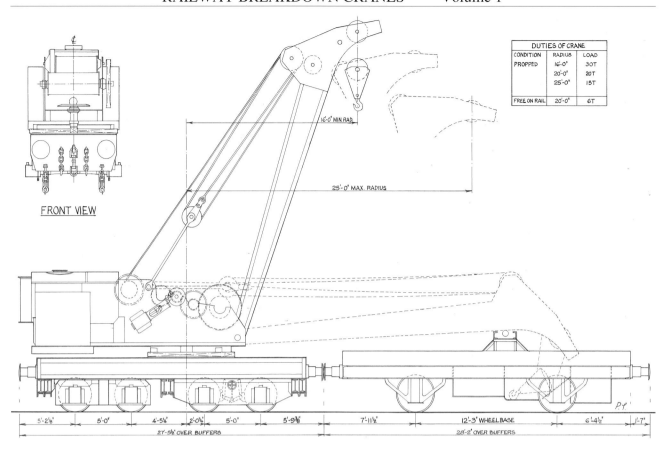

DUTIES OF CRANE		
CONDITION	RADIUS	LOAD
PROPPED	16'-0"	30T
	20'-0"	20T
	25'-0"	15T
FREE ON RAIL	20'-0"	6T

FRONT VIEW

16'-0" MIN. RAD.

25'-0" MAX. RADIUS

5'-2⅛" | 5'-0" | 4'-5¼" | 2'-0¾" | 5'-0" | 5'-9⅜" | 7'-11½" | 12'-3" WHEELBASE | 6'-4½" | 1'-7"

27'-5⅝" OVER BUFFERS | 28'-2" OVER BUFFERS

Figure 50 - *Diagram of Met Rly 20/30-ton Cowans Sheldon steam crane. (Author)*

Outside, No. C604 is seen in the sunshine awaiting disposal. Notice the angle bracing to the jib outside the longitudinal angles of the jib compared with inside on the 25-ton half-sisters. (Author's collection)

A closer view of the crane showing that jacks were fitted to the ends of the propping girders of this crane. Note the circular base-plates for the jacks stowed in pockets on the carriage sides. (Author's collection)

The 30-ton steam crane supplied by Ransomes & Rapier to the London Electric Railway in 1931 for civil engineering works in connection with the extension of the Piccadilly line, photographed lifting a cast iron girder soon after delivery. Note the substantial inverted U-shaped members on top of the carriage into which the propping girders could be fitted to enable them to pass above lineside obstructions, such as platforms or bridge girders. The tail of the crane has to be high enough to pass over these as it slews round. (Author's collection)

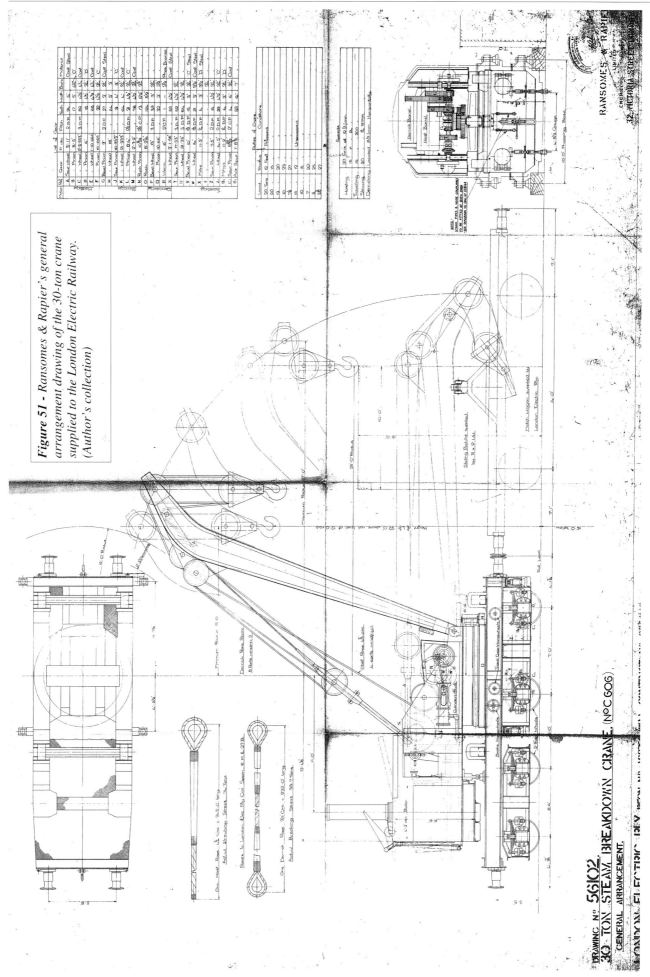

Figure 51 - Ransomes & Rapier's general arrangement drawing of the 30-ton crane supplied to the London Electric Railway. (Author's collection)

Ransomes & Rapier 30-Ton Crane for London Electric Railway

Acquired by the London Electric Railway from Ransomes & Rapier in 1931, justification for the cost of its purchase of this 30-ton crane was primarily based on its use in erecting bridges on the western extension of the Piccadilly line. Nonetheless, it was recognised that it would subsequently be suitable for use on breakdown work and was designed accordingly. It was equipped in the usual locations within the carriage for two pairs of propping girders with screw jacks on the ends. In constricted locations, such as platforms or bridge girders, the propping girders could, however, be fitted into heavy duty stirrups on top of the carriage. This necessitated the superstructure being particularly shallow to enable it to rotate above the stirrups and yet remain within the height gauge of about 12ft 6in. The carriage was also fitted with hinged buffers to improve the portée. The 4-wheel match wagon was provided by the railway company, except for the sliding bolster for the jib to rest on, included in the contract for building the crane. This crane too was incorporated into the LPTB in July 1933.

Another crane of 10 tons capacity was also ordered by the LER from Ransomes & Rapier on 17 March 1931, but this is not thought to have been considered for use on breakdown work.

In 1977 this crane was converted to diesel propulsion by Cowans Sheldon who replaced the boiler, cylinders etc with a General Motors diesel engine. As a result it ended up with an enclosed cab and sported an all yellow livery with diagonal hazard strips on the buffer beams. After testing and training at Neasden, it was transferred to Lillie Bridge with strict instructions that it could go in all roads of the depot except No 9 which, due to the presence of an overhead loading gantry, was of restricted height suitable only for tube stock. All too soon, however, the inevitable happened and the resulting damage was considered so severe that it was cut up at Neasden in early 1978.

Ransomes & Rapier 30-Ton Crane for LER					
Date ordered – delivered	Works No	LTE Nos		Allocation	Disposal
		Crane	Match wagon		
27/2/31 – 1931	D3688	C606	J684	Lillie Bridge 10/5/40	Wdn early 1978

Above - Former London Electric Railway's 30-ton crane and 4-wheel match wagon, as London Transport Executive No. C606 and J684 respectively. The jib and possibly other features are lined out. (JFC Johnson)

Right - A head on view of ex-LER's 30 ton crane and match wagon No. J684 at Neasden on 18 June 1970. (Author's collection)

An unusual approach was taken by the LNER soon after grouping to provide for the need to handle Gresley's pacific locomotives on the East Coast main line. Two 45-ton cranes each on a pair of bogies and with axle loads of 20 tons were acquired from Cowans Sheldon in 1926 and posted to Doncaster and Gateshead. Gateshead's 45-ton Cowans Sheldon steam crane is seen lifting a large rolled steel joist during the renewal of the deck of an over-bridge at Heaton South. Passing through the vertical stiffeners to the carriage of the crane are four small shackles used in the warwicking process to provide a fixing point for additional restraint on the off-side when making particularly heavy lifts. (Author's collection)

11. Unusual Duo

Cowans Sheldon 45-ton crane for LNER of 1926

Shortly before grouping, the Great Northern and North Eastern railways had both witnessed the introduction of 4-6-2 pacific locomotives by Gresley and Raven respectively, later classified A1 and A2 by the LNER. The subsequent multiplication of the former and improvement as A3s, together with the development of the 2-8-2 version for heavy freight trains in the form of the P1s, brought about a requirement for breakdown cranes able to handle loads in excess of 90 tons in the event of a derailment. This need was met in 1926 by the purchase from Cowans Sheldon of Carlisle of two 45-ton steam breakdown cranes (Works Nos. 4524 and 4525), which were allocated to the East Coast main line at Doncaster and Gateshead. North of the border with Scotland the North British had bequeathed a massively constructed 36-ton crane supplied in 1914, also from Cowans Sheldon (Works No. 3310), stationed at St Margaret's, Edinburgh. In the days before one had the Health and Safety Executive endlessly breathing down one's neck, no doubt it would have been used to lift one end of such locomotives as the occasion demanded.

Radically different, these two 45-ton cranes of the 4-0-4 wheel arrangement represented the first serious attempt to improve upon the load capacity of the Rapier 36-tonners. They were interesting in that the resulting axle loads seem to have been of little concern and with these in the order of 20/21 tons, their route availability was considerably curtailed. Under the LNER's route availability scheme, the RA classification was 9, or 7 in an emergency at a reduced speed of 15 mph, together with such other lines within their respective breakdown areas that were listed in the Sectional Appendices to the Working Timetable, having been individually checked out and approved by the Civil Engineer. The cranes were therefore generally restricted to the main lines.

It is interesting to note that apparently Nigel Gresley had considered the possibility of one 120 ton capacity crane to be located at a central point on the system. However, the loss of time negotiating the high density of traffic on so many of the lines meant that working such a crane to the scene requiring its capacity would have negated any advantage. In due course further 35/36- and 45-ton cranes were acquired with a better route availability.

The carriages were mounted on a pair of two-axle cast steel bogies producing axle loads of 20 tons carried on 2ft 6in diameter wheels with 12 by 7 inch journals. Beneath the carriage were mounted three sets of propping girders, one at each end and one in the centre, however those of the centre set were two-part telescopic, enabling them to be drawn out about 9ft 5in from the centre of the crane, compared with 6ft 6in for the outer ones. In the

Doncaster's 45-ton crane No. DE330107 on shed with a set of light metal steps for access to hand. Note the heavy duty cast steel bogie sides. (RHG Simpson)

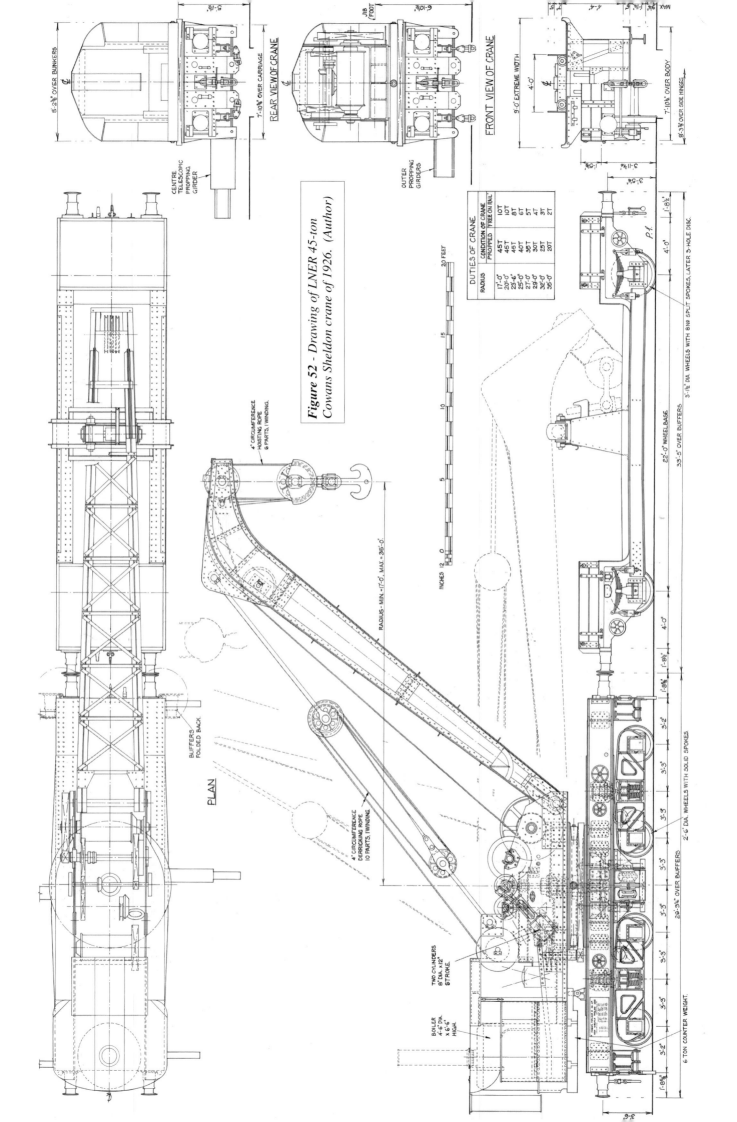

Figure 52 - *Drawing of LNER 45-ton Cowans Sheldon crane of 1926. (Author)*

REAR VIEW OF CRANE

FRONT VIEW OF CRANE

8'-2⅜" OVER BUNKERS

5'-1⅝"

7'-10¾" OVER CARRIAGE

CENTRE TELESCOPIC PROPPING GIRDER

OUTER PROPPING GIRDERS

JIB FOOT

6'-10¾"

9'-0" EXTREME WIDTH

4'-0"

7'-10¾" OVER BODY

8'-3¾" OVER SIDE HINGES

MAX 3⅛"-1'-8⅛"

4'-4"

3'-11⅝"

1'-5⅜"

PLAN

4' CIRCUMFERENCE HOISTING ROPE 6 PARTS, 1 WINDING.

4' CIRCUMFERENCE DERRICKING ROPE 10 PARTS, 1 WINDING.

TWO CYLINDERS 8" DIA. x 12" STROKE

BOILER 4'-6" DIA. x 6'-6" HIGH.

RADIUS - MIN. = 17'-0", MAX. = 35'-0".

BUFFERS FOLDED BACK

DUTIES OF CRANE		
RADIUS	CONDITION OF CRANE	
	PROPPED	FREE ON RAIL
17'-0"	45T	10T
20'-0"	45T	10T
23'-6"	45T	8T
25'-0"	40T	6T
27'-0"	35T	5T
29'-0"	30T	4T
32'-0"	25T	3T
35'-0"	20T	2T

20 FEET

15

10

5

0

INCHES 12

P.A.

4'-0"

22'-0" WHEELBASE

33'-5" OVER BUFFERS

3'-1⅛" DIA. WHEELS WITH 8 No. SPLIT SPOKES, LATER 5-HOLE DISC.

2'-6" DIA. WHEELS WITH SOLID SPOKES

29'-3½" OVER BUFFERS

6 TON COUNTER WEIGHT.

1'-8⅛"

3'-6"

3'-2"

3'-3"

3'-3"

3'-3"

3'-3"

3'-2"

1'-8⅛"

4'-0"

1'-8⅛"

1'-8⅜"

3'-5½"

propped condition, these cranes were capable of lifting their maximum load from a minimum radius of 17 feet out to 23 feet. The 33 foot long jib, although greater than those on most earlier types, was still only regarded as being of medium length compared with that of the GW 36-ton cranes and of all subsequent breakdown cranes which were greater still at 40 feet or more. The jib was supported while in train formation on a 4-wheel match truck of the well type.

The fold down chimney extension was soon dispensed with, while the steam turbine generator on the right-hand side was moved from beside the driver's position to the leading end of the crab. The counter-weight was provided with slots of the type usually associated with the facility to add a detachable weight, but there is no evidence that this was ever done. The yokes to the outer propping girders were presumably replaced at some time, the earlier ones having rounded lower ends, while the later ones are squared up. The Gateshead crane was equipped with four warwicking shackles per side, while the Doncaster crane was fitted with jacks to the outer ends of the two end pairs of propping girders by early BR days. It is assumed it was not practical to do the same to the centre set.

In the late 1960s No. 154 was cannibalised to make one good machine which finished its railway career at Healey Mills and, following withdrawal in 1968, moved to the North Yorkshire Moors Railway.

Cowans Sheldon 45-Ton Cranes for LNER								
Date delivered	Works No	Running No			Match wagon No		Allocation	Disposal
		Group 'ing	1st BR	2nd BR	1st	2nd		
1926	4524	SB1, 39A 941590	(330)107	ADRC 95224	39AA	941751	Doncaster '26, Healey Mills 11/68-12/78	NYMR 4/81
1926	4525	CME 22 901646	154	-	24163		Gateshead '26, Tweedmouth 7/5/64, Darlington 1/10/65, Wakefield 1/5/66, Healey Mills 1/1/67	Wdn '68

Above - *Another view of No. DE330107 on the same occasion. The medium length jib and well type match wagon should be observed. (RHG Simpson)*
Right - *A close up of No. DE330107 on 14 June 1969, after it had moved to Healey Mills. Propping girders were fitted at each end and between the bogies, the latter being, uniquely for a British company, of the double extension type. The jacks at the end of the outer propping girders and the smaller 'I' beam within the box beam of the centre girder should be noted, together with the jacks at the end of the outer propping girders added to this crane. (Author)*

A Lancashire & Yorkshire Railway breakdown train headed by 0-6-0 No. 946 and including a 4-wheeled brake van and a heavy-duty 6-wheeled hand crane. (LGRP, author's collection)

12-ton hand crane No. W210 was built at Swindon in 1902 and still in service at Treherbert in the 1950s and not withdrawn until 1966 from Margam. Note the platform folded up and the arrow on the moveable weight box (indicated) pointing to notice plate for the travelling position. The weight box would have to be wound back so that the arrow was above the right hand notice plate before commencing to lift. (R Holmes)

12. The use of Cranes on Breakdowns

The Early Days

In considering the first use of cranes for breakdown work, one must turn one's mind back to the working of our earliest railways, the size of locomotives and rolling stock in service and their operating methods at the time. By taking these aspects into account, it is possible to imagine the situations likely to arise as they worked the railway in those far off days.

From the time man first set a wagon on a track, which will have been a primitive plate-way, only later becoming the pair of rails we are familiar with today, it seems certain that before long the vehicle will have left the course man had set for it, not least during construction. It will, therefore, have become necessary to restore the miscreant to the track. As a horse was probably the motive power, it would most likely have been used to haul the wagon back onto the rails with a plentiful and cheap supply of labour to assist. Suitable blocks of wood or stone will have been found useful in guiding and lifting the wheel up on to and over the rail head, while levers and jacks may also have been found helpful.

As the development of railways progressed through the first half of the nineteenth century, as we know, iron rails and steam locomotives were introduced, accompanied by improvements in the design and construction of wagons, together with coaches within which to convey passengers. Methods for dealing with derailments and accidents continued much as before, aided by the availability of purpose made re-railing ramps and hand-powered cranes. Many experienced locomotive department supervisors became adept at getting derailed engines and rolling stock back on the track by jacking and packing and the scene cleared up in record time with the minimum of fuss. The train service was thereby soon

resumed and the income stream restored, so that the directors of the company could pay their shareholders a worthwhile dividend.

Introduction of Steam Cranes

It is probable that the introduction of bogie coaches and the increasing size of locomotives to cope with the longer and heavier coaches challenged the capabilities of the simpler methods and gradually led to most of the railway companies recognising the need for higher capacity cranes which were beyond the reasonable abilities of a hand-powered machine. Added to which, whilst a hand crane could hoist and slew a load, altering the radius by derricking under load was not generally practical. Admittedly, though some of the early steam cranes were often restricted in this motion, derricking soon became a feature of steam cranes and its use increased even more as jib lengths became greater.

Tool & Riding Vans

At a local level the first line of defence was the breakdown tool van, either incorporating accommodation for a small gang of men or with an associated riding van. Most vans were redundant revenue-earning vehicles given extra years of life by being converted for further use. Not all depots had a breakdown train and nor did all of those include a breakdown crane, many managing with a converted coach with staff accommodation at one end and tools, jacks and plenty of timber packing etc in the brake end. Such tool vans would be located at any important junction or medium sized or larger locomotive depot and would be capable of dealing with small incidents of which, in the days of steam and loose-coupled wagons, there were many.

The vast bulk of derailments were mundane

An early Inverness & Aberdeen Junction Railway 4-wheeled passenger brake van built by Brown Marshall for the opening of the Highland main line in the 1863 or earlier has been relegated by the Highland Railway as a loco tool van at Perth. Here it resided as spare van until 1903. (Author's collection)

An LBSC Stroudley 4-wheeled brake third, of a type built over a period of 20 years from 1872, has been given an extra lease of life by being used as a tool van for the Locomotive Department at Battersea. (Author's collection)

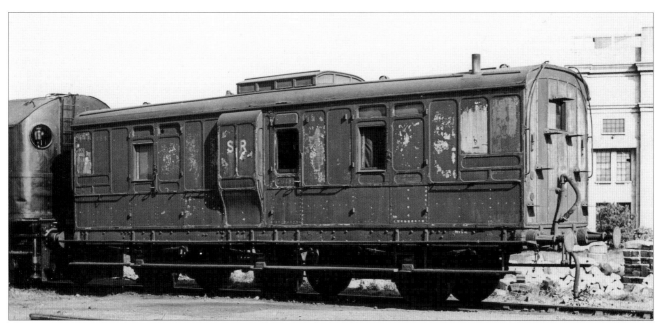

A decidedly tired former SECR 6-wheel passenger brake van No. 485 built at Ashford in 1908, seconded to duty as the tool van No. 1619S at Feltham on 16 May 1948 and coupled to 20-ton Stothert & Pitt crane No. 34S. (JH Aston)

events with a pair of wheels off at split points etc. and for the most of which a tool van and gang of men were more than adequate. If the derailment happened, as too often it did, at the throat of a busy marshalling yard or city goods depot, disruption of other traffic would soon follow and a prompt response was called for. For such trivial jobs, often a traversing jack and some packs, or the re-railing ramps might suffice and, even if a crane were included in the breakdown train, would be quicker. Nonetheless, the full train would be taken out to a known small incident,

because before completing this job it was not unknown for the breakdown gang to be summoned to yet another incident elsewhere. This might mean being sent straight on to perhaps a larger job where the full range of equipment might be required.

By 1970 still only 6% of incidents involved passenger trains, while 90% did not involve running lines. 10,182 were recorded that year, but a decade later this had reduced to 4,843, the reduction probably being largely due to the closure of marshalling yards.

Bedford's 6-wheel breakdown van LMS No. 7304 of Midland Railway origin dating from the 19th century, together with a sheeted open wagon, present at the scene of the derailment of a Stanier 2-6-2T at Cardington on 9 April 1940. Modifications and repairs to van have been carried out in vertical match-boarding. (AE West, courtesy MS King)

On the LNER ex-GNR 6-wheel passenger brake van No. 43840 has been commandeered by the Locomotive Department for Grantham sometime before World War 2. (GY Hemingway, courtesy HMRS)

An entirely new vertically match-boarded body has been built on a 30ft 2in long 6-wheel LNWR carriage underframe as a breakdown train riding van, now No. DM 284681. (Photomatic)

The Caledonian Railway was one of the few companies to construct entirely new breakdown vans for the purpose. Five emergency tool and five riding vans 30 by 8 foot, 6-wheel, were built in 1921 for Perth, Motherwell, Carlisle, Dawsholm and Hamilton. Here riding van No. 354741 has migrated to Helmsdale by June 1949. The tool vans were similar but omitted the pair of fixed windows and had a pair of double doors. (HC Casserley)

The North Eastern Railway too built a range of purpose-made breakdown vans between 1889 and 1895 and this shows 6-wheel tool van No. DE901585 at Starbeck on 25 May 1956, see LNER wagons, Volume 2, Wild Swan, 2007, pages 176 to 177. (RS Carpenter collection)

To handle larger events and major accidents, however, each railway company would have stationed at its main works or other strategic locations one or more hand cranes for breakdown work, together with the associated tool and riding vans. It was not unknown, however, for one company to borrow its neighbour's crane if it had a particularly serious problem. By grouping in 1923, most of the constituents had during the previous three decades acquired at least one steam-powered crane and the larger companies several. Some of the displaced hand cranes will have been cascaded to lesser depots, before eventually being scrapped.

Following grouping, each crane and tool van would be allocated to a defined area, usually set out in the appendices to the working timetable and the first call would always be to the allotted breakdown gang. Should the incident be beyond their ability, then assistance would be summoned from a neighbouring area, particularly if this had a steam crane or a larger capacity crane. In urban areas this could result in a complex network: in the West Riding during the 1950s for example, Wakefield shed covered the ex-L&Y, LNWR and the GN lines of the North Eastern Region, while Leeds Holbeck dealt with the ex-Midland lines. As retrenchment took place under British Railways, areas would be amalgamated and cranes reallocated, with older and smaller cranes being withdrawn.

Apart perhaps from within station and yard limits, by its nature a railway line is not readily accessible to or from the rest of the country's infrastructure, which meant that, if a derailment or accident took place out on the line, apart from the remote possibility of a signal box, the breakdown train had to be self-supporting in respect of such things as the amenities for feeding and rest, not only the breakdown gang, but platelayers, footplatemen waiting for relief, traffic inspectors etc. The properly equipped riding van would, therefore, be able to act as a refuge to these individuals, offering not just cover and warmth from the elements, but sustenance as well.

The standard of facilities provided in both the tool and riding vans developed over the years and by nationalisation the better equipped of the latter might expect to include: a hand brake; an outdoor clothing changing area; a galley in which hot drinks and food were prepared; eating/messing area with tables and chairs/bench; sleeping area equipped with bunks; a toilet and shower; and supervisor's compartment to which he and other officers could adjourn in private.

The tool van would, as its name suggests, contain all the tools and impedimenta that a breakdown gang expected to need for a wide range of circumstances. As well as the previously mentioned jacks of various types and capacity, copious quantities of timber packing, mostly hardwood, was needed to spread under the propping girders of the crane to distribute the load safely into the supporting ground and for other nefarious purposes. Other items would include: oxy-acetylene gas-cutting gear and gas bottles; lamps to illuminate the scene at night; loose lifting tackle, such as shackles and lifting brackets of various shapes and sizes not carried on the match wagon, if any; all sorts of hand tools, such as bars, hammers, saws, shovels etc; marker lights; and signalling flags. Some vans might also be provided with hauling gear to recover items that had ended up some way from the alignment of the permanent way, even after it had been reinstated.

Sometimes a separate packing wagon was included in the breakdown train, but, unless this was also provided with a tarpaulin sheet, there was a tendency with time for the timber to rot and therefore a covered van was preferred.

The floodlighting of the clearing up operations following the accident at Bourne End on 20 September 1945, using paraffin Tilley lamps. (Author's collection)

The Breakdown Gang

The manning of a breakdown train with a steam crane would consist of two groups of men. The crew for the crane would be made up of a foreman, who might have another position within the organisation, such as the mechanical foreman or leading fitter; a dedicated crane driver, who would be responsible for looking after the crane; a slinger; sometimes a van attendant who would also cook; and a few labourers experienced in using the crane. In addition there was the breakdown gang of ten or a dozen men to act as labourers, but nonetheless drawn from among the fitter's assistants at the depot. At large busy sheds, where call-outs were frequent, these would be taken from those men on duty at the time on a rota system.

Such men were paid a special allowance on each occasion they turned out. Even on large jobs, the gangs would tend to stop on the job until the end and this meant that the train had to cater for feeding and housing twelve or fifteen men for up to three days. In the days of meagre wages, membership of the gang was, therefore, a jealously guarded privilege, because it often led to overtime payments.

For bridge work the crane crew would be sufficient, but for a derailment or more serious event they would be supplemented by further men recruited from the shed staff. At Guildford in the 1950s the crane crew

consisted of a foreman, Charlie Wright, a driver, Len Elston and two labourers, who would be augmented by ten or twelve to form a complete breakdown gang. At Stratford shed in London prior to World War 2 men of the breakdown gang were accommodated in a row of houses near the main gate. Each house then had an electric bell which would be operated by the shed to call the men out. The obliteration of this housing by bombs subsequently led to the dispersed men being provided with telephones to enable them to be summoned. They were expected to be away from the depot within half an hour. During 1949 the gang was called out 356 times excluding other pre-planned work.

Calling Out the Breakdown Train

It is the duty of any railwayman witnessing an accident to report the matter to higher authority. Depending upon the nature of the accident, this might mean passing details to the control, who would in turn advise the motive power depot in whose breakdown area the accident had occurred, that the breakdown train was required and make immediate arrangements for the gang to be called and the train despatched. Should a main line be involved, rather than some derailment in a yard, the shed master and district officers were expected to attend.

A breakdown train would usually consist of the crane, if any, often next to the engine, and the tool and

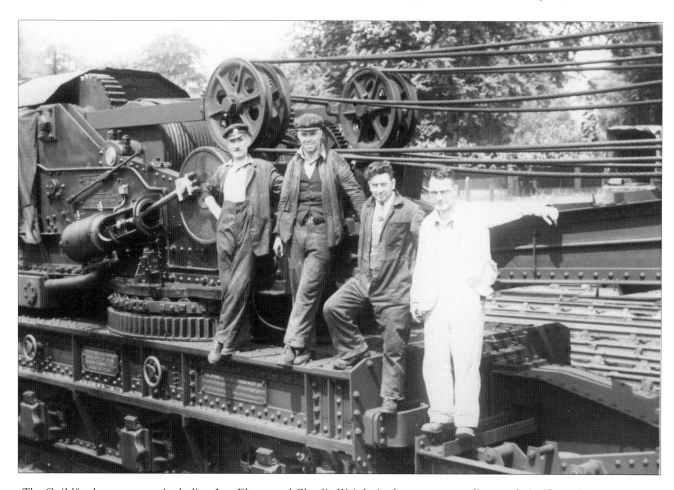

The Guildford crane crew, including Len Elston and Charlie Wright in the centre, standing on their 45-ton Ransomes & Rapier crane No. Ds1561 – this and other modern cranes will be considered in Volume 2. (SC Townroe, author's collection)

mess van with a brake van as the last vehicle. The ideal type of locomotive to haul the train was a six-coupled, usually a tender goods or mixed traffic type, although in the event any suitable engine available was likely to be commandeered. In later days most cranes were at least piped for continuous brakes and of course tool and mess vans became fully fitted, but this had not always been so. On the outward journey the train was entitled to carry the express head code of lamps, one over each buffer.

The G&SWR's breakdown train based at Hurlford behind James Manson's 361 Class 0-6-0 in 1906. As well as the crane itself, a Cowans Sheldon 15-ton steam crane of 1893, the service stock is superannuated former main line stock. The three 4-wheel coaches appear to be Patrick Stirling's with low curved roofs. The match truck and other wagons would be obtained by adapting non-passenger coaching stock or goods wagon underframes displaced from revenue-earning service. (Ian Middleditch collection, courtesy of Glasgow & South Western Railway Association)

MR Johnson 0-6-0 Class 2 No. 3115 near Elstree or Mill Hill ambles by with the Cowans Sheldon 15-ton crane No. 244, later RS1037/15, annotated "London" and with the crane driver aboard, together with a 6-wheel riding van from which a couple of men are waving; a sheeted 4-wheel packing wagon; and a 6-wheel brake/tool van. The train is proceeding under a head code indicating breakdown train not going to clear the line. (Real Photographs, author's collection)

Answering the call for the breakdown train ex-SECR 0-6-0 C Class No. 31719 sets out from Stewart's Lane with Cowans Sheldon 15-ton crane in tow on 27 February 1957. (RC Riley, courtesy Transport Treasury)

THE USE OF CRANES ON BREAKDOWNS

By British Railways' days, speeds were limited to a maximum permissible for breakdown cranes in train formation to 25 mph for those of up to and including 20 ton capacity, 30 mph for those over 20 and up to 29 tons and from 30 to 50 tons 45 mph. This last applied whether the cranes were fitted with or not fitted with weight relieving bogies. Some cranes having articulated jibs, and suitable in other respects might run at 60 mph. Subsequently the new cranes in the 1960s fitted with roller bearings could run at up to 60 mph.

By 1960 the procedure for reporting an accident and ordering a breakdown train depended whether the incident occurred within an area of the system subject to District Control or not. On a controlled line the station master or person in charge would report an accident to the District Control and intimate whether he considered a breakdown train would be required. Control would then decide whether this should be ordered and, if so, make the necessary arrangements.

If the assistance of a breakdown train was required on non-controlled lines it then depended whether the breakdown train was situated at a depot within a controlled area or not. If it was, application had to be made to Control, who would again decide whether to provide it and make the necessary arrangements. If both the site of the incident and depot of the breakdown train were outside any controlled area, the station master or person in charge would make application for assistance through the District Control or direct to the locomotive shed master, which ever was quicker by the most expeditious means of communication, but Control was nonetheless to be fully informed as soon as possible.

Control was responsible for ordering additional breakdown trains whenever they were considered necessary. Nonetheless, if the official in charge of the breakdown train at the site considered such assistance should be given, he was to notify District Control, who would then make the necessary arrangements.

BR (ER) – Route Availability of Travelling Steam Cranes

Crane No	Normally stationed at: On 6 Nov 1961/ 1964	Capacity (Tons)	Route availability	Additional route availability in emergency at reduced speed
131	Stratford/Norwich	35	3	2
132	Ipswich/Ipswich	20	4	2
135	Norwich/March	35	5	3
133	Cambridge/Cambridge	45	3	2
134	March/Stratford	20	4	2
136	Plaistow/Ripple Lane	30	3	2
102	King's Cross/Tinsley	45	3	2
104	Hornsey*/-	15	3	2
110	Peterborough/ Peterboro'	45	3	2
109	Grantham*/-	15	3	2
108	Retford/-	15	7	6
107	Doncaster/Doncaster	45	9	7
103	Grimsby/Immingham	36	4	3
124	Colwick/Colwick LMR	36	4	3
105	Darnall/Wath	20	6	2
125	Mexborough*/-	15	3	2
101	Langwith/Langwith	15	3	2
RS1019/126	Grimesthorpe/Lincoln	30	7	6+
RS1004/159	Holbeck/Holbeck	40	3	-
122	Gorton/Gorton LMR	45	3	2
123	Woodford*/-	35	6	4
54	Neasden/-	35	6	4
112	-/Finsbury Park DD	75	8	-
111	-/Stratford	75	8	Some additional GE routes
967159	-/York	75	8	-
160	-/Wakefield	30	2	-
151	-/Dairycoates#	35	6	-
RS1038	-/Cricklewood	40	6	5
RS1089	-/Nottingham	30	5	-
940215	Doncaster CCE Dept	10	4	3
	All other CCE's cranes	5	2	1

* These cranes must not work over any GE route.
\+ Subject to same restrictions as ex-LM 5MT (4-6-0).
\# This crane must not work over any ex-GE electrified line.

Presumably those cranes marked with an asterisk were barred from GE routes for other reasons, most probably being foul of the loading gauge.

The classification of lines on the Eastern Region for locomotive route availability also applied to travelling cranes, each of which in the list above had been placed in a route availability group, indicated on the crane side (e.g. R.A. 5). All cranes in the groups up to and including, that in which a section of line was placed, were permitted to work over that section, e.g., if a section was in group 4, then all cranes in groups 1, 2, 3 and 4 were permitted over it.

For instance, crane No. 102 was allowed a max speed of 45 mph on RA3 but only 5 mph on RA2.

At busy sheds in the days of steam the fire would usually be alight and light steam maintained in the crane boiler. Some important depots would also have a locomotive in steam ready to take the train out. At Sandhills, on hearing the bell ring the gang would be on the train and moving off within three minutes, the driver normally remaining in the crane cab to build up steam pressure. In more recent times, however, it could sometimes be no mean feat to get the breakdown train away to an incident. A driver and a guard with the necessary route knowledge have to be found to man the train, and a suitable locomotive and path along the line provided. For this reason, some larger depots had a passed fireman passed out as a guard.

Operating Breakdown Cranes

Upon arrival at the scene of the incident, the crane supervisor would liaise with the local signalman or senior traffic person present before he inspected the site and made an assessment of how he proposed to tackle the work of clearing the line. In the event of a serious accident, or one likely to cause substantial delays to traffic, a more senior motive power officer might have been able to make his way to the site by car and put in place arrangements for receiving the breakdown crane, thereby saving time. He might also be able to foresee that a second crane was going to be necessary and make arrangements for it to be called from a neighbouring area with the minimum of delay.

Should any members of the public be involved, whether passengers or otherwise, or staff be hurt, the first priority would be to rescue them and see that they were cared for as necessary. The use of the crane at this point would be inappropriate, because the debris might well be delicately balanced and any movement induced by lifting with the crane could have untold consequences as debris shifted in an uncontrolled manner. Thereafter, the priority would be to clear the line and restore traffic.

The location might present constraints to the use of cranes, such as the presence of an over-bridge, overhead electric traction equipment, or other overhead public utility power lines, which if possible he would have to work round. Overhead telegraph lines might present less of a problem, if they could be temporarily removed and reinstated afterwards. On a tight curve, super-elevation of the track will adversely affect the stability of the crane. The close proximity of lineside obstructions, such station platforms and canopies, bridge girders, retaining walls, signal posts and telegraph poles etc, may limit the scope for manoeuvre and restrict space for the crane's propping girders. Likewise, an under-bridge deck, track drains or steep embankment might not be sufficiently stable to support the propping loads.

Working on steep gradients presents its own particular problems, necessitating particular caution and, if working uphill of a removed bridge span, probably the need for the crane to be permanently coupled to a locomotive. If the work is likely to be protracted, he will need to consider the availability of water and coal to supply both the crane and any attendant locomotives. It might be possible to send the latter off to replenish, but that is unlikely to be feasible for the crane. Again if nightfall is imminent, appropriate steps will have to be taken to provide adequate light to be able to continue the work after dark.

The methods for re-railing he might consider will have included non-crane methods, such as jacking and packing and the use of re-railing ramps. Following World War 2 more sophisticated equipment and methods became available and these will be touched upon in Volume 2. If the crane was selected as the means of carrying out the work, the appropriate lifting tackle would have to be chosen and attached to the crane's hook. As the breakdown train will have left the depot in hurry, the direction of approach will probably not have been considered and so the manner in which the train is split and the way round the crane arrives at the point at which it is to be used may not be the most advantageous. For instance, the match truck may have to be either lifted, if possible, or shunted out of the way. In addition, probably more than half of all cranes were handed, i.e. the portée, or reach in front of the carriage, would be less than to the rear in the normal train formation. If this was a really serious issue, time might have to be taken to withdraw the crane to some point at which it can be turned either by an alternative choice of route or, if available, on a triangle.

Once the strategy for tackling the problem had been agreed, one man, the crane supervisor, should be the only one allowed to give instructions to the crane driver (s), usually by means of a range of standardised hand signals, or a code of blasts on a whistle.

As well as the safe working loads being tabulated at some visible location on the crane, a means of advising the supervisor and crane driver of the actual radius and hence safe load was provided. This was achieved either by a gravity-operated pointer mounted on the jib, or a system of lightweight rods and levers reflecting the inclination of the jib transmitting an indication to a pointer fixed in the driver's view. Both pointers moved across a graduated display on a curved notice plate. The radius shown, however, was only applicable on level track and any super-elevation would invalidate the reading due to the geometry of the tip of the jib being displaced forward or backwards. Failure to appreciate this has led to serious consequences on not a few occasions.

To prepare the crane for use, the spring relieving screws were screwed down on to, or blocks inserted over, each axle-box to render the suspension system inoperative, while the crane driver opened the canopy over his head to afford an improved view. On those cranes fitted with relieving bogies, the load would also be released from the bogies, but not necessarily detached. Following this, the jib would be carefully raised from its support, ensuring that the chains or ropes were bedding down in their appropriate grooves. If necessary, the superstructure would be slewed a little to take any sideways load off the back end lock so that the lock could be released. The selected tackle would then be attached to the hook by the slinger.

The older cranes without self-propelling motion necessarily had to remain coupled directly or indirectly to a locomotive for the duration of the work. On the other hand, those cranes equipped with self-propelling motion would generally have the option of either using this facility, or relying on the attendant locomotive for re-

The gang of GW 36-ton Ransomes & Rapier crane No. 2 tighten the screw jacks on the end of the propping girder prior to making a heavy lift outside Swindon A Shops on 23 August 1971. (Author)

positioning movements. With many cranes, however, engaging the travel gear was not easily accomplished. If a loco was attached, messing about with the travel gear was often considered a waste of time, although a lot depended on the competence of the loco driver, and how attentive he was to hand signals. It was not unknown for the crane to be propelled into a pile of wagons! Also the brakes of the locomotive were far better than all types of crane, except very late in the day the 75-tonne telescopic jib cranes of 1977 to be considered in Volume 2, which have very good brakes.

On gradients of any magnitude it was sensible, and subsequently became obligatory, to keep the locomotive attached to afford adequate braking power. On a line steeper than 1 in 260 it became a requirement to place timbers across the track. On gradients steeper than 1 in 150 it was forbidden to be without a loco coupled to the crane. Nonetheless, where appropriate, the crane could be made self-reliant by using the clutch wheel on the side of the carriage to engage the sliding pinion in the final drive of the travelling gear. Even so, ordinarily the locomotive might be left attached to the remnant of the breakdown train. Depending on how close the crane was going to have to approach the load to be lifted, it might be necessary for the match wagon and, if fitted, one or both relieving bogies to be shunted or lifted clear.

The most important matter was to determine whether any of the proposed lifts could be taken while the crane was 'free on rail', i.e. without having to extend and pack up the propping girders. In an accident of any consequence, propping was likely to be necessary, and failure to do so has been the cause of not a few cranes overturning.

In early days full length propping beams were carried in or under the match wagon. At typically 7 cwt in weight, these must have been quite awkward to insert by hand in the stirrups under the crane carriage, particularly in cramped locations. As the size of the propping girders increased to meet the demands of larger cranes, they were soon, temporarily or permanently, carried in propping

boxes under the carriage and on later cranes ratchets were provided to advance and withdraw the girders. In the end most cranes had screw jacks fitted at the girder ends to tighten down on the previously placed timber packing. It is always good practice to draw out and support the girders on the offside as well in case any sudden release of load throws the crane off balance.

Like locomotives, cranes were subject to a minimum radius of curve that they could safely negotiate. Working on under-bridges was also subject to limitations, mainly the approval of the District Engineer, who would have to ascertain the ability of the underlying structure to safely support the loading of the crane, in particular the concentrated loads imposed by the propping girders and the means of distributing these.

When particularly heavy lifts were to be undertaken, almost certainly beyond the stated capacity of the crane, great care would be taken to ensure that the crane was thoroughly supported. The spread of the packing under the propping girders, particularly nearest the load, needed to be well founded. After briefly taking the strain by lifting the load a small amount and then putting it down again, so as to consolidate the packing and ground beneath, the girder-end jacks or wedges would be re-tightened, prior to making the critical lift. As far as practical, it was good practice to lift the load no further above the ground than strictly necessary, so that in the event of the crane beginning to tip, the load would soon hit the ground and immediately emolliate the situation. The wise supervisor would post a man to the off side of the crane to shout a warning should the wheels of the crane start lifting off the rails.

On the former North Eastern Railway, cranes were fitted with a number of shackles down the side of the crane carriage. To improve the stability of the crane, these could be used on the off side to attach strops which tied the crane down to the adjacent track upon which a heavy locomotive had been positioned, a process known as 'warwicking'.

Conversely on most cranes lighter loads could be

handled at greater speed when hoisting by selecting lower reduction gears. The hoisting tackle on many earlier cranes was usually arranged so that the double chain to the pulley and block to the main hook could be un-reeved and a lighter hook on a single chain used at twice the speed. The smaller hook and no pulley also offered the possibility, if the winding drum would accommodate the extra length of chain, of achieving a slightly greater height of lift.

Should it be necessary to transport a load any distance, such as placing debris into a wagon some way down the materials train or feed bridge components to/ from the bridge span, it was always wise, having picked the load up, propped if necessary, to reduce the radius sufficiently to be safe when free on rail and to slew the jib roughly in line with the track, before releasing the propping girders and travelling to where required. The crane would be more stable in this condition and hence better able to cope with any unevenness in the track, although with long jibs at too short a radius the height of the jib tended to rock the crane.

Lifting and dragging a load with the hoisting rope is risky, because in effect the radius can be increased, and any sideways dragging may strain the jib. Likewise, lifting both ends of a locomotive, long vehicle, or bridge girder using two cranes calls for particular care in coordinating the work of both cranes and avoiding out of plumb lifts. These otherwise can induce unacceptable horizontal forces with the risk of instability. The renewal of under-bridges often requires a crane at each end and the operation of cranes in such conditions is inevitably more tricky than when using only one crane. This is because the supervisor in overall charge must anticipate the effect of one crane's movement upon the other as the load is carefully manoeuvred. Such work is for a very experienced supervisor making small moves of each crane in turn.

On completion of the work, the reverse process was implemented to restore the crane to its running condition coupled up in the breakdown train and returned to its depot. Upon arrival here, any deficiencies in plant or stores would be dealt with without delay, so that the train was ready for its next call of duty.

Left - *Ex-NB 36-ton crane from St Margaret's and LNER 45-ton crane from Eastfield, both Cowans Sheldon, raise a 2-6-0 locomotive that has tumbled down the bank at Inveruglas on the West Highland line in 1947. Note the inclined hoisting ropes.*
(Author's collection)

Opposite bottom *- A Maunsell coach derailed at the throat to the carriage sidings at Clapham Jct is attended to by ex-LSWR 36-ton Ransomes & Rapier crane while officials look on. Note the two pairs of brothers hung from the spreader beam to be able to lift the coach each side of the bodywork.*
(Author's collection)

Above - Two NER 15-ton Cowans Sheldon cranes tackle re-railing the tender of NER 4-4-0 engine No. 725 at Felling
following its derailment on 26 March 1907 as a result of buckled track following a rapid change in temperature. Note that
the right-hand crane has already been fitted with steel wire hoisting rope in place of the original chain still in place on the
left hand one. (Author's collection)

Above and opposite - Ex-Taff Vale 36-ton Cowans Sheldon No. 10 from Cathays and ex-GW 36-ton Ransomes & Rapier crane, probably No. 3 from Landore, prepare to undertake a two crane lift in restoring 650hp diesel hydraulic locomotive No. D 9529 at Glyncorrwg Colliery to the rails on 20 June 1965. (Brian Penney)

The renewal of under-bridges often requires a crane at each end. The operation of cranes in such conditions is inevitably more difficult than when using only one crane, because the supervisor in overall charge must anticipate the effect of one crane's movement upon the other as the load is carefully manoeuvred. Such work is nonetheless good training for re-railing locomotives and bogie stock. Here RS1092/75 from Willesden and the Chief Civil Engineer's own ex-WD Cowans Sheldon 45-ton breakdown crane No. RS1085/45 carry out the reconstruction of an ex-GC bridge. This was on the Marylebone to Neasden line over the Slow lines of the West Coast main line at South Hampstead on 15 November 1964, while the Royal Scot train passes on the Down Fast line. (MS Welch)

13. The Civil Engineer's use of Breakdown Cranes

It cannot have escaped the Civil Engineer's attention that his colleague in the Locomotive Department had, in the form of the breakdown crane, a useful piece of plant, which he too could put to good purpose particularly in the construction and renewal of bridges. Certainly their adoption in this role stretches back to before the turn of the 19th/20th century. It may, however, have been the arrival of the longer jibbed self-propelled high capacity cranes in the first two decades of the 20th century with their greater reach, albeit with a load much reduced below the rated maximum, that particularly attracted the Engineer for use on his bridge works.

It was only the 1960s that road mobile cranes had developed to the point, particularly with the advent of hydraulics and telescopic jibs and, as a result, had grown so substantially in size and capacity that they in any way rivalled the use of railway breakdown cranes for this type of work. More recently still multi-wheeled heavy load movers, developed for the oil and space industry, have been used to remove the old deck complete and install the new one. Even then, this presumes that the site of the work is accessible by road by such large beasts.

Not all rail under-bridges cross highways. Rail intersection and river bridges are, therefore, likely to be inaccessible to road vehicles, especially of the size and weight of the larger road mobile cranes and heavy load movers. Likewise, the underlying ground conditions of the surrounding area will probably be incapable of supporting such plant without major preparatory works. Indeed civil engineers will in the future have to adopt alternatives at inaccessible sites, now that the number of rail breakdown cranes has been reduced to three telescopic jib cranes.

Between the World Wars, the Civil Engineering Departments began to build up substantial fleets of their own travelling cranes. These were, and still are, designed to carry out rather different duties from breakdown cranes. Whereas the latter are capable on occasions of making the extremely heavy lifts when propped, that are often necessary during breakdown and bridge work, the engineer's cranes are intended for a regular and busy schedule. These can be at work six or seven days a week, in the preparation for and the installation of both plain line and points and crossings as part of an ongoing track renewal programme.

Such cranes tend therefore to be of lower maximum load capacity, but very often able to lift this 'free on the rail' as well as propped, if not quite to the same radius. They are robust machines, capable of carrying out several motions concurrently. They are to be found in permanent way pre-assembly yards during the week and out on the line undertaking track renewals, replacement of longitudinal bridge deck timbers, or erection of signal posts, under possession of the line at the weekend. Whilst such cranes had been produced since before the turn of the 19/20th century, their numbers really

began to multiply from the 1930s and 1940s with the introduction of mechanised track relaying by lifting out the old and laying in complete new panels of plain line track. Although twin jib track layers, together with other specialist plant, were subsequently developed for handling panels out on the line, the jib crane continues to be fully employed in the yard making up new and stripping down old panels and for laying in points and crossings. Prior to the arrival of steam and later diesel engineers' cranes, smaller hand cranes would have been available for use particularly in the yard.

For their part, the Locomotive/Mechanical Engineer's Department usually welcomed the opportunity to carry out work on bridges for two very good reasons. Firstly, it was excellent training in the use of the crane and its equipment, the cost of which was borne by another department. Secondly, in the past the men were often glad of the chance to earn overtime and the work was not usually too onerous, there being long spells of inactivity whilst civil engineering activities were carried out. For this reason the young bridge engineer seeking to utilise such a crane on his projects was treated with much consideration and would be looked after during the weekend's work by being invited up into the warm mess van for a break and plied with cups of hot tea or even treated to a cooked meal.

The use of heavy cranes on bridge works calls for careful planning. Even during the design of the bridge, the maximum size of any intended component and the likely radius at which it would have to be lifted will have been considered. Some months before the work is due to be carried out, the weight and size of all the lifts to be made would be carefully calculated and the position of the crane and radius for each load established on a large scale plan to confirm the ability of the crane to perform the work required within its safe capacity. As this was planned work; the latitude in such matters acceptable during the clearance of the line after an accident or derailment would not be tolerated, even in those days.

Possessions of the line between the last train at night and the first in the morning are usually obtainable at a few weeks' notice and much routine work is done under the protection of these, particularly at weekends. To remove the old and install a new bridge deck under the line will, however, almost inevitably involve a greater period and will therefore be classified as an abnormal possession. Because disruption to traffic will as a result be caused, these are only tolerated when absolutely necessary and will have to booked and programmed months in advance as part of the quarterly programme for abnormal possession hammered out with the operating authorities. Temporary speed restrictions, which are required following the erection of an underbridge while the permanent way is fettled, are equally if not more disruptive to traffic and are also considered in the previously mentioned quarterly programme and must

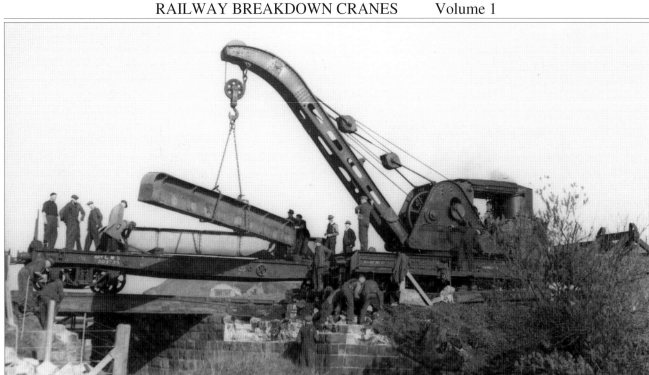

LMS No. RS1023/15, ex-MR 15-ton Cowans Sheldon crane of 1893 at Milton Bridge in 1948 in the process of lifting out a riveted girder prior to loading it on to an ex-WD 40-ton Warflat No. 303735 during a bridge deck renewal. (AG Ellis collection, author's collection)

During a possession of the Up Through and Up Local lines at New Malden over the weekend 10/11 October 1959 the tracks have been lifted between two pre-positioned 45-ton Ransomes & Rapier steam breakdown cranes from Nine Elms and Guildford in preparation for installing 60 foot long temporary steel waybeams. On Sunday work goes ahead by manual labour to prepare the formation for sleeper bearing pads to support the waybeams. (Author)

therefore be booked at the same time.

Speed restrictions may have to be introduced a few days in advance if it is necessary to take out the super-elevation of the track on curves to enable the crane to operate safely on level track. Elsewhere overhead obstructions such as telegraph wires and overhead electrical traction equipment may have to be temporarily removed and subsequently reinstated. The position of the crane's props must be established to ensure that the ground beneath will safely support the load. The unforeseen presence of a drain or other hidden chamber can spell disaster once the crane is under load. Within stations, it may be necessary to cut pockets in the platforms into which to extend the propping girders during the work. When positioned on under-bridges the effect of the concentrated loads during lifting must first be investigated to ensure the structure can safely support them. As a result, occasions have arisen where temporary beams and trestles have had to be provided off which the crane may be propped.

The presence of over-bridges too can seriously hamper crane operations. At least one works inspector, having completed the erection of a replacement precast concrete footbridge adjacent to the one it was in due course to replace, discovered to his horror when it was time to pack up and go home that it was necessary to partially dismantle the new bridge in order to be able to lower the crane jib and re-erect it from the other side, before giving up the track possession. In complex and confined situations, it has been known for models to be used to confirm the practicality of the proposed work in advance, such as the clearance to the jib and tail from obstructions in a range of positions, in an attempt to avoid such embarrassing occurrences with the possibility of being unable to complete the work, or seriously overrunning the possession.

Nearer the event, meetings will be held with the works contractor and all the departments involved to run through the work envisaged and to agree all the details. One or more material trains will be required and the order in which these are made up, routed to and arrive on the site will be given considerable thought to ensure that suitable wagons are available and can be accessed at the appropriate point in the complicated sequence of events envisaged. Trains may be travelling from different points to arrive one side of the bridge or the other. During the

Gateshead's 45-ton Cowans Sheldon steam crane No. CME 22 has been carefully positioned and propped up prior to lifting out the second main girder of a life-expired over-bridge at Heaton South. Note the short length of the slings from the girder to the rams-horn to maximise the height of lift. Also the large diameter pipe has temporarily been propped at mid-span and disconnected from the girder while the latter was replaced. The first of the old girders lies on the track until such time as it can be loaded on to a wagon. ((Author's collection)

The renewal of the superstructure of the Pirbright flyover carrying the Up line from Alton over the four tracks of the West of England main line between Brookwood and Farnborough on the afternoon of Saturday 6 April 1963. The old steelwork over the two Up lines has been removed and Ransomes & Rapier 36-ton steam breakdown crane No. Ds80 from Guildford moves forward with the first new precast concrete slab. With the assistance of Nine Elms' 45-ton crane, hidden from view, the new concrete deck has yet to be installed and the whole process repeated over the other two roads, the track on top reinstated and available for traffic by Monday morning. (Author)

On 25 November 1945 two LNER Cowans Sheldon steam cranes undertaking the removal of an underbridge deck of Dunston Bridge No. 6 on the Newcastle to Carlisle line. The near crane is No. 901719 of 45-ton capacity from Darlington, whilst the other is a 35-tonner from Tweedmouth, but both of similar design with long jibs. One of the materials trains can be seen in the background. (BR, NER, author's collection)

work, the track may be severed and each wagon must be on the correct side of the opening once this happens. The crane and vans often travel from their home depot in their own train with the jib pointing in the direction required by the work, which may mean routing the train by the less than obvious line to ensure it arrives the appropriate way round. On arrival, it may be necessary to shunt, or lift off the track, the match wagon and/or one or even both of the relieving bogies.

Carrying out such work on single lines causes further complications in that the crane cannot run up and down alongside a materials train and new items will have had to have been previously off-loaded beside the track and redundant materials placed there for removal afterwards.

Once on site with its jib raised the crane will move cautiously forward to the correct point of work. Most modern cranes are capable of propelling themselves at slow speed at the scene of operations and therefore ordinarily do not need a locomotive constantly attached. Once the track is broken an upturned sleeper or wheel scotch should be placed across the rail ends. Particular care needs to be exercised when operating on steep

gradients, however, because not only may a runaway occur but also the crane may fall into the gap created by the bridge works.

The renewal of decks to under-bridges of any size usually requires two cranes, one on each side. Larger lifts, such as the removal and installation of main girders, will often be performed as a two crane lift, either to or from a suitable wagon standing on an adjacent track, or temporary stillage erected beside the bridge span and upon which the new girders have previously been placed prior to severing the track. Alternatively the new superstructure may be assembled complete alongside on a pair of adjacent trestles parallel to the line of the bridge abutments and subsequently rolled horizontally into final position.

Breakdown cranes are not normally used for handling track, being too slow and cumbersome, but in the case of bridge work they may remove and subsequently replace the odd track panel or two to enable the work to proceed without resort to manpower, or the need for an additional smaller crane.

During bridge renewals, the hook of the crane would be attached by means of suitable chains, strops, or

Above - *The exception that proves the rule that breakdown cranes do not ordinarily lift track is seen here as Cowans Sheldon 30-ton diesel hydraulic No. DB 965183 swings a track panel clear during the renewal of longitudinal timbers at Kew Bridge on the line from Richmond to Old Oak Common on 25 April 1965. Note the crane supervisor standing on the crab side directing the driver. (Author)*

purpose-made clips etc. to each element to be lifted. In the case of removal of structural elements, these would often have to be separated from adjoining members, by means of oxy-acetylene torches for metalwork; saws for timber; and pneumatic breakers for concrete with torches to cut any reinforcement, or occasionally thermic lances. Care is needed to ensure that the element to be removed is fully separated from its neighbour before hoisting away. Otherwise, the crane may attempt to lift much more than intended with the risk of an overload.

Further care is needed in handling plate girders once they cease to be, or until they become part, of a larger framework. Temporary props and/or lifting girders may be required to ensure that the girders remain structurally stable and do not buckle until adjacent members are connected to them, or they are cut up into smaller pieces for carting away. Following the demolition and removal of the old bridge deck, attention is usually required to the abutment and pier tops to prepare for the bedding down of the new elements. New structural members will generally be installed in reverse fashion to the removal of the old. Skill is required in operating the crane to position and land the new members to tight tolerances, particularly when two crane lifts are being carried out. Steam and diesel hydraulic cranes are well suited to holding heavy loads just above their final position while the engineer checks the setting out before allowing the unit to be lowered those last fractions of an inch, or millimetre or so, and is a very similar operation to positioning a vehicle over the track and landing it on the rails with the wheel flanges in the four-foot.

In some ways work on over-bridges, footbridges and signal gantries is not quite so easy, because the crane is positioned well below where most of the activity is taking place and the slope of the jib can easily present an obstruction. The earlier short-jibbed cranes will have been of little use in these circumstances and whilst longer jib cranes have been employed for many years, the availability of road mobile cranes following World War 2 quickly showed themselves more suitable once their

Opposite page - *Cowans Sheldon 75- and 30-ton diesel cranes from Wimbledon Park, formerly at Nine Elms, and Feltham meet at the London end of Raynes Park station on the main line into Waterloo on 15 October 1967 in preparation for the installation of temporary waybeams in the Up Local line in connection with the renewal of a highly skewed under-bridge. Note the pair of 'brothers' hanging from the rams-horn of both cranes. In addition, the propping girders are not fully extended on the side nearest the camera due to the presence of the conductor rail and adjacent track and along which the material train is about to arrive. (Author)*

Two generations of Cowans Sheldon crane are depicted here working together on placing the first of three large bridge girders for a new over-bridge. Ex-NER 35-ton Cowans Sheldon crane No. CME 1 assisted by LNER 45-ton crane No. 901719 prepare to lift a 70 ton riveted steel plate girder into position at Billingham-on-Tees, located on the Stockton to Hartlepool line on the north side of the estuary, on 3 October 1943. The difference in length of jibs is clearly apparent. Both cranes have their propping girders extended and packed up. The older crane only has timber packing and folding wedges, whilst the younger one has jacks screwed down onto the packing. The additional packing under the front of this crane and under the frames of the other confirms that the lift is particularly heavy one and near the limit of the cranes' capacities (Author's collection)

capacity became adequate, because they could more often be positioned at the level of the work. They could also be brought to the site in advance of the possession and positioned as soon as this was obtained, compared with waiting until the train bringing a rail crane had arrived.

The attachment of the crane's hook or rams-horn

The long jib of the 75-tonners was an asset when it came to handling large girders to over-bridges. Here Carlisle's No. RS1094/75 removes half the North face girder of Bridge No. 4, Trinity Street, at Bolton station on the line to Euxton on 30 March 1969 during its reconstruction. (MS Welch)

75-ton crane No. RS1092/75 from Willesden installs a new precast concrete footbridge in March 1962 at the site of Bridge No. 81 at Apsley as part of the preparation for electrification of the West Coast main line. The propping girders can be seen obstructing the adjacent line and will have to be withdrawn before a train can be allowed to pass. (MS Welch)

to the load would often be by the means of two chains on a ring with hooks at end of each length of chain, known as a pair of brothers. When removing redundant material following demolition, the arms of the brothers would frequently be passed round the member. New components require more careful lifting to ensure that they are truly vertical and can be accurately positioned. Small steel sections and rails can usually be lifted by purpose-made clips over the flanges or rail head. In the old days of riveted girders, it was usual to leave out four or more rivets towards the end of the girder and through which a lifting cleat would be temporarily bolted. Following erection the bolt holes would be permanently filled by site rivets or bolts.

Precast concrete members need to be constructed with a means of lifting, such as loops of projecting reinforcing bars or steel strand, that can be subsequently be burnt off and the concrete made good with mortar, or sockets into which a lifting eye can be screwed and subsequently removed. Because pre-stressed concrete beams rely on their self weight to balance the applied

prestressing forces, they must be lifted from each end and may, therefore, need special lifting beams to enable them to be hoisted from their ends, thereby maintaining acceptable internal stresses.

Not all metal or timber bridges have ballasted track across their decks. In years gone past, to save weight and/or restrict the depth of construction, longitudinal timbers were often used and from time to time these need replacing. Although Engineers' travelling cranes are more usually used for this kind of work, breakdown cranes have sometimes been called in when there is a shortage of the more appropriate travelling cranes.

The installation and renewal of locomotive turntables is really a very similar operation to the renewal of bridge superstructures and breakdown cranes have been used in the same manner on such occasions.

In making breakdown cranes available for bridgeworks, the owning department laid down the stipulation that in the event of an emergency call being received for the use of the crane, then this must be given

During the weekend of 13/14 June 1965 bridge renewal work was undertaken at Vauxhall station, one stop short of Waterloo. This involved the replacement of the underbridge carrying the Up Main Through and Down Windsor Local lines over Upper Kennington Lane. The 75- ton crane from Nine Elms No. DB 965186 and 30-ton crane from Feltham No. DB 965183 were used. They are seen here having recently lifted out one of the old main girders; meanwhile men with pneumatic jack hammers cut down the existing abutment tops to receive new precast concrete bearing units. As the work was within the platforms, the canopy roofing had to be removed to permit the cranes to operate in the station area. The new girders have already been off-loaded prior to the removal of the deck and can be seen between the cranes temporarily placed behind the new platform girder. (Author)

priority. In view of the protracted arrangements that had to be made for bridgeworks, the possibility that the crane might be withdrawn at short notice was of some considerable concern to the civil engineers. Whilst it is possible to envisage the crane being called away just before the bridge work was due to start, with consequent disruption to the work, following the setting up of the crane on the site and particularly once the existing bridge had been opened up, the potential delay to railway operations by removing the crane at this crucial stage one hopes was enough to dissuade the authorities from being so rash. In reality, one trusted, an alternative crane would have been found from an adjacent district to cover for it and deal with any such emergency.

During long weekend possessions steam cranes can exhaust their supply of feed water. Somewhere in the breakdown train there is therefore likely to be a tank of further water. Alternatively most civil engineering sites will have a temporary source of supply for its own activities and arrangements easily could be made with the contractor for a water hose from his supply to be run out to feed the crane's tanks.

Despite all the plans of mice and men, occasionally things go awry. On multi-track lengths of line work was likely to be confined to not more than two tracks, with between train possession of the adjacent line being taken to allow for the swing of the tail of the crane when slewed round or lifting close by. On the Southern Region, at a time when every night there were newspaper trains from London to the provinces, such were hauled by steam or later diesel locomotives and several would pass during the small hours of the morning.

On one such occasion during the renewal of the deck to the Chertsey fly-under at Byfleet Junction on the West of England main line in the autumn of 1964, the first down multiple-unit electric train on Sunday morning, a Portsmouth Slow, highlighted firstly that an oxygen bottle had been left proud in the six-foot way between lines and secondly that the packing timbers supporting the crane's propping girders on the off side were just foul of the third rail electrical pick-up shoe and beam mounted on the bogie.

The oxygen bottle was severely dented, but fortunately not punctured, otherwise your author might not be here to tell the tale. Rather than try and explain the dent to the British Oxygen Co. on its return, the bottle was quietly buried at the bottom of the embankment. The crane driver was shaken by the nudge given to the crane by the shoe hitting the support to the propping girder, while the electric train was found, when it stopped at the next station, West Weybridge (now Byfleet and New Haw), to have lost its leading pick-up beam.

Again nine months later, at Vauxhall in preparation for the renewal of the deck to the Up Main Through and Down Windsor Local, much thought had been given to the operation of the cranes in such a confined space. This led to the excavation of pockets in the platform for the propping girders, the temporary reduction of the track super-elevation and the removal of a complete section of the roof canopy in the vicinity of the bridge. What had been overlooked, however, was that these then relatively new 75-ton and 30-ton cranes had an extensive canopy over the machinery between the crab sides and that with the jib raised and when running back down beside the materials train on the adjacent track, the crane's canopy marginally fouled the guttering to the remaining platform roof. Some time was spent, therefore, at the beginning of the possession hurriedly removing long lengths of cast iron guttering. A full description of this work will be found in *Backtrack* magazine for April 1999.

Making lifts near the limiting capacity of the crane tests the ability and nerve of the crane crew, especially the supervisor. Such lifts will naturally be at a short radius and with the propping girder jacks well screwed down. The load will be initially taken up very gently and put down again, and the girder supports checked for possible settlement with the jacks being re-tightened if necessary. New components usually arrive in a wagon and are not therefore very far above the ground, and anyway if dropped will only fall back into the wagon. Again at Byfleet at least one 20-ton Grampus wagon had an unintended dynamic spot check on its suspension system when the crane driver, unfamiliar with the controls of his new diesel crane, fumbled with the main hoist brake and consequently dropped a 15 ton precast concrete bridge deck unit from a height of about 15 feet. Fortunately, the wagon seemed none the worse for its experience.

Occasionally it is necessary to lift and/or remove large and heavy items from some height, where once the crane has taken up the load there is a long way to go before reaching ground level. One such occasion was during the widening of the A3 Kingston Bypass trunk road between Raynes Park and New Malden, when the existing reinforced concrete parapet beam to the over-bridge had to be removed. The density of concrete cannot be predicted with great accuracy and anyway in those days tended to be underestimated, as the increase in density due the presence of significant quantities of steel reinforcement was frequently ignored. Once the 75-ton Nine Elms crane working at minimum radius, started to take the load, it was soon realised that the 72 tons calculated was well short of the actual weight and there was much relief once the beam was safely on the ground, where it could be cut up into smaller pieces and loaded up for removal.

Occasionally the engineer has his own emergencies requiring the use of breakdown cranes. More spectacular than most was the partial collapse of the signal bridge carrying Clapham Junction A Box on 10 May 1965, when, as a result of corrosion, an end tension diagonal of the London side lattice girder parted company with the gusset plate connecting it with the lower chord member. The result fortunately was not a total collapse of the bridge across all the lines into Waterloo but the dropping of the girder on the failure side by about 4 feet, causing some of the mechanical interlocking frame to seize up and the lower chord to foul many of the tracks below.

To secure the existing lattice girder in its precarious position and prevent further downward movement, arrangements were made to bring up the 75-ton Cowans Sheldon diesel breakdown crane from Nine Elms. This was worked round the West London Extension lines so as to approach the signal box bridge from the London side with jib leading, the match truck having been detached and lifted or shunted to one side a little short of

Following the partial collapse of Clapham Junction Signal Bridge at 8.36 am on 10 May 1965, the first phase of remedial work was to bring up the 75-ton diesel breakdown crane from Nine Elms MPD. This was attached to the second node of the lattice girder to prevent the possibility of any further downward movement. Beyond the bridge, a diesel shunter brings up a bogie bolster wagon loaded with military trestling to be off loaded by a Grafton 10-ton travelling steam permanent way crane behind the trestle. Once complete, a pair of jacks on the trestle were used to restore the girder to its correct position. (Author)

the site. The hook of the crane was then attached by means of a heavy duty chain to the second node from the support of the lattice girder. Whilst the strain was taken up, no attempt was made at this point to raise the girder by lifting on the hoist rope of the crane. Instead, two small towers of steel military trestling were erected under two nodes of the main girder. From these trestles, the defective girder was raised by means of small portable hydraulic jacks until the bottom chord of the girder was restored to its proper position and the crane released. Further details of this event will be found in *Backtrack* magazine for December 1997.

As can be seen the breakdown crane, as well as being an essential item of equipment for clearing the line following accidents, collisions and derailments, is also very useful to the civil engineer for his bridge works. Breakdown cranes were sometimes used around the main works handling locomotive boilers out in the yard.

Occasionally they were used too by the traffic department to assist in loading and unloading heavy items such as electrical transformers or stators, or even adjusting the position of out of gauge loads during the journey.

On a more frivolous note, before World War 2 the LNER was in the habit during the summer of holding open days in some of its larger goods yards. At these weekend events, as well as placing on display the latest Pacific locomotive, coaches and wagons etc, offered rides in an open goods container suspended from the hook of a steam breakdown crane. The Guildford 45-ton crane even starred in the Ealing comedy film *A two way stretch*, when on the branch from Brookwood to Bisley rifle range, it lifted a motor van loaded with gold bullion away from the pursuing Police and into the thieves clutches. When so employed on such diverse activities, cranes can go some way to earning a living and offsetting their high initial capital, maintenance and operational costs.

NER 25-ton Craven steam crane on hand to adjust the tilt of an out-of-gauge load as it approaches a through girder bridge having just passed under a signal gantry at Dunston. The load was a large steel casting for the rudder post of RMS Aquitania. (NER, author's collection)

Interim Conclusion

In this volume we have explored the development of the steam breakdown cranes for use on British mainland standard gauge railway lines, starting from humble beginnings in 1875 at 5 ton capacity on four wheels through to 25 or 30 tons on three or four axles by 1906. From there on greater capacity, and in some cases a longer jib, required one or two more axles, thereby rendering the size of the carriage a hindrance to approaching close to the load to be lifted.

The Great Western Railway's high expectations in 1908 for a 36-ton crane with a length of jib capable of enabling a load to be lifted over and above any obstruction on the ground set new standards which were maintained until the introduction of telescopic jibs in 1977. Ransomes & Rapier's design was a challenge to which for some time other makers struggled to compete. It can be seen from Figure 52 that most achieved the capacity, but not the maximum reach. Only with Cowans Sheldon's response to the LNER's requirements in 1926 were the stakes raised to 45 tons capacity, albeit by means of a very high axle load.

Long before that, however, the solution to the weight versus the minimum number of axles/axle-load and hence the length of the carriage had been resolved by none other than Ransomes & Rapier themselves by the patenting of the Stokes detachable relieving bogie in 1904. Although the first crane utilising this was built for an overseas railway in 1906, it was to be 1916 before the first was delivered to a British railway and this remained unique for another 15 years. It is this feature, together with some more modern smaller cranes that will be the topic of Volume 2 and which will also contain a bibliography, references and an index.

Graph depicting the load outreach capabilities of cranes built since the introduction of the GW's 36-ton Ransomes & Rapier crane in 1908. Whilst many of its competitors achieved comparability at minimum and out to 30 foot radii, only in 1926 was it significantly exceeded, by the LNER 45-ton Cowans Sheldon design. (Author)

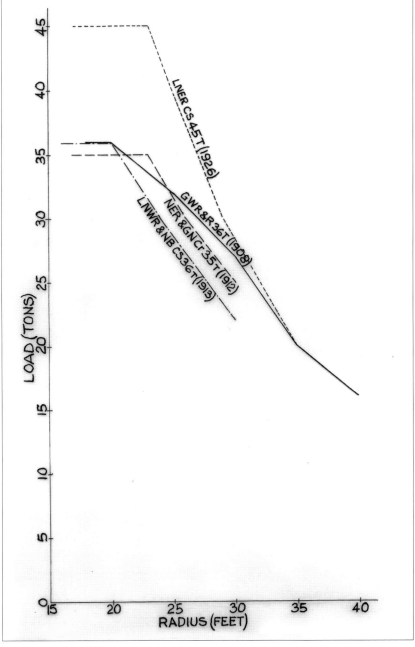

Appendix 1 - Mechanical Details

Maker	Purch'd by	Year built	Works/ Order Nos (No if not clear from wks Nos)	Max load @ radius (Tons/ft-in)	Wheel Arrg't	Cylinders dia. X stroke (inch)	Boiler		Jib length (ft-in)	Tare Wt (T-c)	Notss
							Pressure (lb/sq in)	Dia. X ht (ft-in)			
Appleby	MR	1874-5	(4 or 5)	5/	0-4-0						
Appleby	LSWR	1875-80	(2)	10/17-0	0-6-0		60		22-0/S	33-17	
Forrest	NBR	1882	(1)	20/18-0	0-6-0	9 x 12			22-0	49-0	
Chaplin	TVR	1884	2303	20/12-0	0-6-0	7 x 12			20-6/S	45-9	
GER	GER	1885/3	(3)	12/18-1½	0-6-0			3-6 x 5-9	21-7	32-16/ 34-4	
CS	GER	1892-9	(3)	12/	0-6-0						
Dunlop &Bell	LSWR	1885	(1)	15/19-0	0-6-0				21-6/S	38-17	
CS	CR	1886	1436+1?	15/20-0	4-4-0			4-3 x 7-6	22-0/S	51-10	
CS	HR	1887	1485	15/25-6	4-4-0	8 x 14		4-3 x 7-9	26-0/S	60-0	
Smith	GNR	1892	4164-5	15/16-0	0-6-0	8 x 12		4-6 x 7-6	23-6/S	50-15	
CS Mk 1	M&SLR	1893	1847	15/22-0	4-4-0				26-6/S	52-10	
CS Mk 1	MR	1893	1854-7	15/22-0	4-4-0	8 x 14	60	4-3 x ?	26-6/S	52-18	
CS Mk 1	NER	1893	1858-9	15/20-0	4-4-0			4-3 x ?			
CS Mk 1	GSWR	1893	1890	15/20-0	4-4-0				24-2	52-0	
CS Mk 1	NSR	1895	1965	15/	4-4-0				26-0/S	56-8	
CS Mk 2	NBR	1897	2117	15/22-0	4-4-0	8 x 14		4-5 x ?	26-6/S	50-9	
CS Mk 2	NER	1897	2118	15/20-0	4-4-0	14	70/80		25-0	58-9	
CS Mk 2	GCR	1898	2119-22	15/20-0	4-4-0				26-6/S	52-10	
CS Mk 2	LBSCR	1898	2181-2	15/20-0	4-4-0			4-5 x 7-0	26-0S	55-2	
CS Mk 2	MR	1899	2234-7	15/22-0	4-4-0						
CS Mk 2	GNR	1899	2246-7	15/20-0	4-4-0				26-0/S	52-8	
CS Mk 2	SER	1899	2250	15/20-0	4-4-0		60	4-5 x 7-0	26-0S	55-2	
CS Mk 2	MR	1901	2421	15/22-0	4-4-0	8 x 14					
CS Mk 2	GWR	1901	2449+2?	15/20-0	4-4-0	8 x 14		4-5 x 6-3	26-0S	57-10	
CS	L&YR	1902	2545	20/22-0	4-4-0	8 x 14		4-9 x 6-7½	26-0S	68-6	
CS	GWR	1903	2614-5	20/20-0	4-4-0	8 x 14		5-0 x 8-0	26-0	67-14	
LNWR	LNWR	1904	(1)	20/23-0	0-8-0	8½ x 14	100			54-6#	
CS	MR	1904	2617	20/22-0	4-4-0	8 x 14					
CS	FR	1904	(1)	15/18-0	0-6-0	7 x 10	Loco	Loco	20-0		
Jessop & Appleby	AD (N&SW)	1904	(1)	20/20-0	0-4-4?	9 x 12			32-0S	64-8	
CS Mk 2a	LTSR	1906/1	2933	15/22-0	4-4-0		60	4-3 x 6-8	26-0	53-0	
CS	L&YR	1906	2954	30/17-0	4-4-0	8 x 14	80	4-6 x 7-0	25-10	58-8#	
Craven	CR	1907	8117(2)	20/21-0	2-4-2	8 x 14	120	4-9 x 7-0	25-3	65-0	
Craven	GCR	1907	8138(1)	20/21-0	2-4-2	8 x 14	120	4-9 x 7-0	25-3	64-0#	
Craven	NER	1907	8152(3)	25/23-0	2-4-2	8 x 14	120	4-9 x 7-0	25-9	76-13	
S&P	LSWR	1908-9	T89(2)	20/21-0	0-4-4				29-9	55-11	
CS	LNWR	1908	2987	25/22-0 30/17-0	4-4-0	8 x 13	80		25-10	59-19#	(1)
GER	GER	1908	(2)	20/20-0	0-8-0		100	3-11½ x 7-7⁷/₈	22-10	56-8	
Wilson	GWR	1908	(1)	12/15-0	0-8-0	9 x 10	100	4-6 x 8-0	39-0	48-18	
R&R	GWR	1908	4411(1)	36/20-0	0-6-4	9 x 14	80	4-8 x 7-2		91-10	
S&P	GWR	1909	(1)	36/20-0	0-6-4	10 x 12	100	4-6 x 7-6		85-10	
R&R	LNWR	1909	5049	36/20-0	0-6-4	9 x 14	80	4-8 x	41-1½	80-9#	
CS	TVR	1911	3143	36/22-0 50/20-0	4-4-4	9 x 14		4-3 x 6-9	35-0	94-2	(2)
R&R	GWR	1911	6113(1)	36/20-0	0-6-4	9 x 14	80	4-8 x 7-2		91-10	
Craven	L&YR	1911	9158(1)	35/17-0	2-6-2	8 x 14	120	4-9 x 7-0	29-6	65-12#	

Railway Breakdown Cranes – Mechanical Details

Maker	Purch'd by	Year built	Works/Order Nos (No if not clear from wks Nos)	Max load @ radius (Tons/ft-in)	Wheel Arrg't	Cylinders dia. X stroke (inch)	Boiler Pressure (lb/sq in)	Boiler Dia. X ht (ft-in)	Jib length (ft-in)	Tare Wt (T-c)	Notes
Craven	NER	1912	9372(2)	35/23-0	2-6-2	8 x 14	120	4-9 x 7-0	25-3	74-10	
CS	LNWR	1913	3221	36/20-0	4-4-4	8 x 14	120	4-3 x 6-8	34-0	83-17#	
Craven	GNR	1914	9780(1)	35/23-0	2-6-2	8 x 14	120	4-8 x 6-6	25-3	71-0	
CS	RR	1914	3235	35/17-0	0-6-4	8 x 14		4-9 x 6-5¼	31-0	65-0	
CS	NBR	1914	3310	36/20-0	4-4-4	8 x 14		4-3 x 6-9	34-0S	85-16	
R&R	GER	1915	7478	35/23-0	0-6-4	9 x 14	100	4-6 x 6-3	29-10¼	72-4#	
CS	NER	1916	3335	35/23-0	4-6-0	8 x 14	100	4-3 x 6-9	29-1	75-5	
CS	LNWR	1917	3765	36/23-0	4-6-0	8 x 14	100	4-6 x 8-6	30-9	70-19#	
CS	WO	1918	3855-6	25/20-0	4-4-0	8 x 14	100	4-3 x 6-3	28-8		
R&R	LSWR	1918	7999	36/20-0	0-6-4	8 x 14	80	4-6 x 6-6	41-10S	82-12$	
CS	WO/NER	1918	4047	25/20-0	4-4-0	8 x 14	100	4-3 x 6-3	28-8		
CS	Barry Rly	1919	4099	25/20-0	4-4-0	8 x 14	100	4-3 x 6-3	28-8	58-0	
R&R	GER	1919	413	35/23-0	0-6-4	9 x 14	100	4-6 x 6-3	29-10¼	80-0	
CS	LSWR	1921	7199	36/20-0	0-6-4	8 x 12	100	4-6 x 6-6	41-6S	85-6	
CS	Met Rly	1924	4475	20/20-0 30/16-0	4-4-0				28-6S	57-1#	(1)
CS	LNER	1926	4524-5	45/23-6	4-0-4	8 x 12		4-6 x 6-6	32-6	81-17	
R&R	SR	1927	C6553(2)	36/20-0	0-6-4	9 x 14	100	4-6 x 6-6	41-10S	78-2	
R&R	London Electric	1931	D3688(1)	30/12-0	0-4-4	8½ x 12	120	4-3 x 6-6	27-6	51-0	

Note: Jib length measured from pin at jib foot to pin of main hoist.
    #   Jib resting on match wagon
    S   Scaled from drawing or diagram
    $ Jib resting on match wagon + counter wt & propping girders in place
    (1)   Up-rated
    (2)   Under special conditions with extra counter weights.

Appendix 2 - Speed of Motions

Railway Breakdown Cranes – Speed of Motions

Maker	Purchased by	Year built	Works/Order Nos	Max speed lifting (ft/min) Max load	Max speed lifting (ft/min) Reduced load	Max speed travelling (ft/min)	Slewing 1 revolution. (min)	Raise Jib (min)	Remarks
Wilson	GW	1908		12T @ 30	? @ 100	432	½		
R&R	GW	1908/11	4411/6113	36T @ 10	12T @ 30	80	1½		
CS	Taff Vale Rly	1911	3143	36T @ 15		100			
Craven	NER	1912	9372	35T @ 15	17½ @ 30	450	1	4	
CS	LNWR/NB	1913/4	3221/3310	36T @ 15	18T @ 30	60	1		(1)
CS	Rhymney	1914	3235	35T @ 15	-	302	1	4	
R&R	GER	1915/19	7478/413	35T @ 10	9T @ 30	346	½		
CS	NER	1916	3335	35T @ 20	17½ @ 40	350	½	10	(2)
R&R	LSWR	1918	7999	36T @ 10	12T @ 30	80	1½		
CS	WO/NER/Barry	1918	3855-6/4047/99	25T @ 20	-	150	1½	2½	
CS	LSWR	1921	7199	36T @ 20	12T @ 40	150	1⅝		
CS	LNER	1926	4524-5	45T @ 12	15T @ 40	300	2		(3)
R&R	SR	1927	C6553	36T @ 10	12T @ 30	80	1		
R&R	London Electric Rly	1931	D3688	30T @ 12	15T @ 24	200	1¼		

Note: (1)   Auxiliary hoist 1T @ 200 ft/min.
       (2)   Auxiliary hoist 2T @ 200 ft/min.
       (3)   From 35ft to 23ft 6in radius in 2 minutes.

Railway Breakdown Cranes – Lifting Performance

Maker	Purchased by	Year built	Works/ Order Nos	Crane Propped			Free on Rail		Remarks
				Max load @ radius (Tons/ ft-in)	Min rad. (ft-in)	Load @ max radius (Tons/ ft-in)	Max load @ radius (Tons/ ft-in)	Load @ max radius (Tons/ ft-in)	
Appleby	LSWR	1875-80		10/17-0	16-0	/22-0	4/16-0	2/22-0	
Forrest	NB	1882		20/18-0		2/24-0	4/18-0	2/22-0	
Chaplin	Taff Vale	1884	2303	20/12-0		12/18-0	10/12-0	8/18-0	
Dunlop & Bell	LSWR	1885		15/19-0	14-0	11.85/24-0		4½/24	
Smith	GN	1892	4164-5	15/16-0	16-0	6/26-7			
CS Mk 1	GSWR	1893	1890	15/20-0		10/26-0	6½/18-0	3/26-0	
CS Mk 2	NB	1897	2117	15/22-0		10/26-0	5.15/22-0		
CS Mk 2	NER	1897	2118	15/20-0		5/28-0	5/20-0		
CS Mk 2	GC/ GN	1898/9	2119-22/2246-7	15/20-0		6/28-0	6½/18-0	2/27-0	
CS Mk 2	LBSC/ SER	1898/9	2181-2/2250	15/20-0	15-0	6/28-0	7½/16-0	2/28-0	
CS Mk 2	MR/ LTSR	1899/ 1901/6	2234-7/2421/ 2933	15/22-0		10/28-0	5/22-0	2/28-0	
CS Mk 2	GW	1901	2406/48-9	15/20-0		10/26-0	5/20-0	3½/26-0	
CS	L&Y	1902	2545	20/22-0		9/28-0	6/22-0	4/28-0	
CS	GW	1903	2614-5	20/20-0		14/26-0	7/20-0	4/26-0	
LNWR	LNWR	1904		20/23-0	16-10				
CS	FR	1904		15/18-0	18-0	12/21-0	7½/18-0	6/21-0	
Jessop & Appleby	AD (N&SW)	1904		20/20-0		14/26-0	7/20-0	4/26-0	
CS	L&Y/ LNWR	1906/8	2954/2987	25/22-0 30/17-0	17-0	20/25-6	6/22-0	4/29-0	
Craven	CR/ GCR	1907	8117/8138	20/21-0	15-0	10/27-0	10/15-0	4/27-0	
Craven	NER	1907	8152	25/23-0	17-0	16/27-0	10/17-0	4/27-0	
S&P	LSWR	1908-9	T89	20/21-0	14-0	16.8/25-0			
Wilson	GW	1908		12/15-0		6/30-0	6/15-0	3/30-0	
R&R	GW	1908/11	4411/6113	36/20-0	18-0	16/40-0	14/20-0	4½/40-0	
S&P	GW	1909		36/20-0		15/40-0	7½/20-0	1½/40-0	
R&R	LNWR	1909	5049	36/20-0		18/40-0	14/20-0	4½/40-0	
CS	Taff Vale	1911	3143	36/22-0	16-0	8/35-0	11½/16-0	1½/35	
Craven	L&Y	1911	9158	35/17-0	13-0	10/32-0	14½/13-0	3/32-0	
Craven	NER	1912	9372	35/23-0	17-0	25/26-0	6/23-0	4½/26-0	
CS	LNWR/ NB	1913/4	3221/3310	36/20-0	16-0	22/30-0	9½/20-0	4½/30	1T (1)
Craven	GN	1914	9780	35/23-0	17-0	25/30-0	12/17-0	6/23-0	
CS	Rhymney	1914	3235	35/17-0	17-0	18/30-0	8/17-0	3/30-0	
R&R	GER	1915/19	7478/413	35/23-0	15-0	4/33-0	14/15-0	5/30-0	(2)
CS	NER	1916	3335	35/23-0	15-0		7½/23-0		2T (1)
CS	LNWR	1917	3765	36/23-0	15-0	16/32-0	7/23-0	3/32-0	2T (1)
R&R	LSWR/SR	1918/27	7999/C6553	36/20-0	18-0	16/40-0	14/20-0	4½/40-0	
CS	WO/NER	1918	3855-6/4047	25/20-0		15/26-0		4/26-0	
CS	Barry	1919	4099	25/20-0		12/26-0	8/15-0	5/26-0	
CS	LSWR	1921	7199	36/20-0	18-0	16/40-0	14/20-0	4½/40-0	
CS	Met	1924	4475	30/16-0	16-0	15/25-0	6/23-6		
CS	LNER	1926	4524-5	45/23-6	17-0	20/35-0	10/20-0	2/35-0	
R&R	London Electric Rly	1931	D3688	30/12-0	12-0	7½/27-0	15/12-0	3¾/27-0	

Note: (1) Auxiliary hoist.

(2) Free on rail without detachable tail weight, 17T @ 15'-0" and 6½T @ 30'-0" with tail weight.

(3) Over the years the stated capacity shown on the maker's drawings and details and subsequently adopted by the owning railways sometimes varied, due in some cases to a reassessment of capacity and/or the deterioration of the crane with age. The original has been quoted, where known.

Appendix 4 - Glossary of Terms

Articulated jib	A design of jib, which when in the lowered position, is capable of lateral angular movement relative to the crane as it passes round a curve in the track.
Bevel gears	A set of gear wheels, usually of different diameter, meshing at an angle, usually a right angle, with each other.
Block	The arrangement of pulleys at the foot of the hoisting tackle and their connection to the hook.
Blocking up	Propping the crane by use of the propping girders.
Bogie	A sub-frame carrying four or six wheels on axles able to rotate in plan and often move laterally, usually constrained, relative to the carriage it supports.
Bridle gear	The fixed length portion of the derricking gear connecting pulley wheels to either the superstructure or jib head.
Brothers, pair of	Two chains fastened at the top end in a single ring and at the bottom each to a hook.
Cant	See super-elevation.
Carriage	That portion of the crane below the superstructure that incorporates the wheels and running gear, together with the propping girder boxes, outriggers, or yokes.
Counter-weight	Ballast weight attached to the underside or at the rear of the tail of the superstructure to provide counter- balance to the applied load. Sometimes detachable.
Crab sides	Side frames to the machinery on the superstructure.
Derricking	The motion of raising the jib from its travelling position to a working radius and vice versa, also known as luffing.
Dolly jack	Vertical downward facing jack usually attached at the four corners under the carriage frame behind the buffers.
Folding wedges	A pair of matching hardwood wedges placed one upon the other with opposing slopes to provide a flat surface, so that when positioned between parallel surfaces and driven home they tighten in the gap.
Four-foot	The space between the rails, approximating to 4ft 8½in.
Heavy lifter	LSWR term for a breakdown crane.
Horse	Sometimes used to describe a jib rest on a match wagon.
Lattice girder	Girder, such as jib, fabricated from longitudinal angles braced apart by flat or angle sections.
Live ring	A race of multiple conical steel rollers between a pair of cast steel roller paths upon which the superstructure revolves on the carriage.
Loading gauge	The maximum dimensional parameters for a given route within which all parts of a locomotive and any rolling stock must be contained under all conditions of motion.
Luffing	See derricking.
Match truck	The wagon that accompanies the crane primarily to act as a guard truck to the jib in its lowered position when travelling in train formation. Frequently the jib is lowered on to a bolster. Other paraphernalia is often also carried.
Mitre gears	A set of bevel gear wheels of same diameter meshing at a right angle with each other.
Moment(s)	The product of a force by the lever arm perpendicular to its line of action about the point of rotation.
Outriggers	Vertically hinged outriggers on the carriage provide an alternative to propping girders.
Parts (of chain or rope)	One chain or rope in either the derricking or hoisting tackle, also known as a fall.
Pinion	Small toothed gear wheel.
Portée	Usable distance from edge of carriage to point of lift.
Propping girders	Two or three sets of transverse beams either inserted in yokes under the carriage, or incorporated in boxes under the carriage and drawn out telescopically. In both cases these are then supported by robust packing on the ground to enhance the propping base thereby improving the stability and hence the lifting capacity. Alternatively hinged outriggers may be used.
Radial axle	Two wheels mounted on an axle which is able to move radially relative to the carriage.
Ram's horn hook	Double-sided hook often used on large capacity cranes, sometimes includes a central eye hole.

Rail clip	A pair of claws and screw coupling mounted on the end plate of the carriage that can be clamped around the rail head.
Relieving bogies	Small bogies at each end of the carriage to which a proportion of the crane's weight is transferred, by beams and jacks, for travelling in train formation, but detachable prior to commencing lifting operations.
Roller path	The path upon which rollers supporting the superstructure permit it to revolve on the carriage. Teeth are usually cast on either the inside or outside to form the slewing rack.
Safety chains	A pair of chains additional to the draw gear used between adjacent vehicles, particularly the crane and match wagon.
Skillet	A LSWR term for match wagon.
Slewing	The motion of revolving the crane superstructure on the carriage.
Slip pinion	A pinion gear capable of being slid along a keyed shaft to mesh with a spur wheel.
Snatch-block	The block incorporating the lower pulley wheel to the hoisting tackle and the hook suspended there from.
Spreader beam	A lifting beam hung from the hook to spread the points of lift and from which chains, or a pair of brothers are hung so that they pass over the width of a vehicle.
Structure gauge	The minimum dimensional parameters for a given route outside which all fixed items along the line must be constructed and maintained.
Super-elevation	The raising of the outer rail above the inner rail on a curve to counteract centrifugal force of a train traversing the curve at speed, also known as cant.
Superstructure	That part of the crane that revolves on the carriage.
Tackle	System of chains or ropes rigged around pulleys to achieve a motion, such as derricking, hoisting, etc.
Truck (Pony)	A sub-frame carrying two wheels on an axle able to move laterally relative to the carriage.
Warwicking	Attaching strops to tie down the offside of a crane to the adjacent track upon which a locomotive is standing to prevent uplift of the crane carriage when lifting heavy loads.
Winding (of chain or rope)	The chain or rope acted upon by either the derricking or hoisting barrel.
Worm	A spirally threaded gear wheel that engages with the worm wheel.
Yoke	Metal strap fixed to the underside of the carriage through which the propping girders are threaded.

Acknowledgements

No project of this nature is undertaken without the assistance of a great many people over the years and some contacts were so long ago that I may have overlooked one or two. Initial help came from the Public Relations & Publicity Officer of the London Midland Region at Euston and subsequently the other regions. Access was granted to the archives by the CMEEs of the LM, ER, WR and Scottish Regions at Derby, York, Swindon and Glasgow respectively. Permits to visit motive power depots were issued to myself and others, thereby enabling photographs to be taken of breakdown and other cranes. Facilities were also afforded by Cowans Sheldon; Herbert Morris Cranes (Craven Bros); and Ransomes & Rapier; together with the National Archives at Kew and its predecessors the Public Records Office and British Transport Historical Records; National Archive for Scotland in Edinburgh; the librarians of the Institute of Civil Engineers, Institute of Locomotive Engineers (now incorporated in the Institute of Mechanical Engineers), Science Museum and University of Surrey; and various county records offices, including Cumbria and Suffolk County Records Offices.

Over the years correspondence has been entered into with various fellow enthusiasts and railwaymen of whom perhaps the late Jack Templeton, Duncan Burton, Stephen Townroe and WM Roscoe Taylor deserve special mention. More recently Chris Capewell, Roger Cooke and David Withers as founder members of the Breakdown Crane Association have been of great help and encouragement. Assistance has also been received from many individuals, sometimes members of the Cumbria Railway Association, Great Eastern Railway Society, Great Northern Railway Society, Great North of Scotland Railway Association, Historical Model Railway Society, Industrial Record Society, LMS Society, LNER Study Group, LNWR Society, NERA, Railway Preservation Society of Ireland, Stephenson Locomotive Society, or Welsh Railways Research Circle: together with Messrs Paul Bartlett, Mike Blakemore, Noel Coates, Alan B Collins, Chris Dean, JM Dunn, John Edgington, Bob Essery, Keith Fenwick, Len Elston, Ron & Allan Garraway, Ken Hoole, Mike King, Barry Lane, John Lewis, Peter Lund, Jim MacIntosh, Robin Mathams, Ian Middleditch, Tony Miller, Eric Mountford, K Noble, Ken Norris, Dave Pennington, Brian Penney, Ron Shepherd, Allan Sibley, Jack Slinn, Tony Sparkes, Robin Tunstall, Charles Underhill, John Watling, Martin Welch, Peter Wright and Derek Young. My thanks are due to them all for thus enabling me to offer this work.

One of the major milestones to occur in the development of the railway breakdown crane was taken by the Great Western Railway during the first decade of the 20th century, when it commissioned a pair of long jib 36-ton cranes. Not only did these embrace a 20% increase in maximum lifting capacity over that achieved to date, but a 30 to 50% increase in jib length meant this new class of crane could out perform previous designs by a wide margin and remained the norm for fifty years. Here GW No. 2, the product of Ransomes & Rapier in 1908, stands outside A Shop at Swindon on 23 August 1971. (Author)

By comparison the GW's previous largest class of crane was the pair of 20-ton cranes supplied by Cowans Sheldon in 1903. No. 5 was also photographed at Swindon Works on 23 July 1961, still fitted with its chain hoisting and lifting tackle. (MS Welch)

By 1908 when this 30-ton crane was supplied to the LNWR, Cowans Sheldon had taken their highly successful range of cranes about as far as was possible on four axles. This was a development of the 20-ton crane in the previous illustration itself derived from and both should be compared with the 15-ton version within the book and in colour illustration on the front cover. Renumbered RS1020/30 by the LMS in May 1941, upon withdrawal this crane was set aside for the National Collection. After periods in store at Preston Park and restoration to working order at Steam Town, Carnforth, it was transferred to the Churnet Valley Railway and has recently moved to Crewe Heritage Centre. (J Woolley)

Opposite page (upper and lower) - Cravens Bros had entered the breakdown crane market with three 20 and three 25-ton cranes in 1906. Illustrated is No. RS1053/20, one of two supplied to the Caledonian Railway that year, soon followed by another for the Great Central, together with three 25-ton for the NER. In the upper view No. RS1053/20 was photographed at Eastfield on 6 June 1965 in BR black livery, while by 28 May the next year the same crane had been repainted in red. (Both MS Welch)

Above - Another view of GW No. 2 Ransomes & Rapier 36-ton crane at Swindon on 23 August 1971 in the process of raising its jib off the match wagon prior to attaching appropriate lifting tackle in preparation for making a lift. On being withdrawn from main line service in 1975, this crane was acquired for use on the Dart Valley and South Devon railways. In 1989, however, it was sold to a private buyer, and currently awaits restoration on the East Somerset Railway. (Author)

Opposite page - As well as obtaining a 36-ton crane off Ransomes & Rapier, the GW turned to Stothert & Pitt of Bath for an example to the same specification delivered in 1909. As in 1912 a repeat order went to the former maker, one must conclude that the latter was not quite so successful. Nonetheless, as No. 1, it survived until late 1967. It is seen here at Swindon on 23 July 1961 following an overhaul. (MS Welch)

Above - Rival crane manufacturers' response to the challenge set by the GW's super-crane was initially a little heavy handed. Cowans Sheldon's first attempts at a 36-ton crane resorted to a rather long carriage supported by six axles, making it difficult to approach close to the load to be lifted. As well as the two pairs of propping girders, the dolly jacks under each corner of the frame can be seen. Illustrated is No. RS1062/36, also annotated DM1062 and its capacity as 36,576 klgs, supplied to the North British Railway in 1914. In 1979 this crane too found its way into the hands of the Scottish Preservation Society, first at Falkirk and in 1993 at Bo'ness.   (J Woolley)

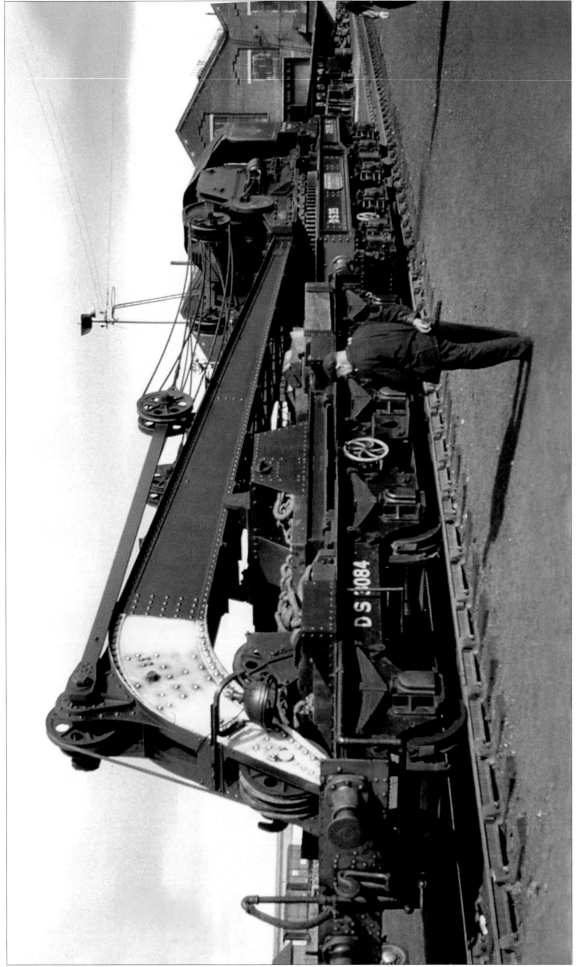

Leaving aside the Midland Railway, which acquired the first crane equipped with relieving bogies to be considered in Volume 2, the Great Eastern and LSWR were not slow to recognise the merits of the long jib 35/36-ton crane, as espoused by Ransomes & Rapier for the GWR in 1908. Although ordered in March 1915, the other demands on industry for war work delayed delivery of the latter's 36-ton crane until 1918. This, as No. Ds35, was photographed by Stephen Townroe at Eastleigh probably in the late '50s/early '60s. (Colour-Rail)

Following the grouping of the railways in 1923, the Southern Railway ordered two more similar 36-ton cranes from Ransomes & Rapier. These were delivered the following year and allocated to the Central and Eastern sections. Nonetheless, in due course No. Ds80 had found its way to Eastleigh, where it was photographed on 26 July 1961. Note that these two cranes were provided with purpose built bogie match wagons rather than the lash-up of a couple of redundant 4-wheel locomotive tender underframes provided for the LSWR crane. (L Elsey)

The summons to deal with a derailment, often of a minor nature, sometimes took breakdown trains into some obscure locations, where not infrequently the standard of track was not all it could be. Typical was Eastleigh's call in February 1953 to assist the Royal Navy in their ammunition depot at Bedenham, near Gosport. After dealing with the minor incident, on the way out, the crane itself became derailed on some lightly laid flat-bottomed track. The propping girders were extended to improve stability while the crane was jacked up and its wheels restored to the rails. (Both SC Townroe, courtesy Colour-Rail)

Right - Eastleigh's 36-ton crane was on occasions specially fitted out with a half-size version of its own jib placed at the top of the full-size one to extend the reach sufficiently to be able to replace the chimneys to the boiler house at the Works. When ever undertaking this task, the crew dreaded the possibility arising that they would receive a call to an incident, because to it was a lot of effort to disassemble this special rig and reinstate it again to complete the work. (SC Townroe, courtesy Colour-Rail)

Bottom - Eastleigh's 36-ton Ransomes & Rapier crane No. Ds35 in the centre was joined by the Cowans Sheldon 36-ton crane from Salisbury No. Ds37 on the left to deal with an ex-SR 2-6-0 N Class No. 31816 which had come to grief at Tipton Yard, Eastleigh South on 19 November 1962. No. Ds37 was to the same performance specification as No. Ds35, but, according the latter's driver Bill Bishop, not as efficient. (SC Townroe, courtesy Colour-Rail)

With the withdrawal of steam from the Southern Region following the electrification of the line to Bournemouth in July 1967, Guildford's 36-ton Ransome & Rapier crane No Ds80 was sent to Doncaster for overhaul. By June the next year it had arrived back at Stewarts Lane in pristine red livery but still lettered Guildford despite the fact this shed had closed with the end of steam. (Author)

Both ex-SR cranes of 1927 survived longer enough to be renumbered in the CEPS scheme. Close up pictures of No. ADRR 95201, formerly Ds81, were taken at Stewarts Lane on 5 December 1980, nearly six years before withdrawal and its preservation on the Kent & East Sussex Railway. The design of the roof to the shelter extended at little further on this crane compared with its sister. (Both P Bartlett)

Above - *In 1926 the LNER took an alternative view regarding the route availability when it ordered two 45-ton cranes from Cowans Sheldon. Instead of the time consuming methods of keeping the weight down and hence maximum axle loads adopted by some other companies, the limitation of a 20-ton axle load was accepted allowing these cranes to be mounted on a pair of 4-wheel bogies. By 14 June 1967 No. 330107 was stationed at Healey Mills and exists to the present time on the North Yorkshire Moors Railway. (Author)*

Left and opposite - *On 6 June 1970 an electro-diesel hauled coal train got out of control on the 1 in 122 downhill gradient to Tonbridge and derailed a number of 16-ton all steel mineral wagons. On a hot summer Saturday afternoon No. Ds80, by now a little faded, set about restoring the errant vehicles to the rails. (Author)*

Steam cranes were still in use during an abnormal track possession over the weekends of 13/14 and 21/22 October 1985 to carry out the replacement of the deck of Market Place Bridge within Haywards Heath station on the London to Brighton main line. Closest to the camera is Ransomes & Rapier 36-ton No. ADRR95201, formerly Ds81, while at the other end is Ransomes & Rapier 45-ton No. ADRR 95210, once Ds1561. (John Goss Photographs)

Looking down on ex-Caledonian 6-wheel breakdown riding and tool vans at Dalry Road shed in September 1959 with a couple of ex-CR 0-6-0s and a diesel shunting locomotives parked on the far end. (Colour-Rail)